NORTH EAST INDUSTRIES

THROUGH TIME

Stafford M. Linsley

AMBERLEY

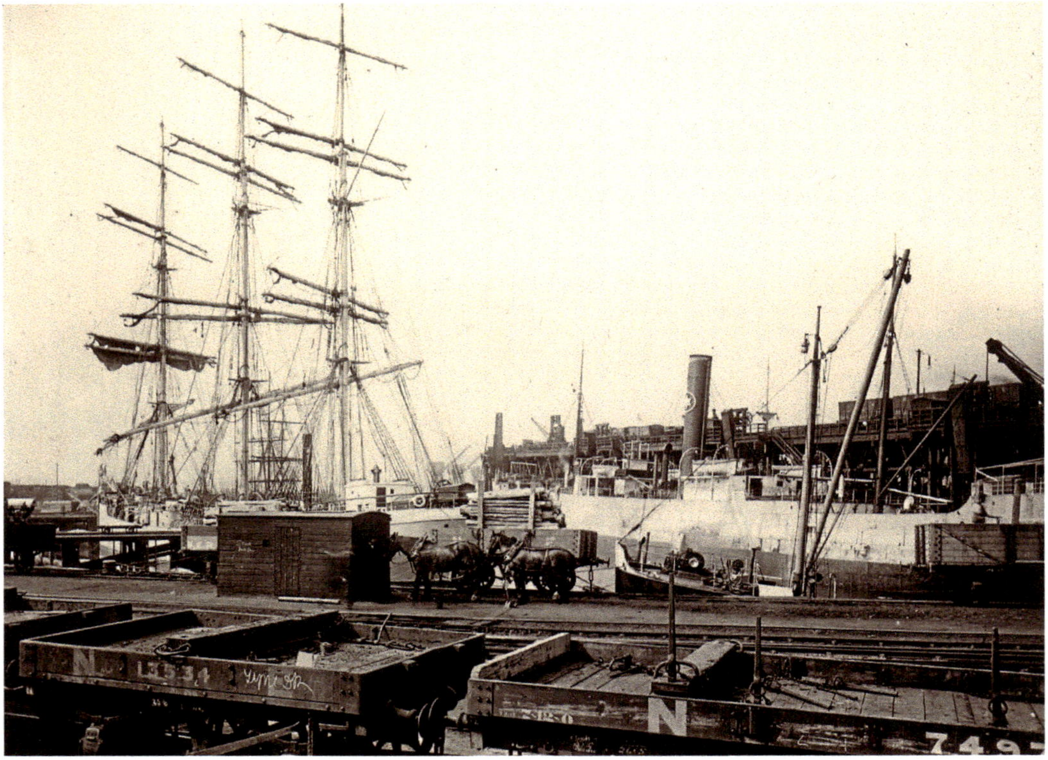

Tyne Dock, South Shields, NZ 352 654
At its zenith, Tyne Dock (built in 1859) shipped over 7 million tons of coal in one year, and it is reputed that, in total, more coal was shipped from it than from any other dock in Britain. It lost its coal staiths soon after 1967, and the dock was filled in during 2011. But here we see it in its busy heyday, *c.* 1890.

This book is dedicated to both my families, all twenty-six members of them, and to the memory of my late friend and colleague Bob Rennison

First published 2011

Amberley Publishing
The Hill, Stroud
Gloucestershire, GL5 4EP

www.amberley-books.com

ISBN 978 1 84868 683 0

British Library Cataloguing in Publication Data.
A catalogue record for this book is available from the British Library.

Typeset in 9.5pt on 12pt Celeste.
Typesetting by Amberley Publishing.
Printed in the UK.

Introduction

The industrial fortunes of North East England were built on its coal, lead, iron and other mineral resources, its shipbuilding, heavy engineering and chemical industries, a host of lesser smokestack industries, its agriculture and those industries that the rural areas supported. But the collieries, brickworks, gasworks, steel mills and so on, together with much of their formerly necessary transport infrastructure, have largely gone, only to be replaced by more sanitary commercial activities such as business parks, call centres, service industries and leisure and tourism facilities. We await, perhaps with some trepidation, the outcome of a society that is primarily based on a service economy, and on global inward investment to the neglect of home-grown businesses. There have of course been some recent industrial success stories, such as the Nissan car manufacturing plant at Sunderland, the growing number of hi-tech and computer software industries, and the newer offshore engineering technologies, but these have none of the visual impact of the older industries – our present industrial landscapes are much less fascinating than they once were. Moreover, many of our former industrial sites are now simply manicured grassy spaces, or remain as gaps within the built environment, as at Startforth, Barnard Castle, for example, where the present imprint of Ullathorne's Mill resembles nothing more nor less than a missing tooth.

I have lived most of my life in the North East, and the changes in its industries and society have been considerable. What has gone? For me personally, the coal mine where my father spent his working life (the site is now a nature reserve), one of the colliery rows that I grew up in, my primary school, the mineral railway that bisected my village, the Miners Institute where I learned the green-baize arts, the Electric Palace where I watched Saturday morning matinees, the wooden hut where I learned how to march in formation and play the bugle in the Boys' Brigade, the large engineering works where I served my apprenticeship; I could go on. Our world and its environments inevitably change, whether through the planned or unplanned activities of humankind, or through the disinterested actions of nature.

Until relatively recently, most of the industrial relics around us were the chance survivors of an uninterested society, and while there is little to be gained by bemoaning the fates of those that failed to survive, it was fortunate at least that industrial decline was accompanied by a growing interest in the industrial heritage. The study of industrial archaeology and creation of industrial museums have been a valuable by-product of this trend. So windmills and watermills have been preserved, as have railways, pumping stations, and colliery buildings, while other industrial structures have been incorporated into museums, or adaptively reused; several such projects are illustrated in these pages. But, understandably, there has been little interest in re-using a defunct tar distillery for example, or a tannery. Perhaps the best we can hope for is to be able to influence the ongoing changes in our working environments in such a way that we can retain a few valued reminders of our industrial past to enhance our lives in the future. The images in this book represent a world we have left behind, for good or ill. By contrast they also show the world that we now inhabit; a very different world but one where we can still find reminders of a not-too-distant industrial past.

The photographic sequence deals first with the coal and coal products industries, and then the railways to which the coal industry gave birth, changes in land transport, and the ports and harbours that both the roads and railways served. This is followed by examples of other industries of North East England, and of its industrial housing. Locations have been noted using their grid square reference. If there appears to be an emphasis on the county of Durham, this is simply because that county was more industrialised than its neighbour Northumberland; 'Tyneside', straddling the two counties, was of course the most heavily industrialised part of the whole North East, and here receives its fair share of attention.

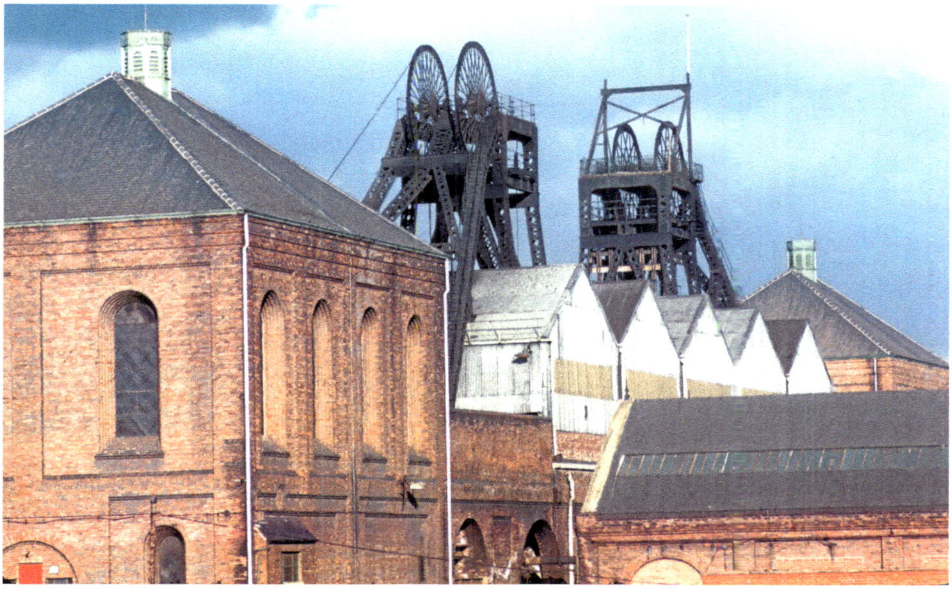

Hylton Colliery, NZ 366 528

This colliery was opened in 1900 by the Wearmouth Coal Co. Ltd. and employed some 1800 men by 1930. The two coal-drawing shafts originally had steam winding engines but these seem to have been replaced by electric winders around 1936 within the same engine houses, as seen here. The pit was closed in 1979, and a retail park was subsequently built on the site – from coal mining to Comet. Photographs 1973 and 2011.

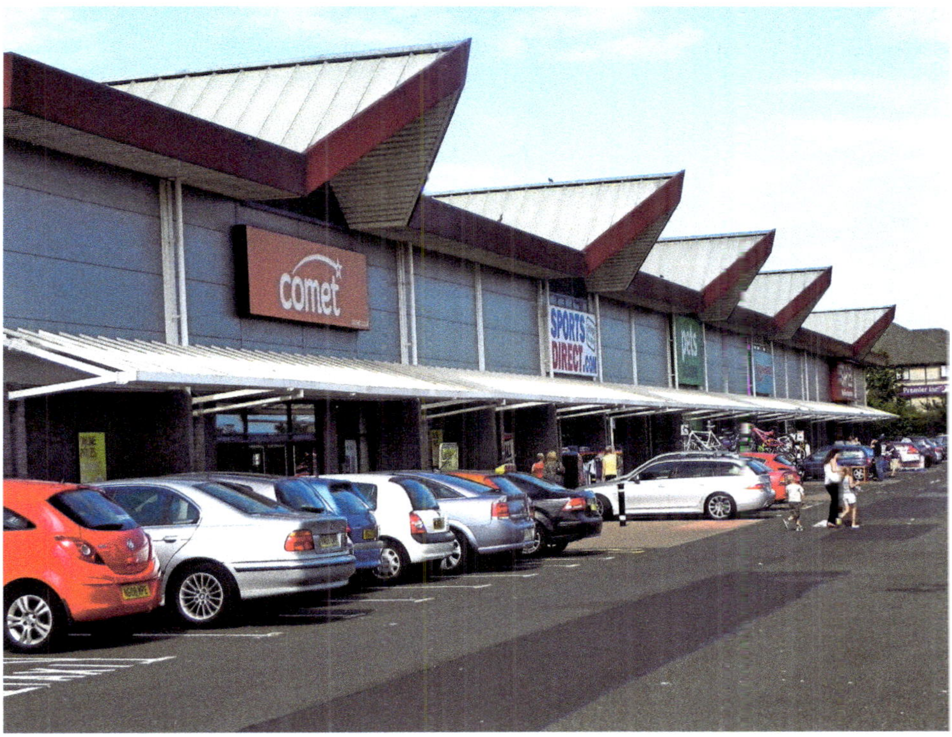

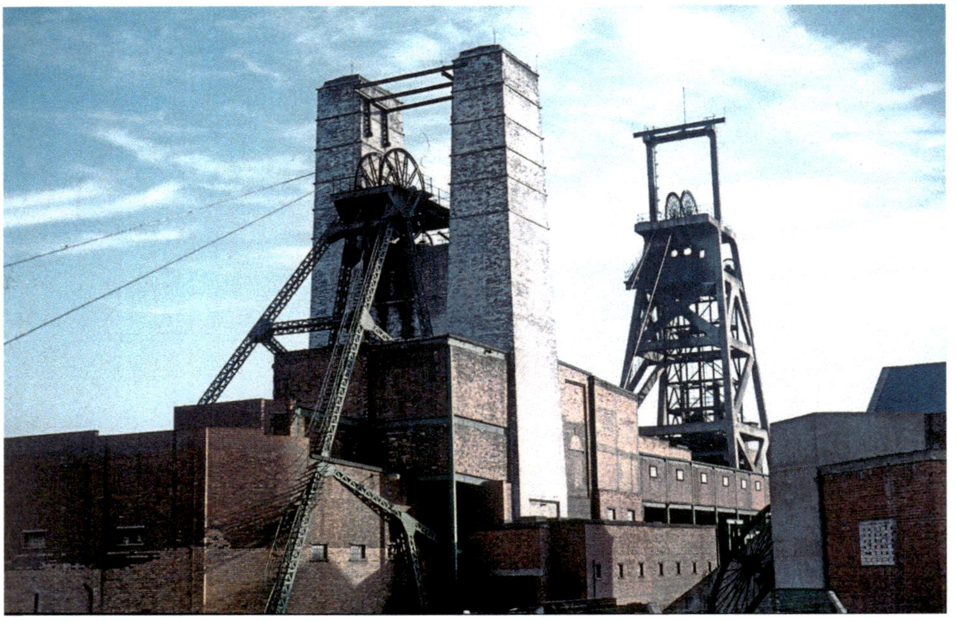

Silksworth Colliery, NZ 376 540

Silksworth Colliery opened in 1872, then one of the largest coal mines in County Durham. It closed in 1971/2, when it was one of very few to retain its ventilation chimneys. After closure the mine buildings were demolished while the large spoil heaps and partially flooded areas of land were converted into a major sports centre for Sunderland, dominated by an all-year ski and snowboard slope. There are also angling lakes, football pitches, an athletics track, and indoor and outdoor tennis facilities.

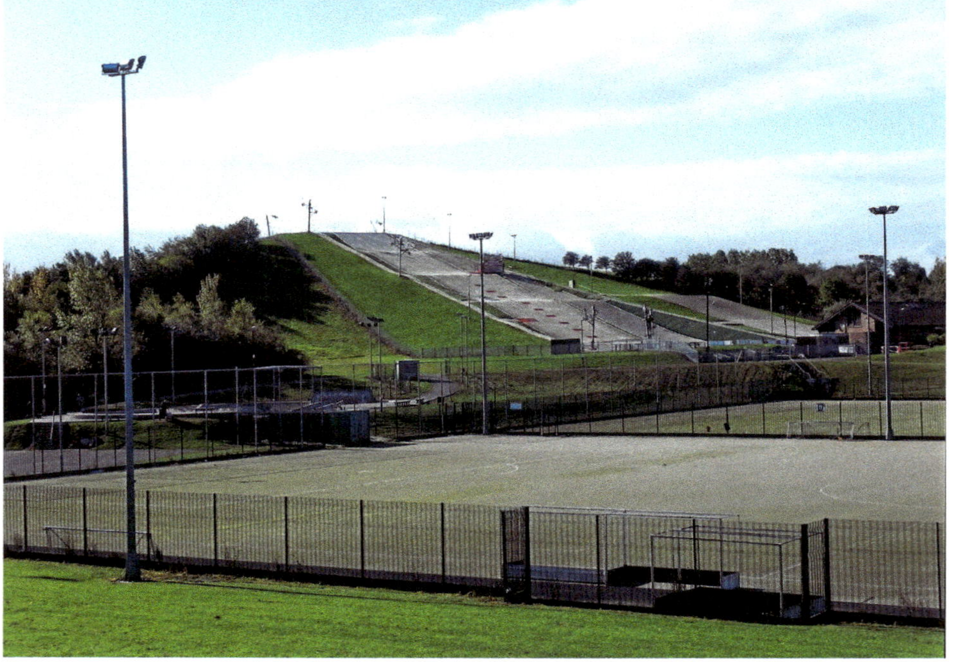

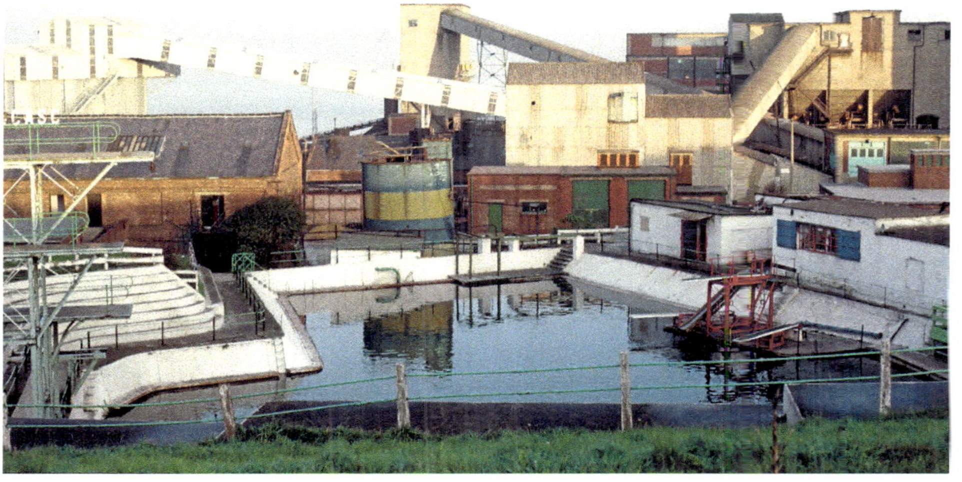

Dawdon Colliery, NZ 436 479

An unusual feature of Dawdon Colliery, which opened in 1907 to exploit undersea coal reserves, was its heated open-air Olympic-standard swimming pool of 1951, with terraced seating for spectators and a bandstand. This was all abandoned when the pit closed in 1991, and the only swimming facility at Dawdon now is the unheated North Sea. The pit site is now marked by what may look like a fairly ordinary array of windsocks, but is actually a piece of public art called 'The Sky Field'. A large new business park has also been created overlooking the former colliery site. Photographs 1986 and 2010.

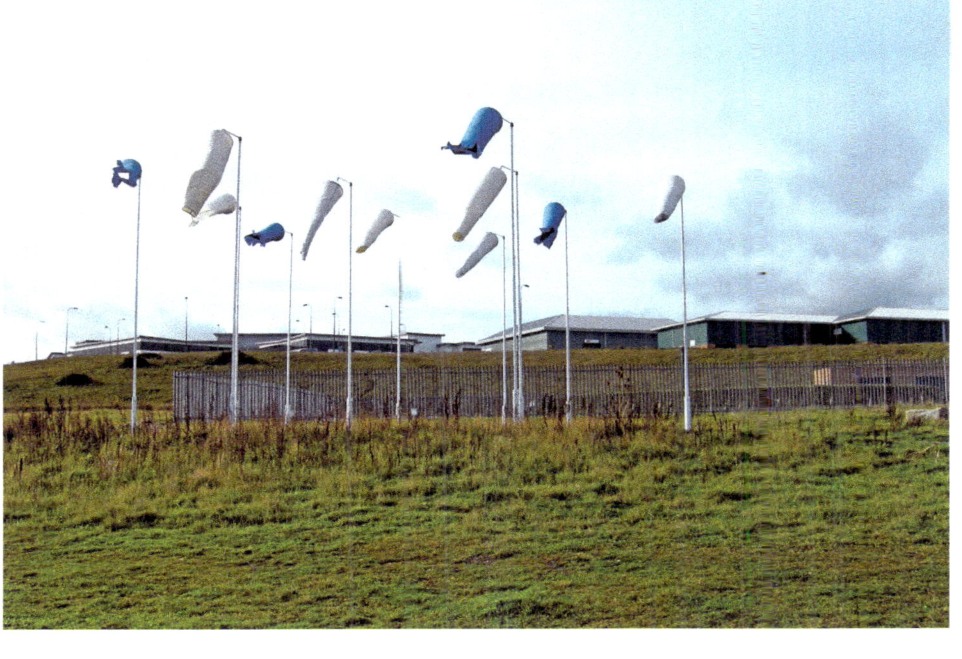

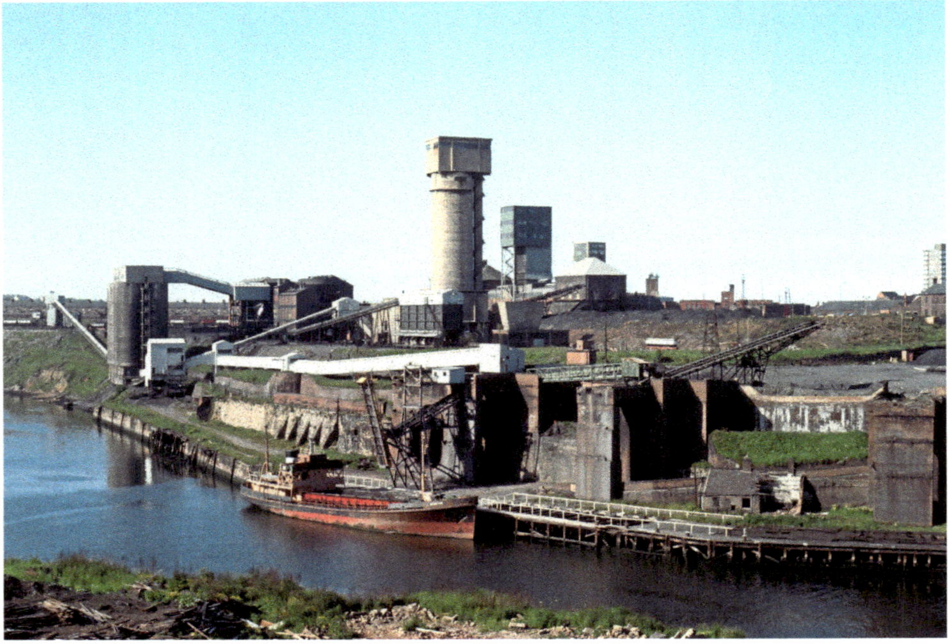

Wearmouth Colliery, Sunderland, NZ 394 578

Sunk between 1826 and 1834, Wearmouth was one of the pioneering deep mines of the North East. A major surface reconstruction of the colliery was carried out in the 1960s, but the pit closed after the 1984/85 miners' strike and the site was completely cleared soon after, only for the Sunderland AFC's 'Stadium of Light' to be constructed there, opening in 1998. Some of the former staith supports remain on the river bank as tangible reminders of former mining activity. Photographs 1986 and 2011.

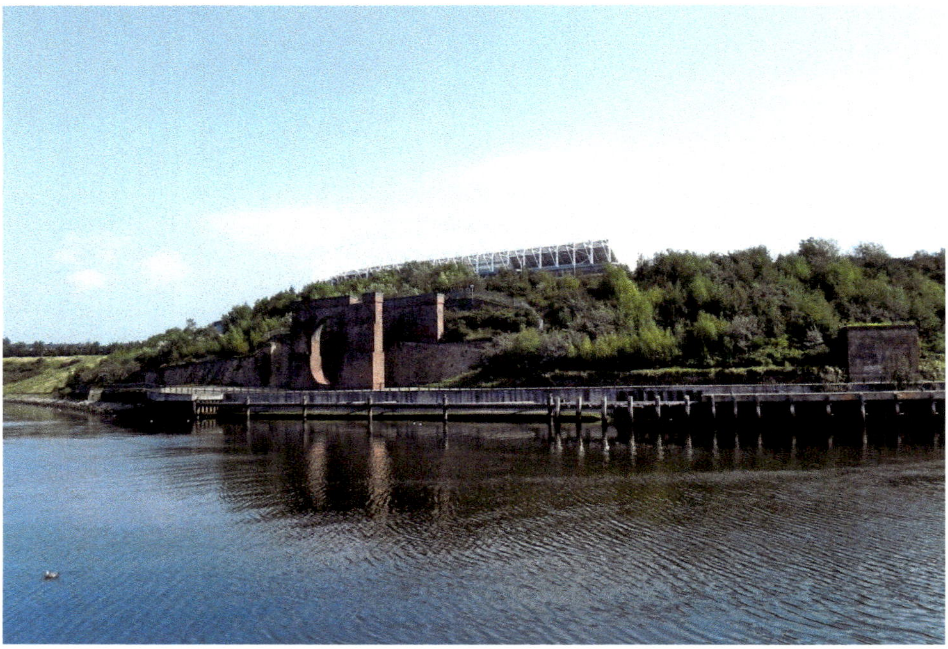

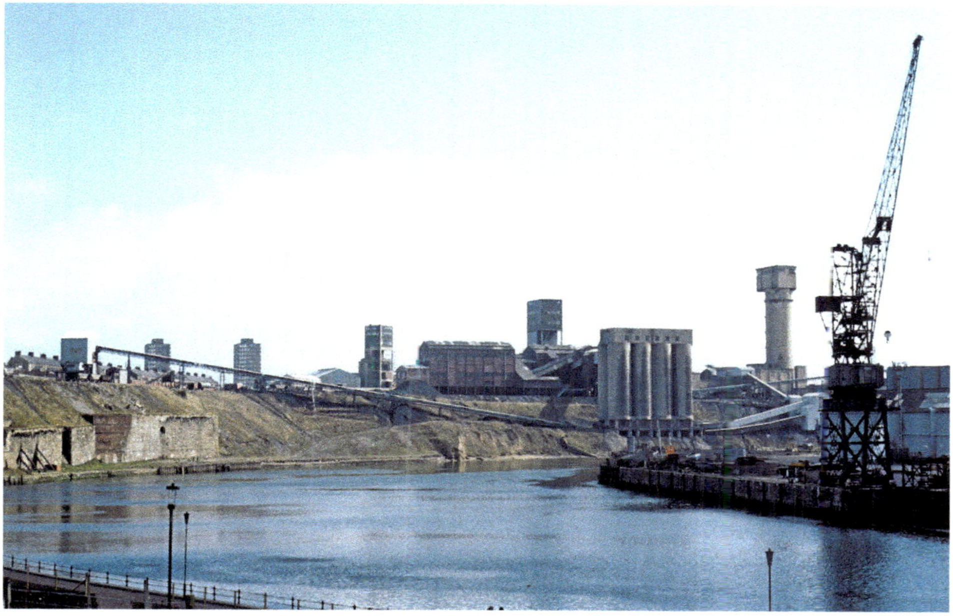

Wearmouth Colliery, Sunderland, NZ 394 578

Another view of Wearmouth Colliery with an enormous bank of disused limekilns beneath it. These kilns carry 1821 and 1872 dated keystones. The colliery faces Laing's shipyard across the river, but neither colliery nor shipyard would remain open much longer in 1973 and both sites had been transformed by 2011. The old limekilns have been restored and the Sunderland Aquatic Centre stands alongside the Stadium of Light. Photographs 1973 and 2011.

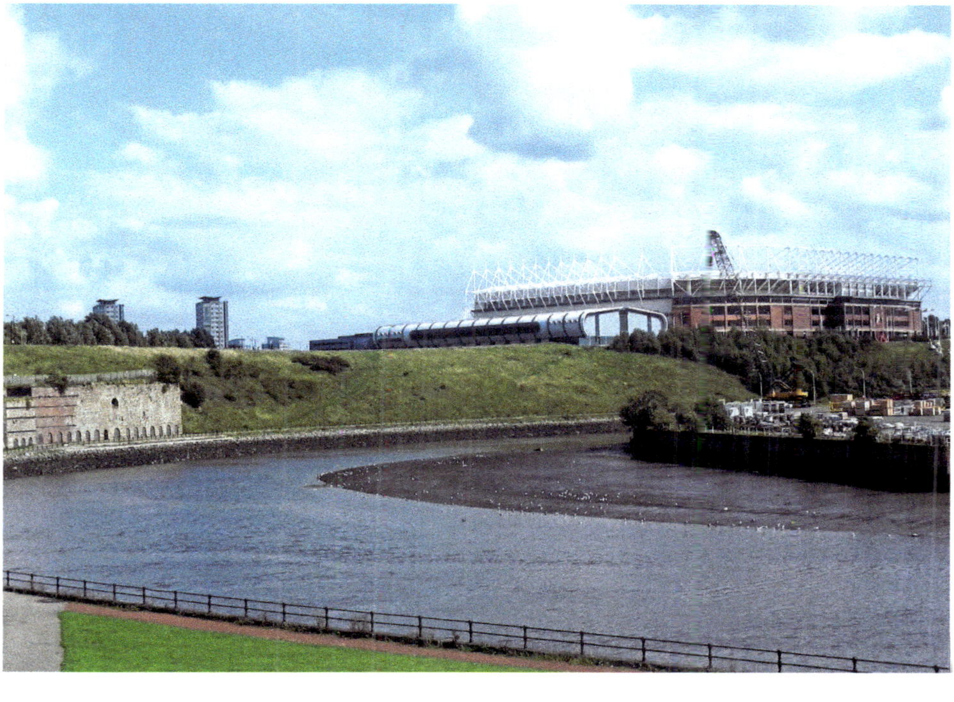

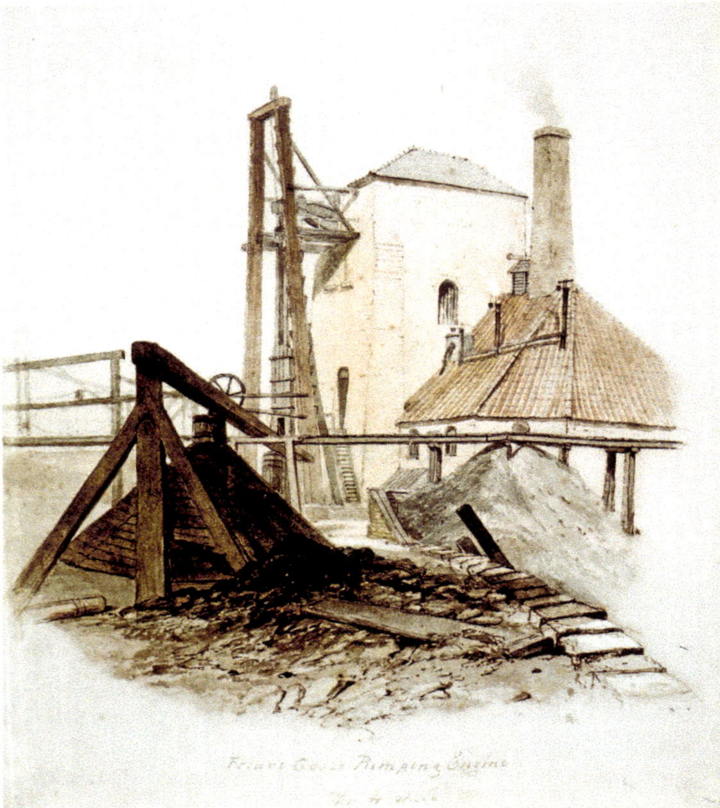

Friars Goose Engine House, Gateshead, NZ 278 632

A problem arose at some Tyneside coal mines due to the synclinal geology of the Tyne coal basin where water drained down the dip to form a vast subterranean reservoir. This led to a succession of powerful pumping engines at Friars Goose to dewater pits on both sides of the Tyne, one of which is depicted in Thomas Hair's watercolour. Probably dating from about 1823, the final remains of the engine house have been preserved. Watercolour 1839/40; photograph 1972.

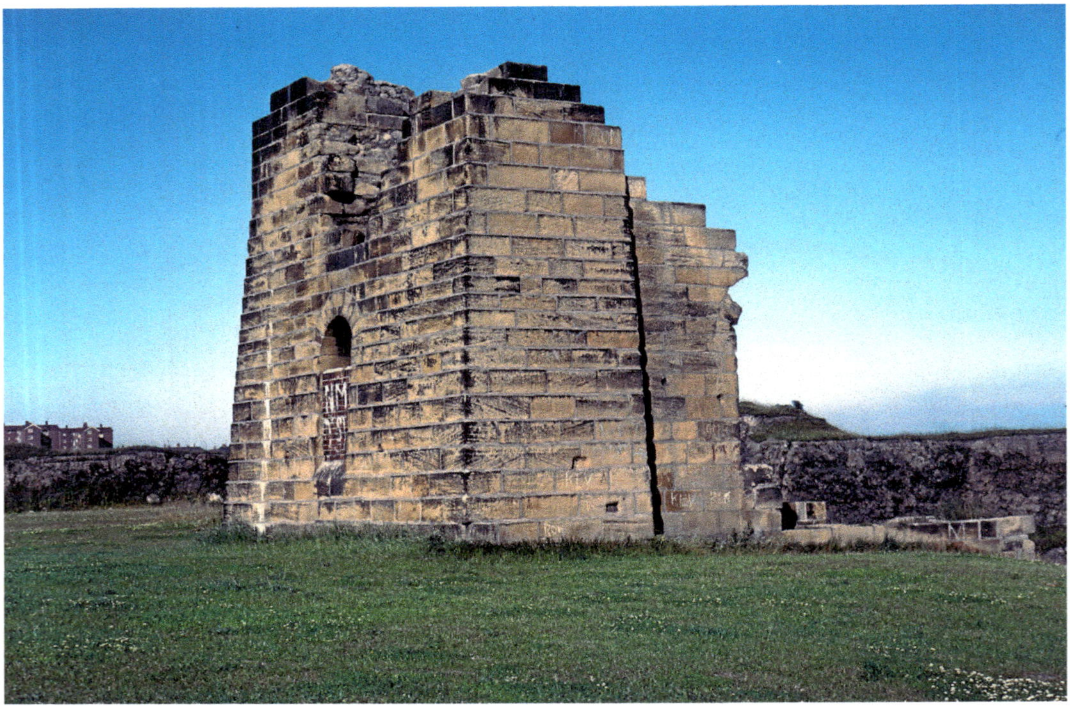

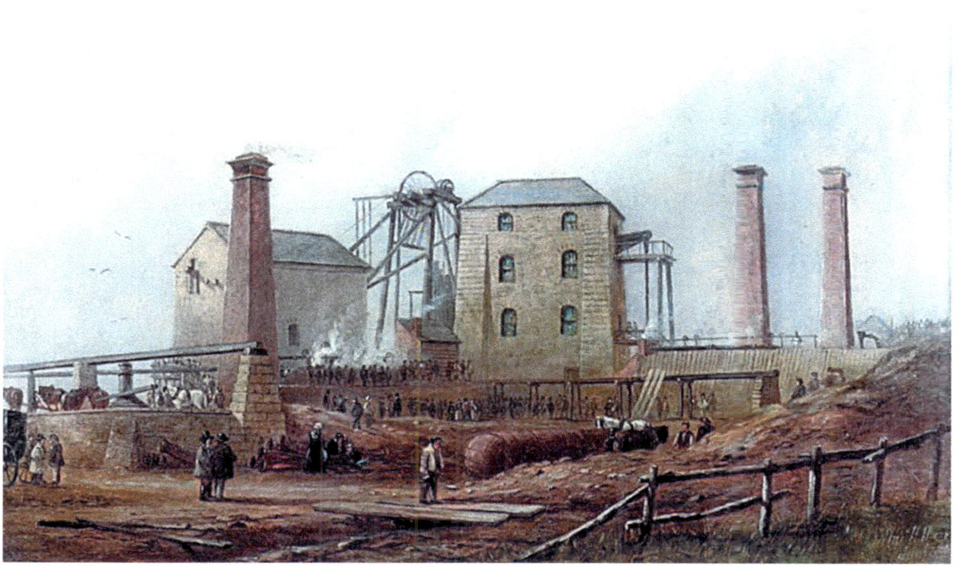

The Hester Pit, New Hartley, NZ 312 768

An accident at the Hartley Hester Pit in 1862 resulted in the deaths of 204 men and boys – the worst single accident in the country up to that time. The pit was subsequently abandoned, and only fragments of the shaft heads remain, as a memorial, behind the houses on the west side of Hester Gardens. A more formal memorial stands in Earsdon churchyard. Painting of the Hester Pit *c.* 1862 (John Clayson, Newcastle Discovery Museum); photograph 2010; 2011 (inset).

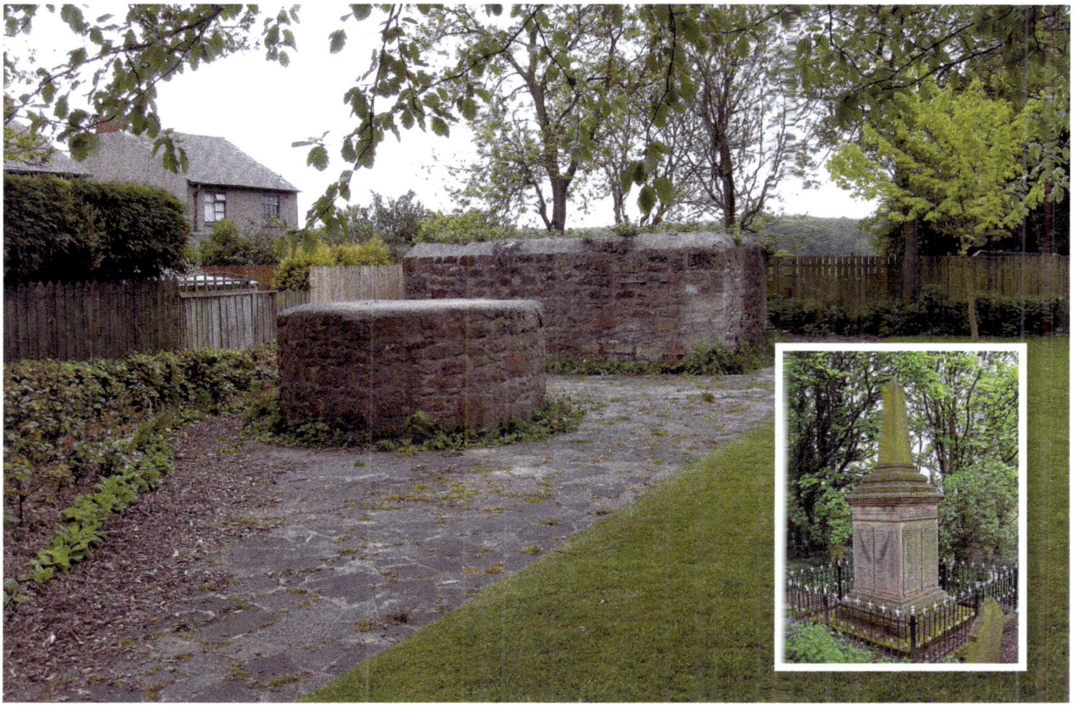

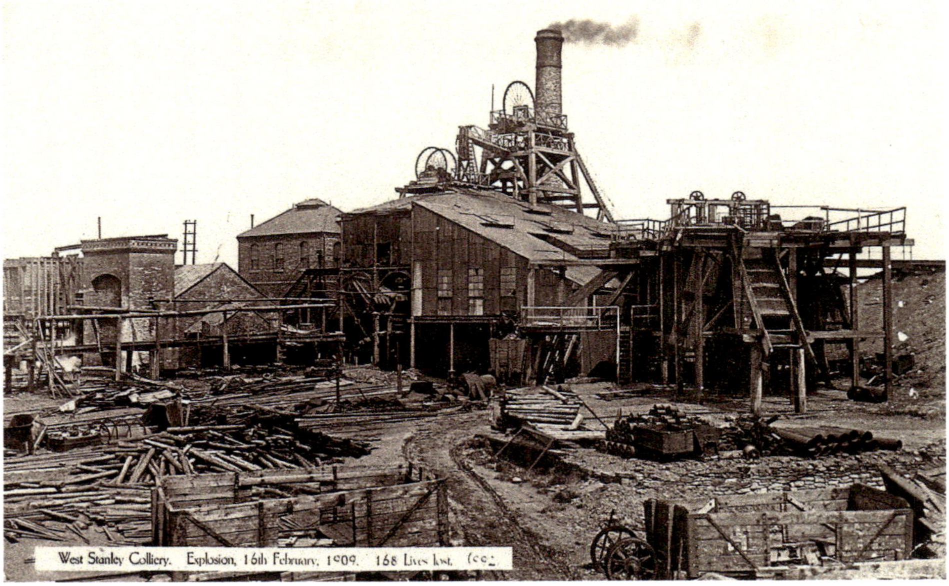

West Stanley Colliery, NZ 200 529

Sunk in 1832, this coal mine was prone, as many were, to explosions. Two men died in 1865, thirteen in 1882, and most catastrophic of all, 168 died in February 1909. The pit was then closed down for a while but was reopened to continue until 1936. The memorial structure on the site of the pit was formally opened by the footballer Kevin Keegan, whose grandfather was one of the few pitmen at West Stanley who survived the disaster. Postcard *c.* 1909; photograph 2011.

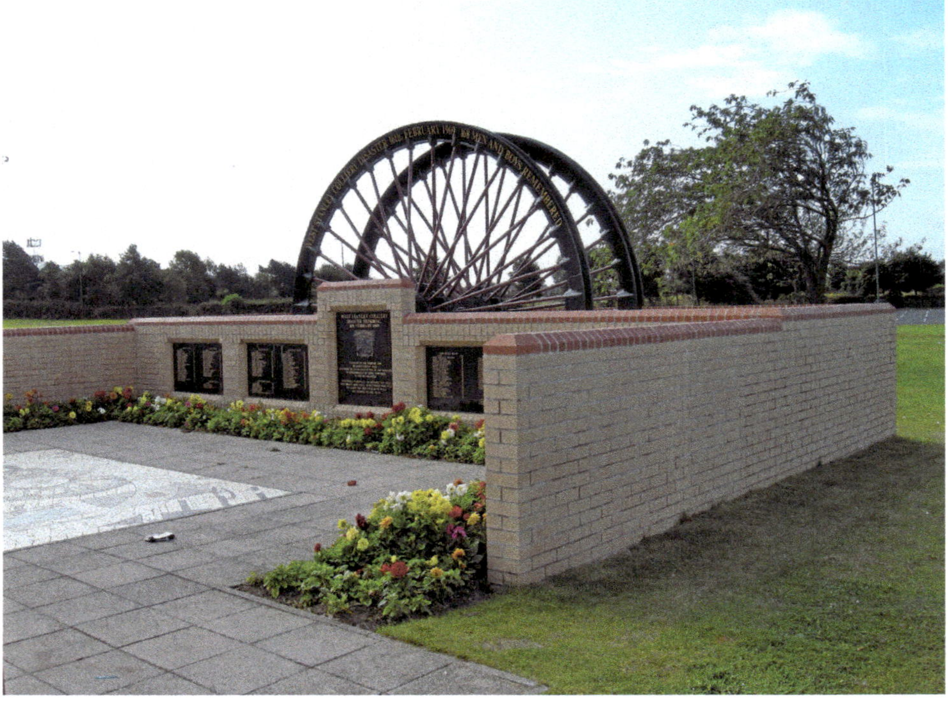

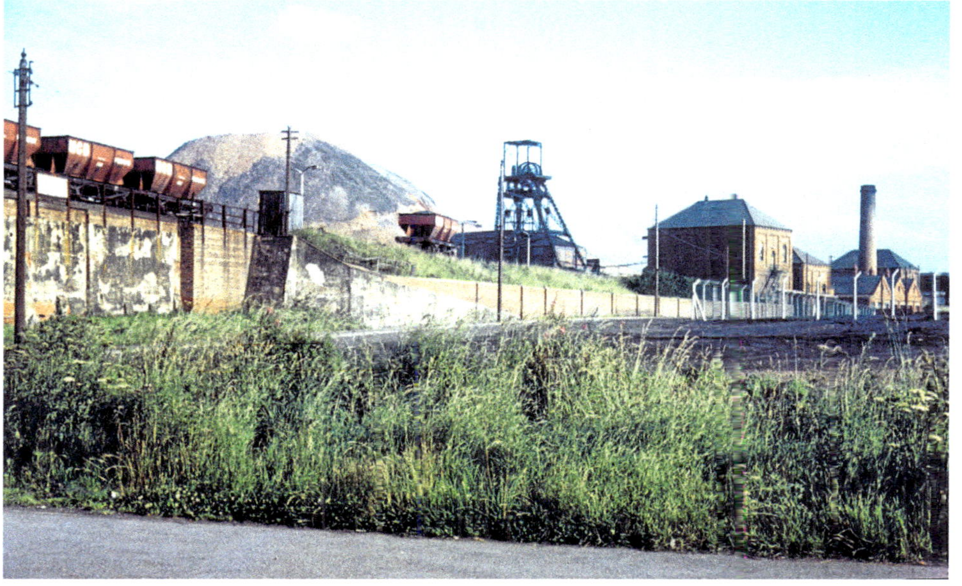

Washington 'F' Pit, NZ 303 575

One of the oldest working pits in the country at the time of its closure in 1968, having first won coals in 1777/8. It had two shafts, each worked by a steam winding engine at its closure, and one of these engines, together with its engine house and headstock, was retained as a heritage feature for Washington New Town, the last obvious vestige of mining in the Washington area. As can be seen, however, the widespread but not universal desire for sanitisation and tree planting has again prevailed. Photographs 1968 and 2010.

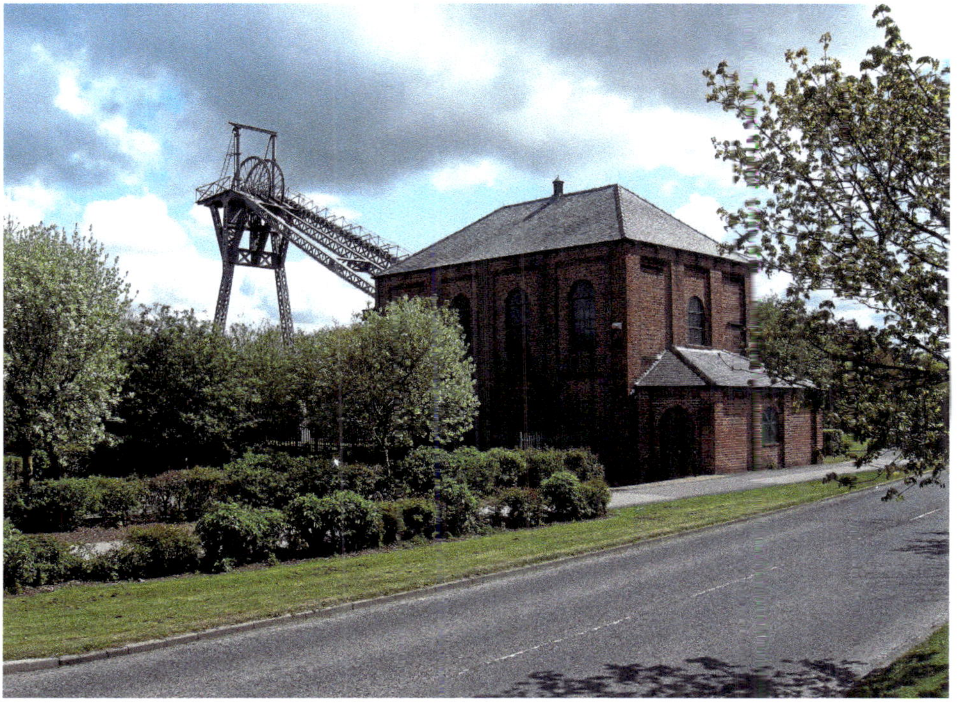

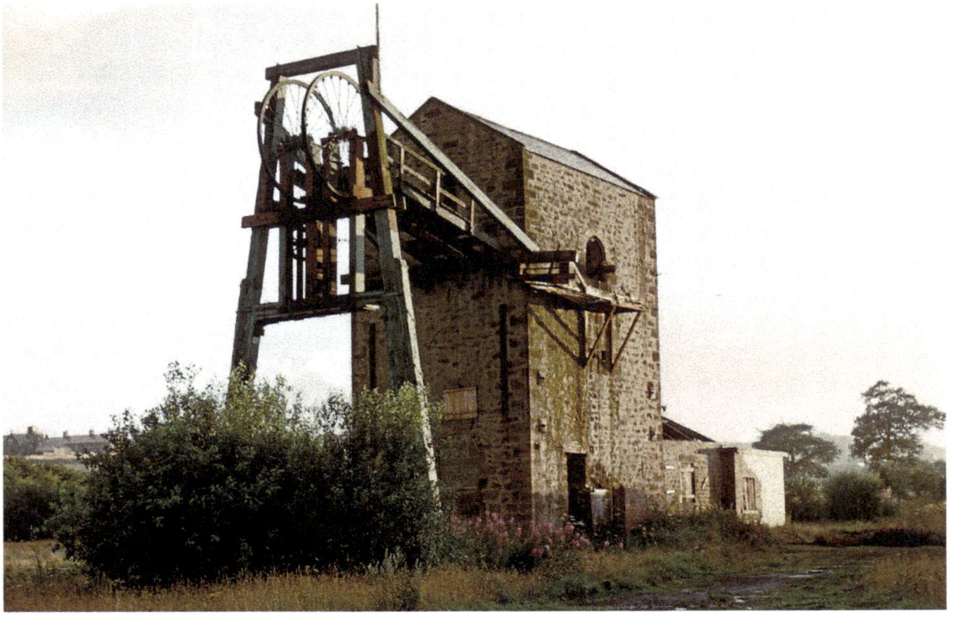

Beamish Second Pit, near Stanley, NZ 221 536 and 219 543

There were numerous coal mines in the Beamish area, some coal seams being so shallow, it was said that you could hear the mooing of cows in the fields above while working underground. The Beamish Second Pit, sometimes known as Chophill, was sunk around 1784. It continued working until 1962, and thereafter the colliery buildings and the small associated village, were generally allowed to decay. The vertical winding engine house and its 1855 Newcastle-built engine were, however, removed and reconstructed at the nearby Beamish Museum.

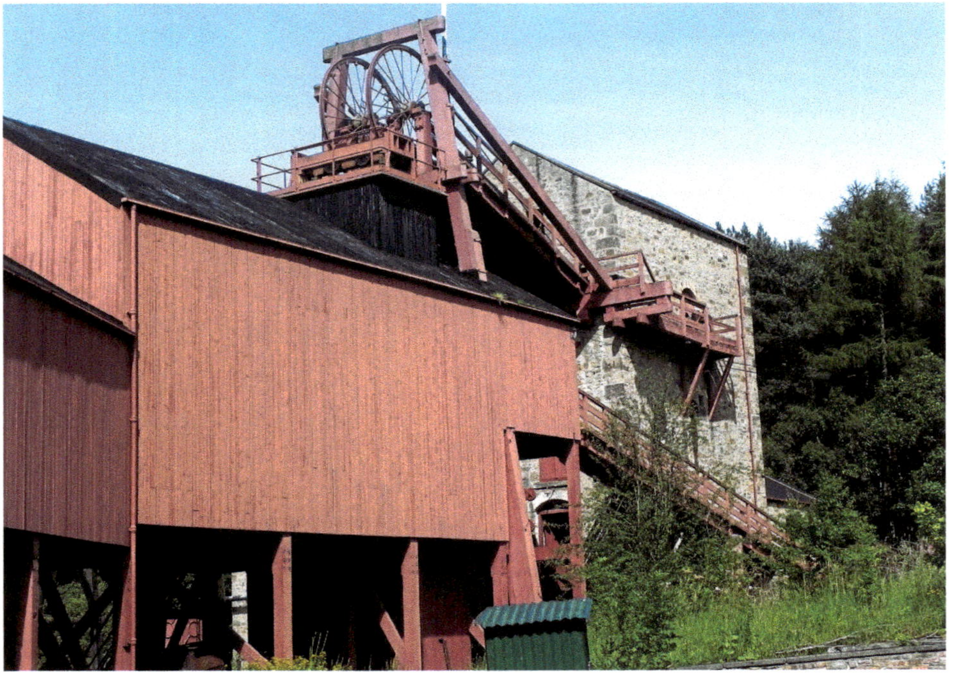

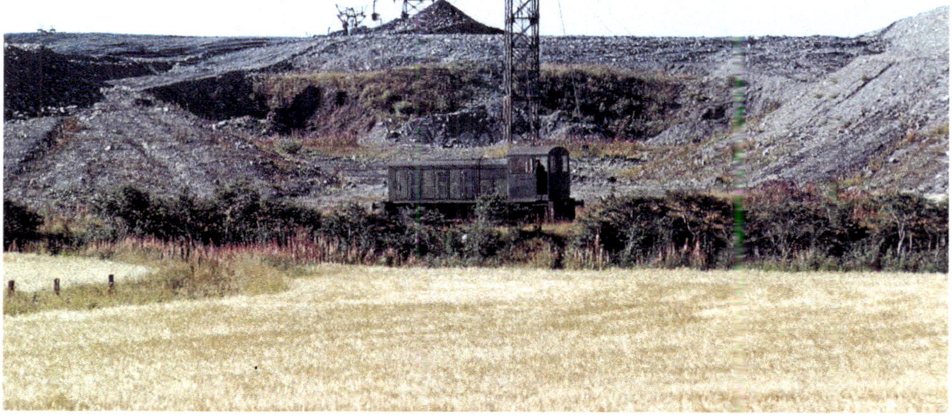

Murton Colliery Aerial Flight, NZ 400 472

Murton Colliery opened in 1838 after a particularly difficult sinking through waterlogged Magnesian Limestone strata. The aerial flight, which probably dated from the 1950s, carried waste from the mine to large spoil heaps about half a mile away. The mine closed in 1991 and the slag heaps were subsequently landscaped, and provided with artworks and footpaths within the curtilage of the Dalton Park Outlet Shopping Centre. Photographs 1972 and 2010.

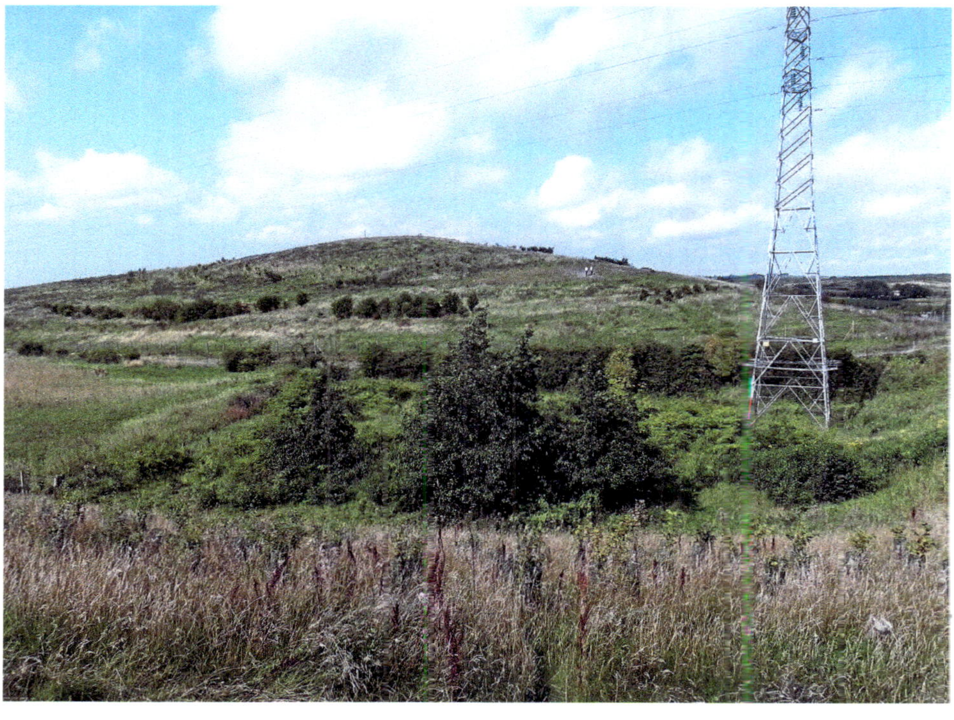

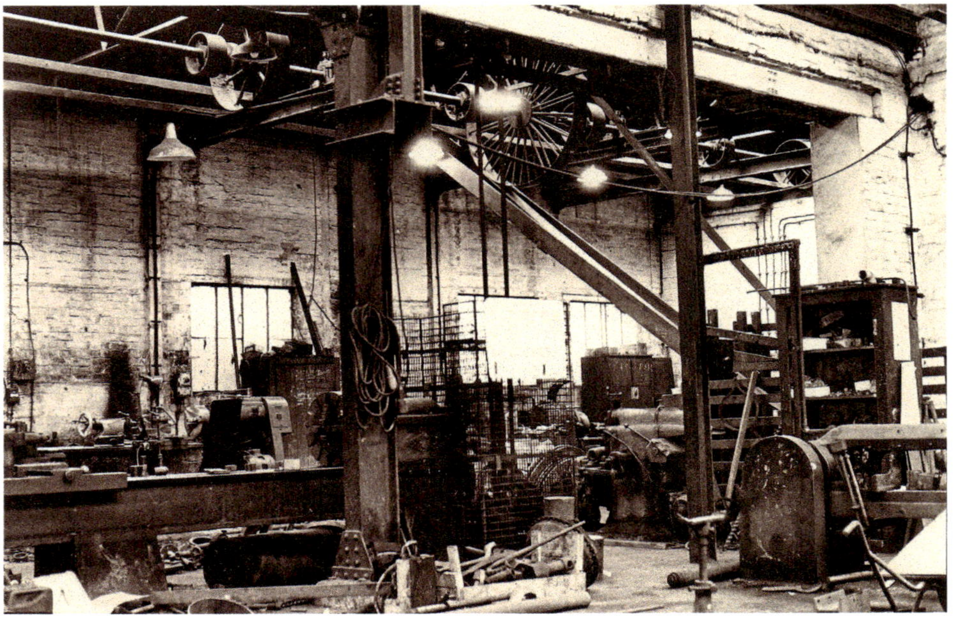

Backworth Eccles Pit Workshops, NZ 306 720

The Eccles Pit opened in 1907, then the deepest pit in the Northumberland Coalfield, and closed in 1980. It had, like most larger collieries, an extensive range of workshops. The site, including the fitting shop shown here, was largely cleared after closure, but some former workshops remain as part of the Backworth Business Park. Thus CW Tents occupies what seems to have once been a paint shop, while a motor repairer, a motor valeting business and a pizza outlet occupy some other former workshop buildings. Photographs 1980 and 2010.

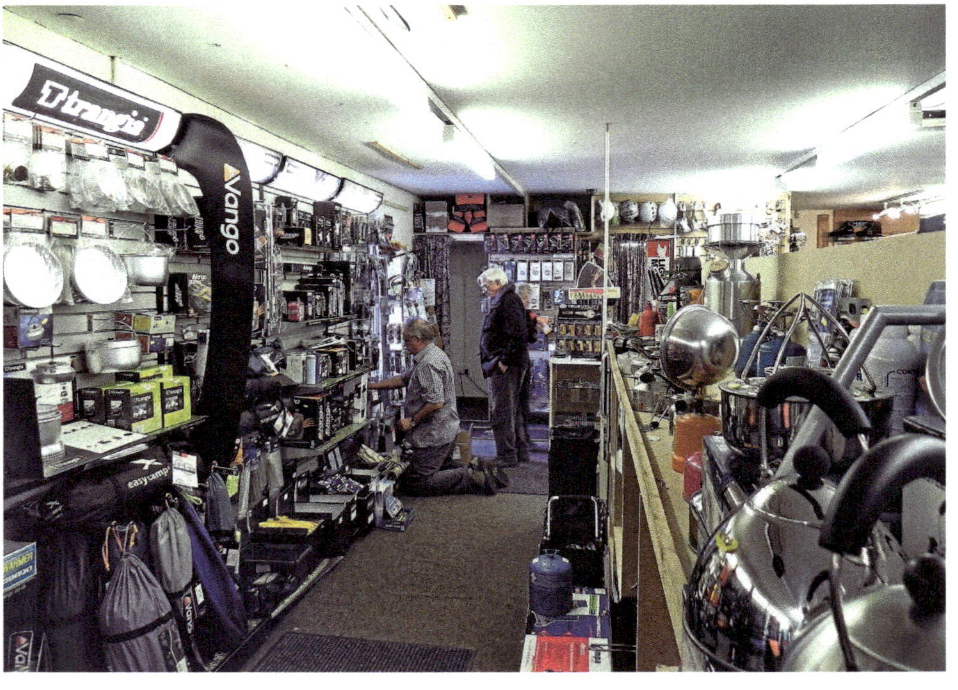

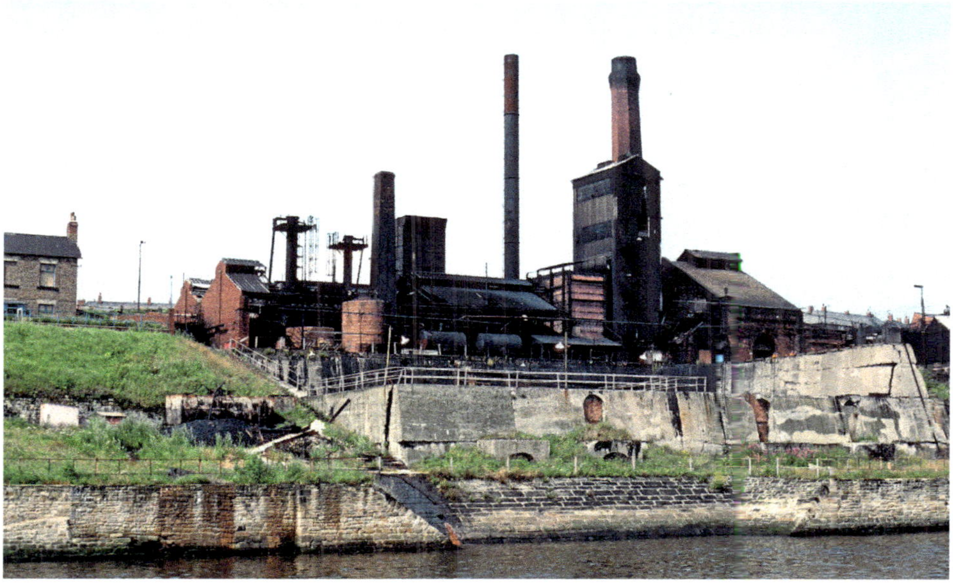

St Anthony's Tar Works, NZ 287 629

A works for the manufacture of tar and its derivatives was established here in the nineteenth century. Later known as 'Thomas Ness', a wholly-owned subsidiary of the Nationl Coal Board (NCB), the works was closed in around 1979 and its site subsequently reclaimed for leisure purposes – cycling, walking etc. Although contaminated earth was removed from the site up to a depth of 25m, tar products continue to seep into the adjacent River Tyne, producing glistening, rainbow-coloured streaks of oil on the river surface. Photographs 1980 and 2011

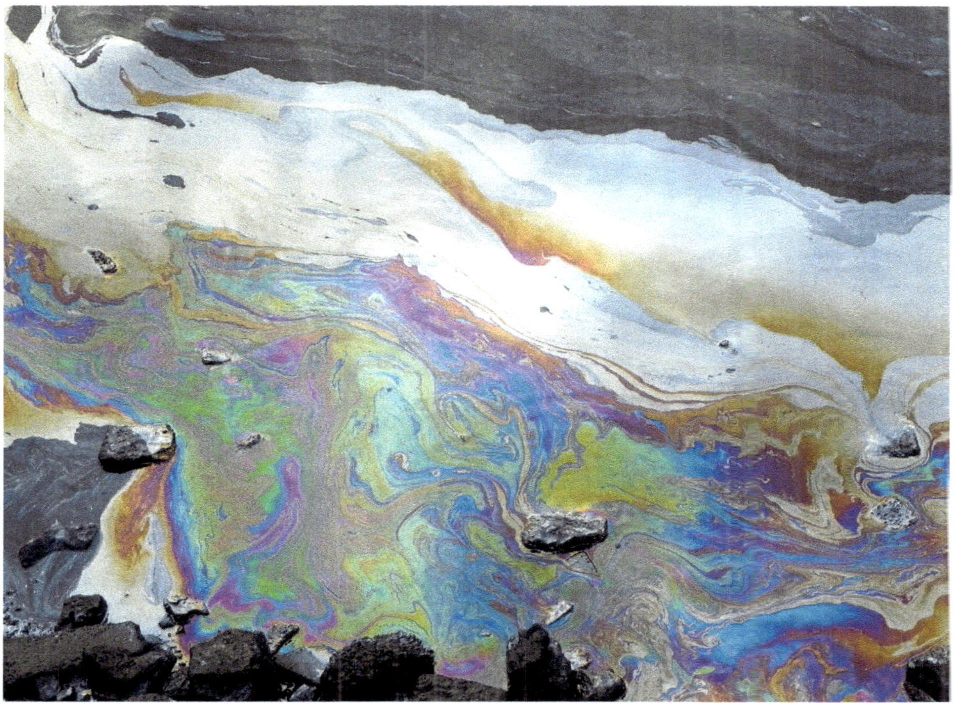

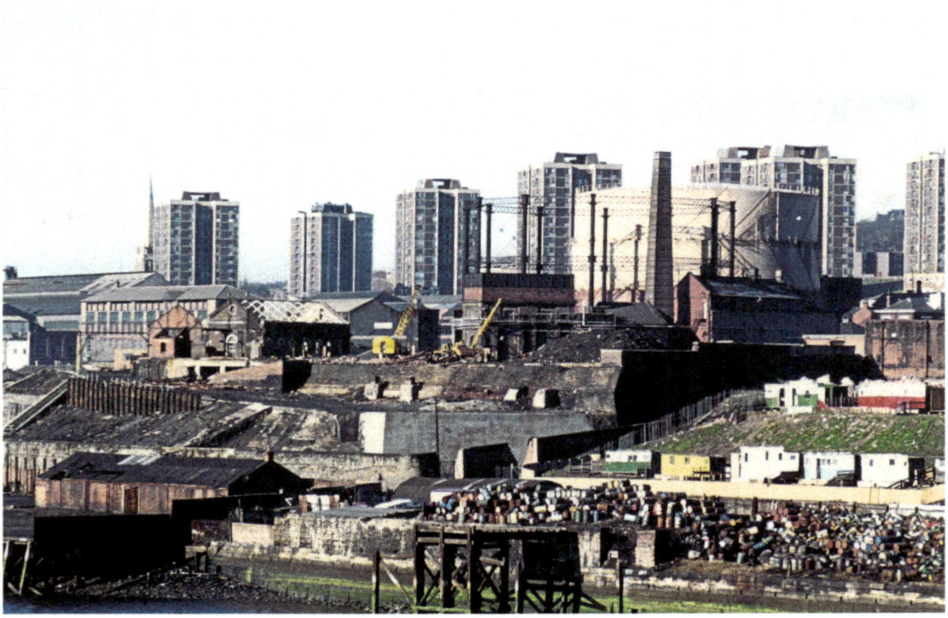

Elswick Gas Works, Newcastle, NZ 240 630

The early Tyneside gasworks were all built on constricted urban sites, but the demand for gas was growing faster than anyone had foreseen by the mid-nineteenth century, and much larger sites were required. One such was at Elswick where a large new works opened in 1859/60. The national switch to natural gas in the period 1967–1977 saw the writing-off of all UK gas manufacturing plants but, as can be seen, a gasholder still remains. Photographs 1976 and 2009.

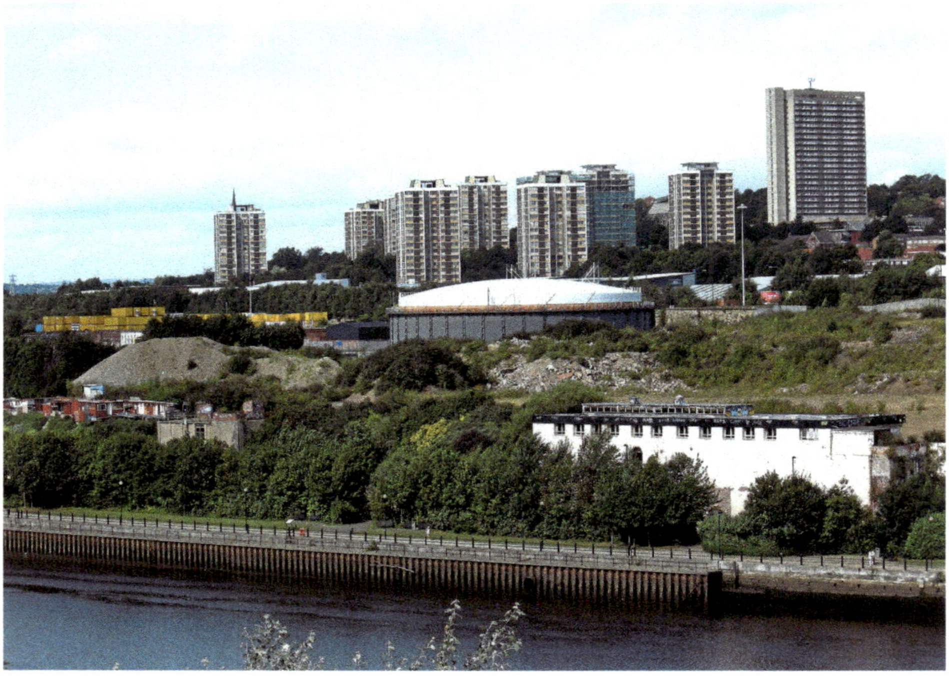

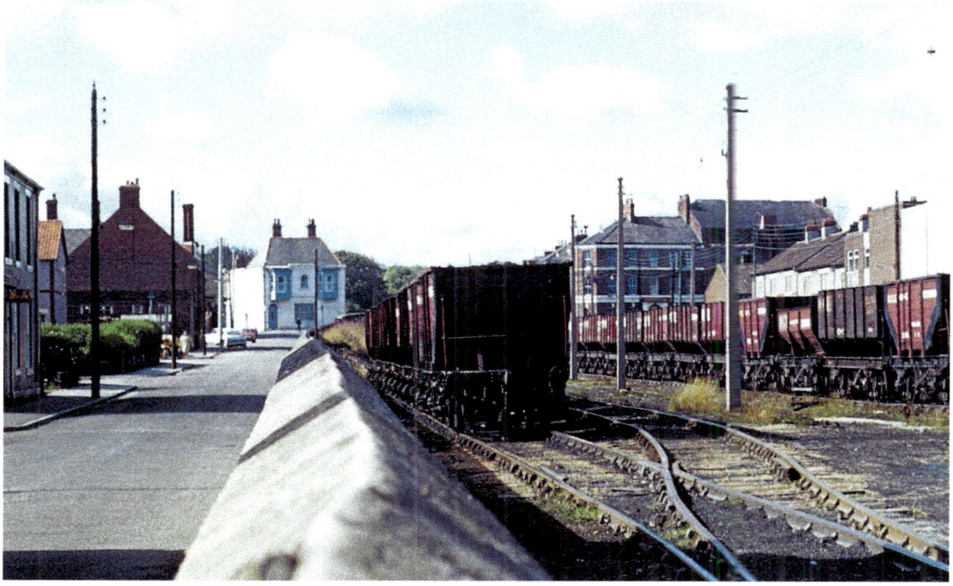

Rainton & Seaham Railway, Seaham Harbour, NZ 430 494

This was the first railway to the new harbour at Seaham, and it was originally entirely rope-worked, hence the unusual road sign. It opened to Seaham, where the town was built around it, in 1831, to carry coals for shipment from the harbour, which was just a few hundred yards behind the camera position. Seemingly the wall to the left of the line was built in 1870 to prevent accidents to people wandering onto the lines. This section of the line closed in 1984/85, and it was replaced by a walkway, green spaces and car parks. Photographs 1972, 1984 (inset) and 2009.

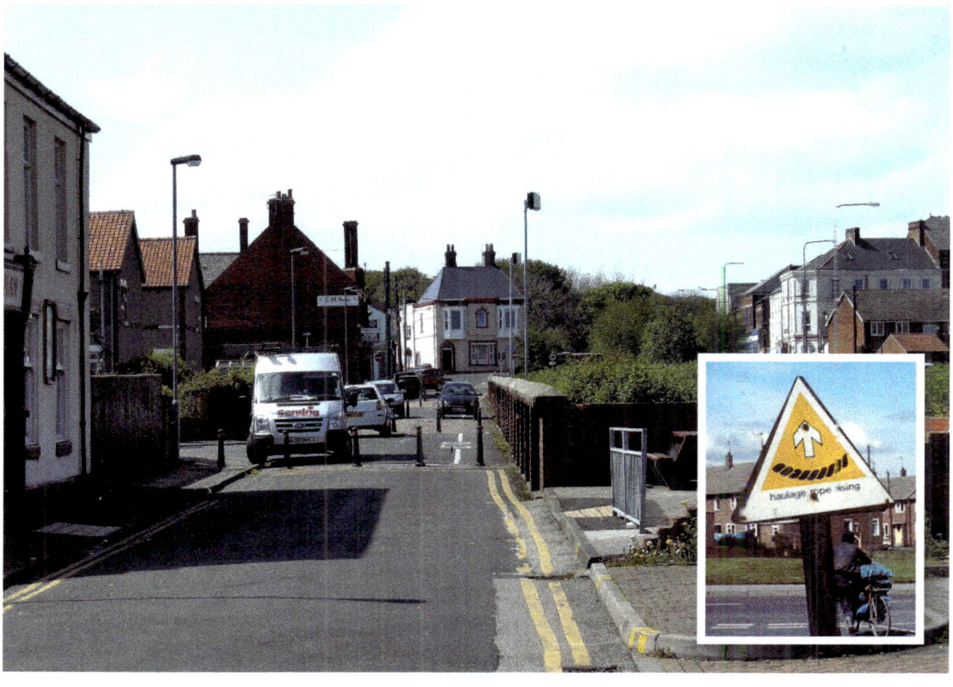

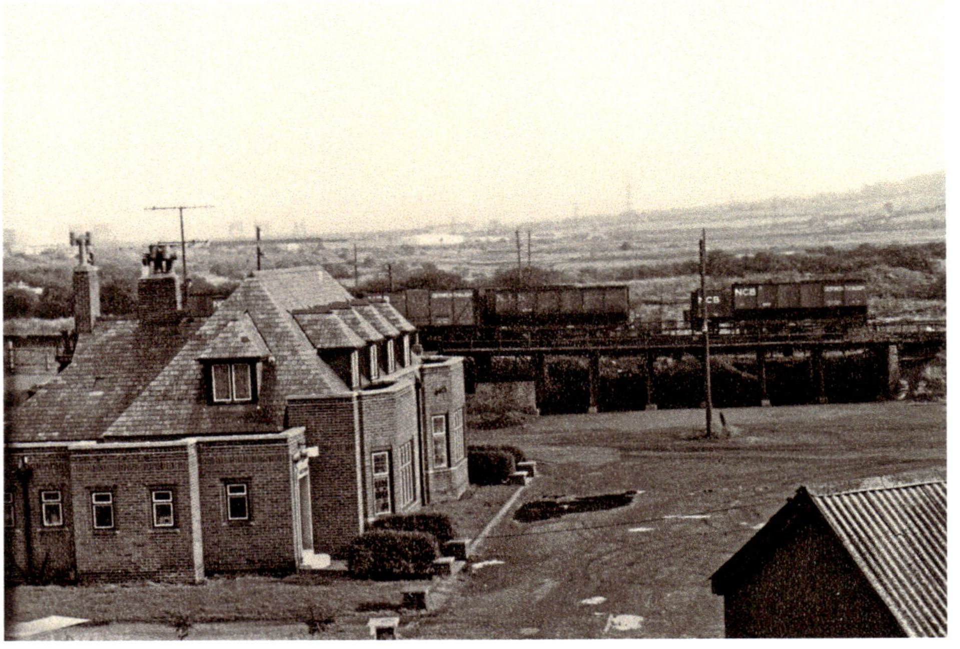

The Skiff Inn, Derwenthaugh, NZ 203 633

The rather attractive inn, a 1938 rebuild of an earlier version of the same name that had once been in the ownership of Harry Clasper, the notable Tyne oarsman, stood marooned amid industrial decay in 1968. Behind it the mineral line to Derwenthaugh staith was still functioning, and would do so for a few more years. But the entire area has since been transformed, especially by the creation of the Gateshead Metro Centre, said to be the largest shopping centre in Europe. A Holiday Inn now stands behind the Skiff Inn, while offices are to its right. Photographs 1968 (Mike Longbottom) and 2011.

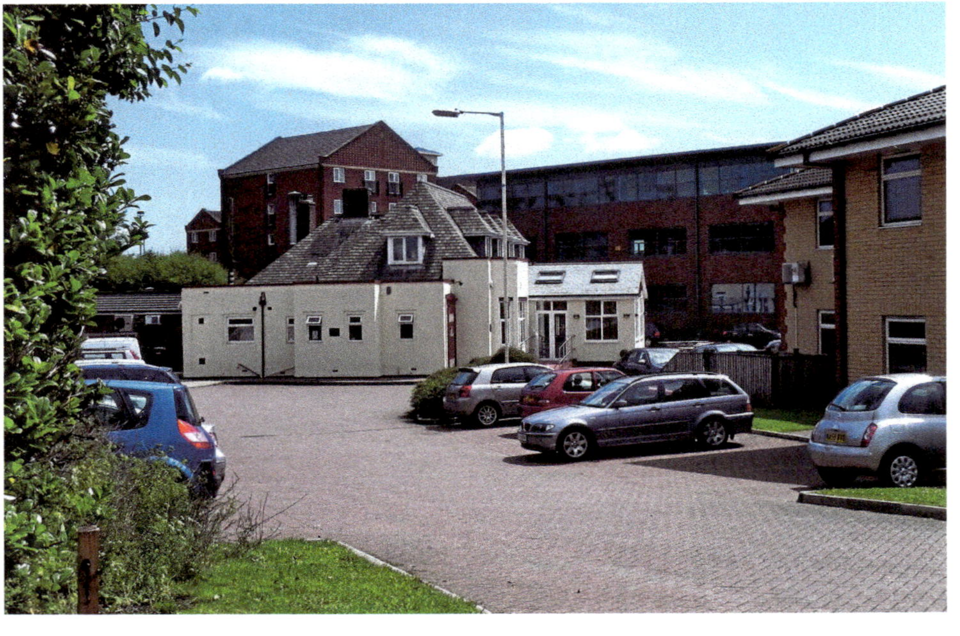

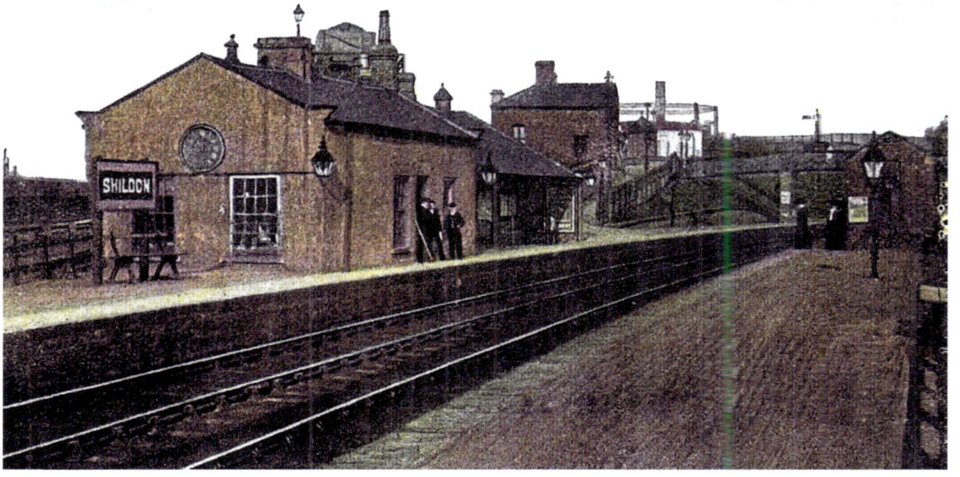

Shildon Railway Station, NZ 236 256

The town of Shildon, as we see it today, owes its existence to the Stockton & Darlington Railway, for which Shildon marked the original limit of locomotive working and the location of the company's first locomotive-building works. The station offices shown in the postcard probably mainly date from the 1840s, and although they were largely extant in the 1970s, the station now just has simple bus shelters. Postcard *c.* 1905; photograph 2009.

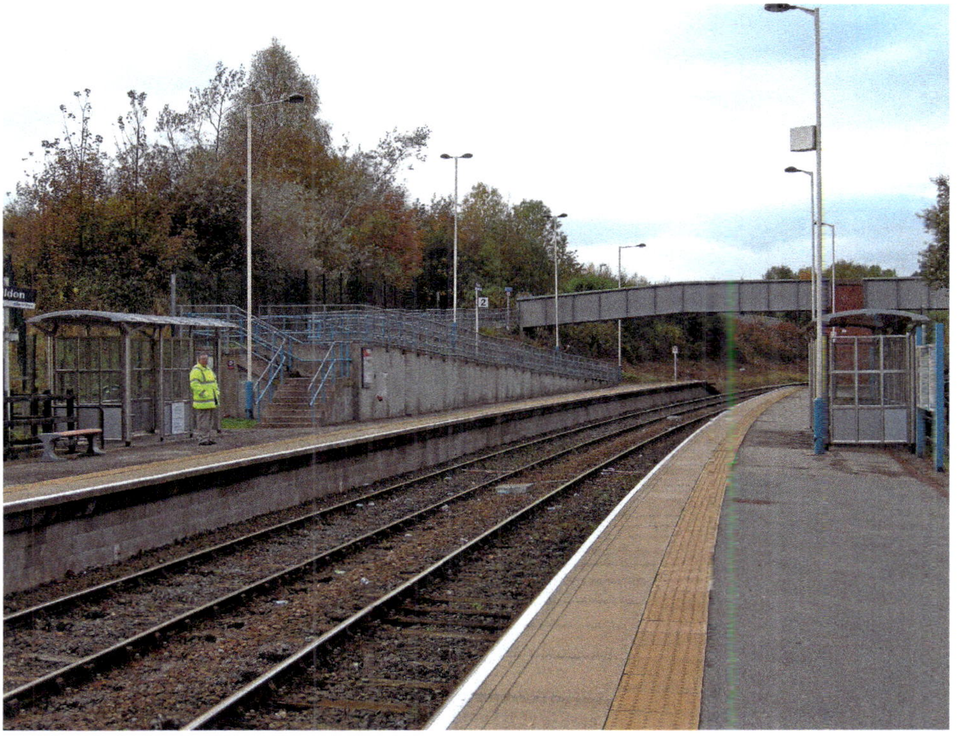

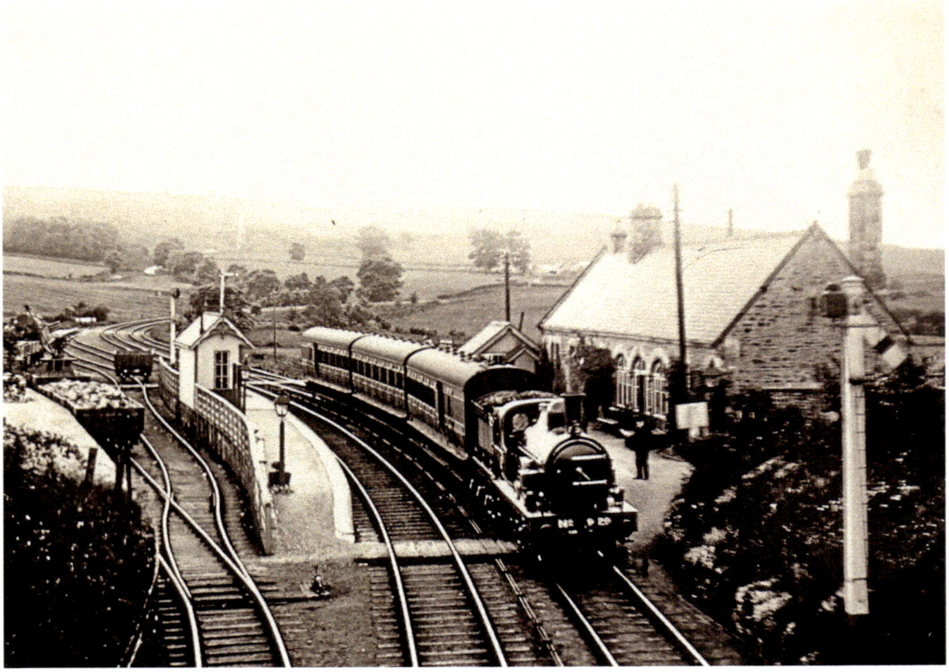

Cold Rowley Railway Station, near Castleside, NZ 087 478
This station was opened by the Stockton & Darlington Railway in 1845. Originally called Cold Rowley its name was wisely shortened to Rowley in 1868. The station closed to passengers in 1939 and to goods in 1966, and although it subsequently suffered general decay by neglect, sufficient of its main structure survived into the early 1970s to make its rescue feasible. Postcard *c.* 1925; photograph 1969.

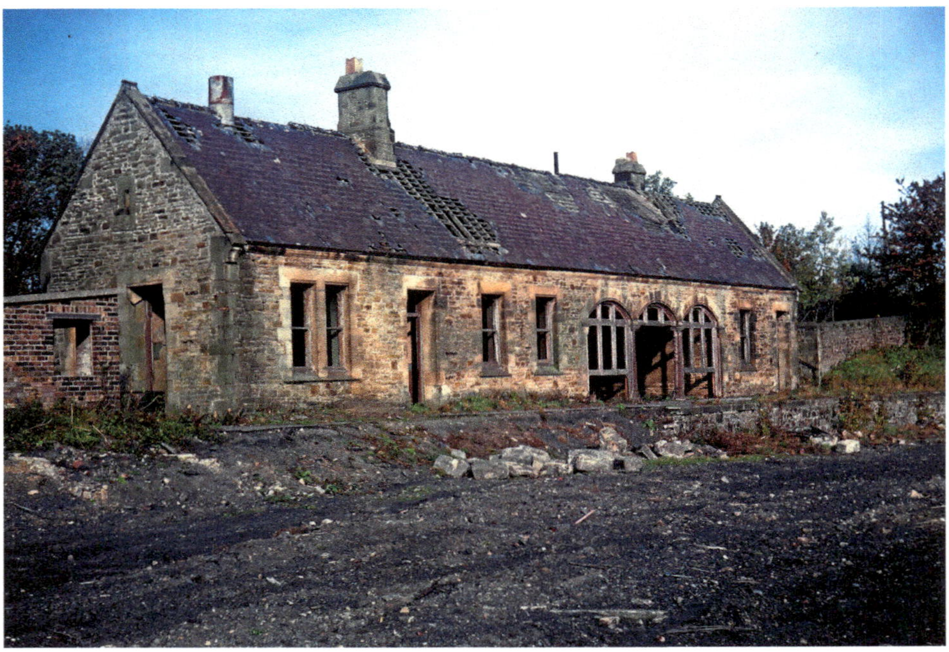

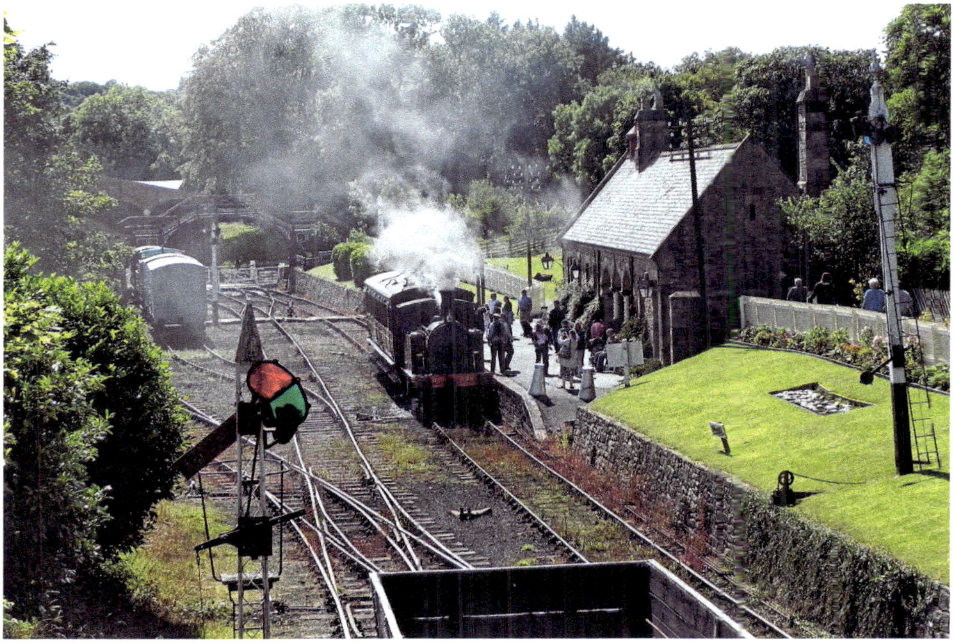

Cold Rowley Railway Station at Beamish, NZ 217 549

The main station building at Rowley was dismantled and re-erected at the Beamish Open Air Museum, being formally opened there by the poet, writer and broadcaster Sir John Betjeman in 1976, where it forms part of a comprehensive if eclectic North Eastern Railway display. Photographs 2011.

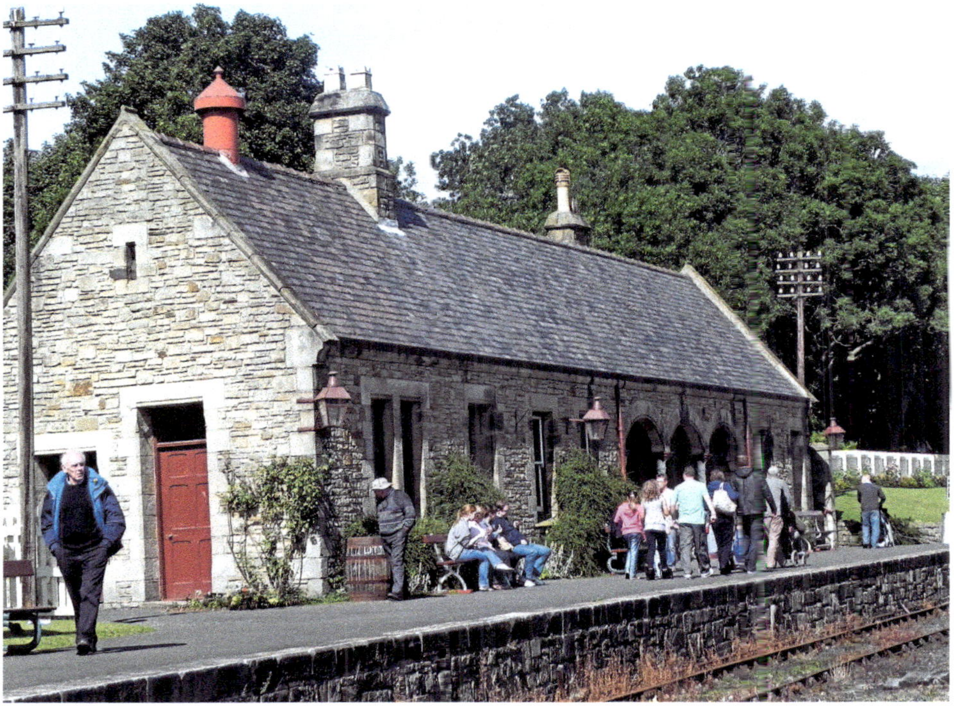

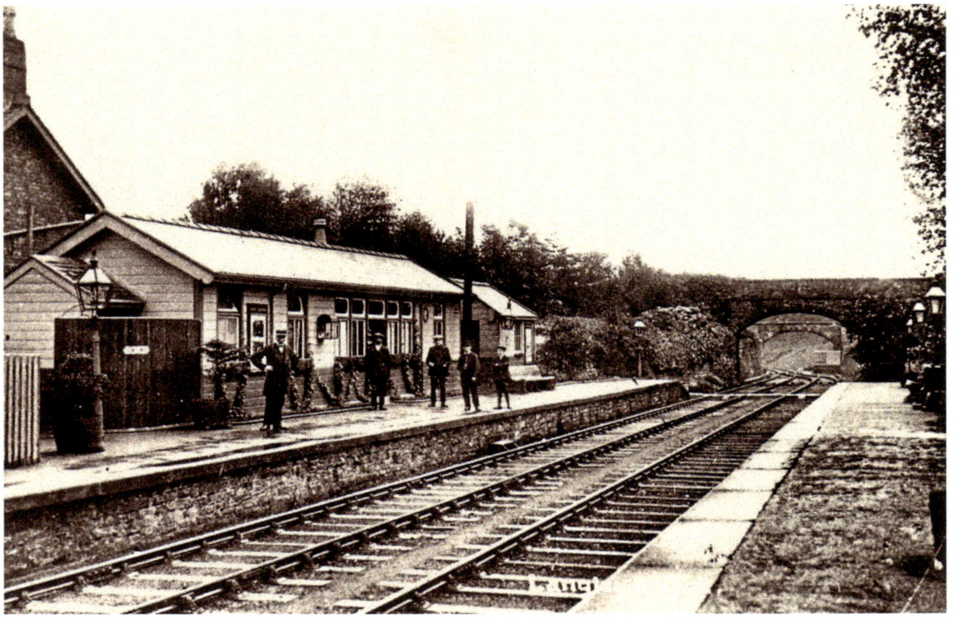

Langley Railway Station, near Hexham, NY 829 612

The Hexham & Allendale Railway opened in 1868/69, only 13½ miles long, and with few intermediate stations, whose platform offices were very simple and mainly wood-built. The line was very attractive scenically, but much less so financially. Yet it was a long time dying, finally closing in 1950. From about 2004, the Langley station platform buildings have functioned as the Garden Room, where plants and coffees are sold, and from which there are pleasant walks. Postcard *c.* 1905; photograph 2010.

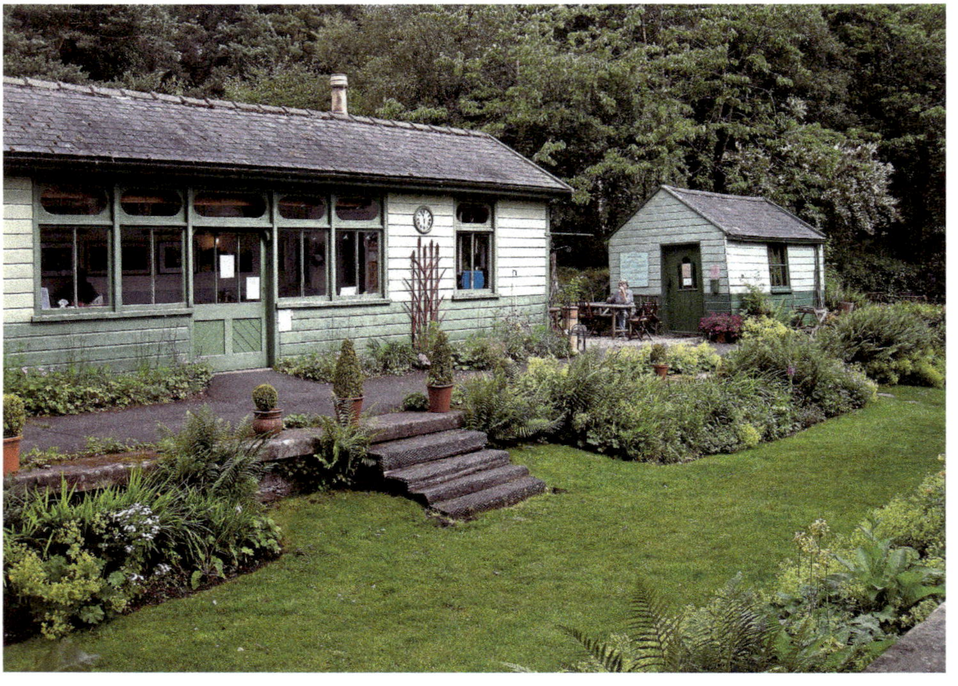

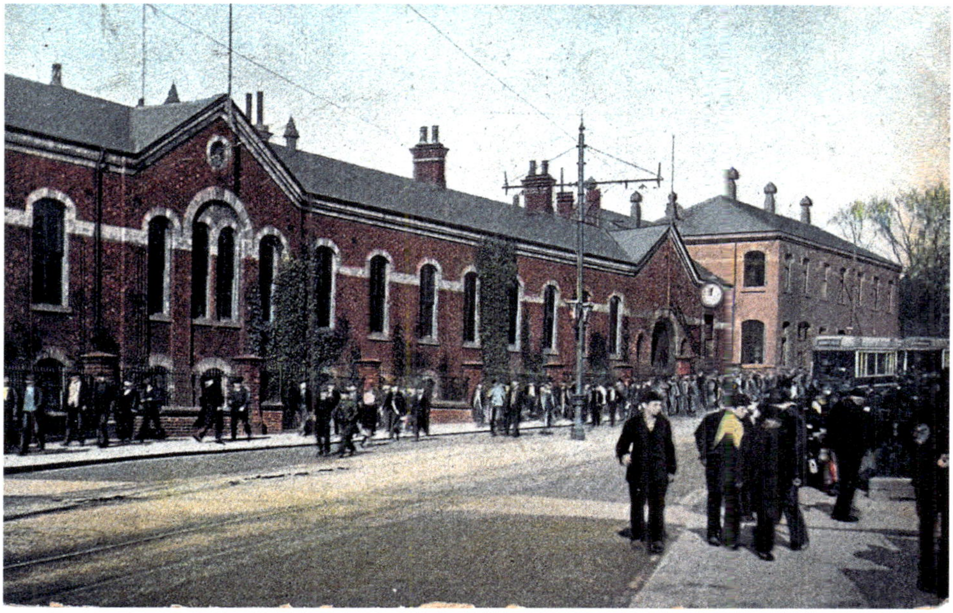

Darlington North Road Locomotive Works, NZ 289 162

The North Road Works of 1863,was a locomotive building works for the Stockton & Darlington Railway and subsequently for the North Eastern Railway. At its peak, the works built some fifty locomotives and performed classified repairs to some 700 locos each year, employing a workforce of about 3,500. The works was closed down in 1966 and a supermarket and bowling rink built on the site. Note that the works' clock was rescued, enhancing an otherwise architecturally bland Morrisons of 1980. Postcard *c.* 1907; photograph 2011.

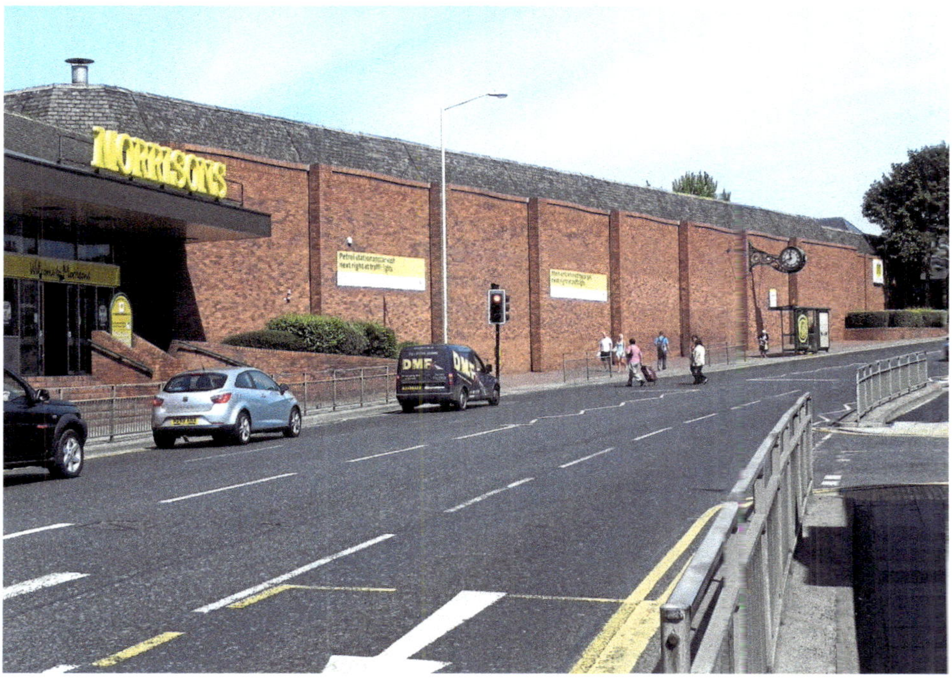

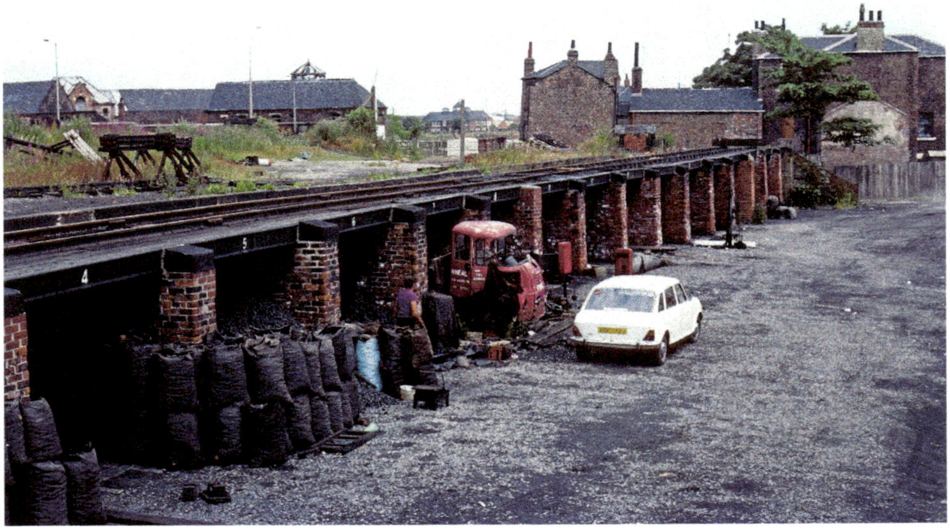

Stockton Coal Depot, NZ 446 183

Most of the larger railway stations in the North East operated coal depots, and very often these were within the patronage of the stationmaster. Stockton's coal depot was adjacent to the original terminus of the 1825 Stockton & Darlington Railway, and the rears of some of the terminal buildings appear in the photographs. The line passed from here to the Stockton Corporation Quay, the last train doing so in 1967. No doubt a use will soon be found for the land once occupied by the depot. Photographs 1979 and 2011.

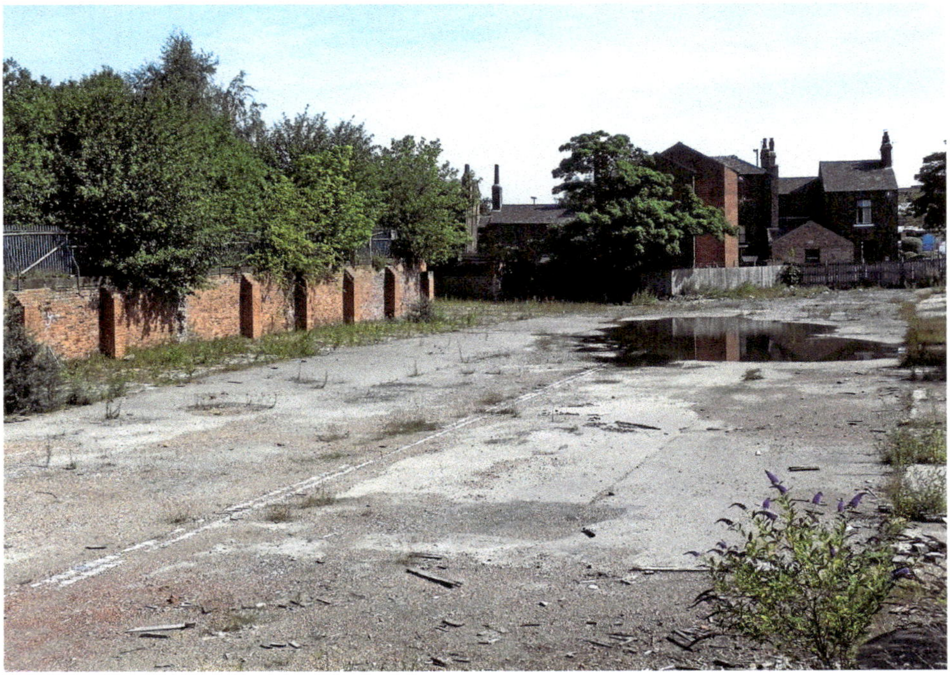

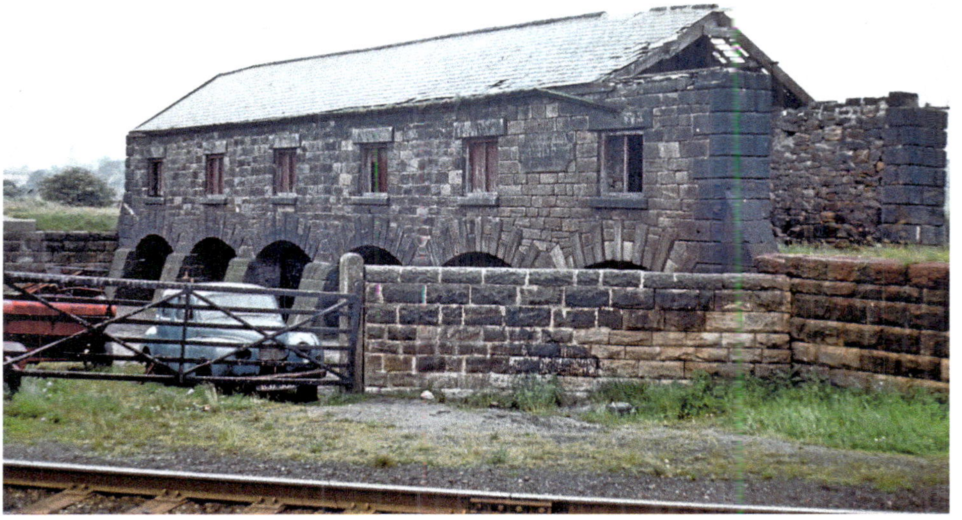

West Boldon Coal & Lime Depot, NZ 343 609 and 217 549

Built by the Stanhope & Tyne Railroad Company for the land sale of coal and lime, this depot was only a small part of a very ambitious undertaking designed to carry limestone from Weardale and coal from north west Durham to the Tyne at South Shields for export. The railway was completely closed in 1985, but the depot had been dismantled around 1972 and was subsequently substantially rebuilt at the Beamish Open Air Museum. Photographs 1971 and 2011.

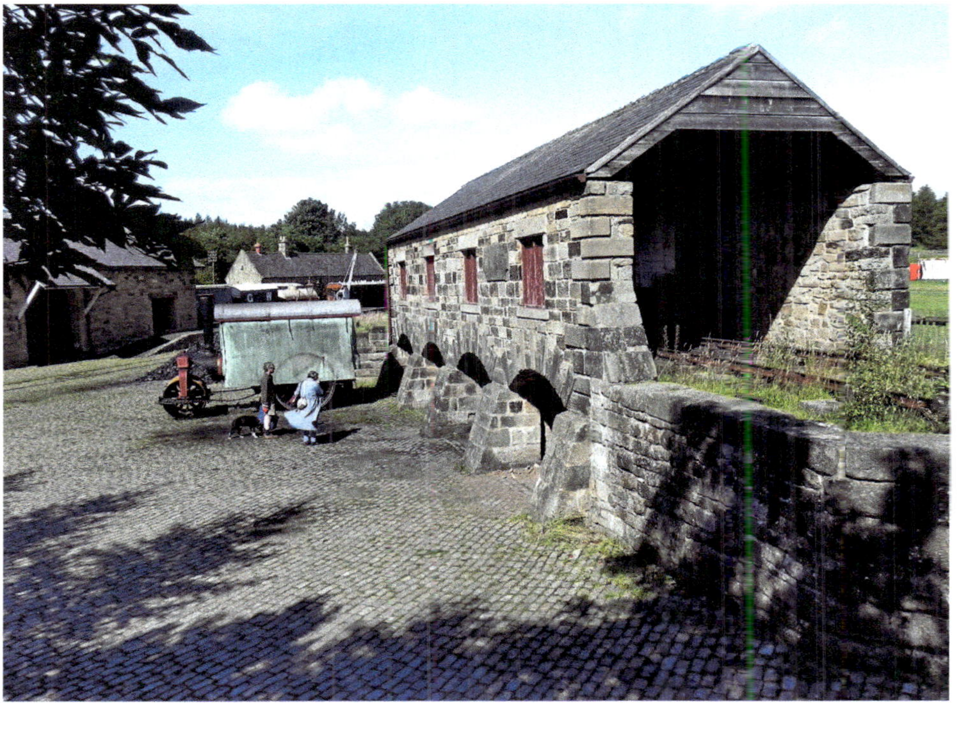

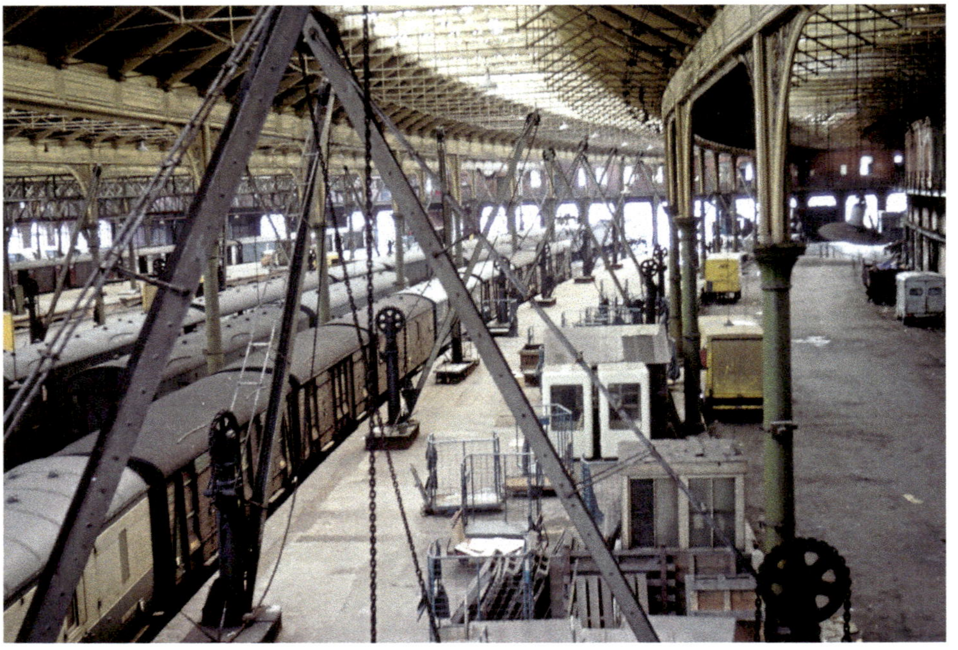

Forth Goods Shed, Newcastle, NZ 243 635

The goods shed at the Forth in Newcastle was completed in stages between 1871 and 1874, and extended in 1891–93. Still a busy centre of local freight distribution in 1971, its tracks full of goods wagons and its platforms lined with hydraulic cranes. It was demolished 1972/3 and its site is now merely a private car park, but the curves of the former platforms are clearly discernible. Photographs 1971 and 2011.

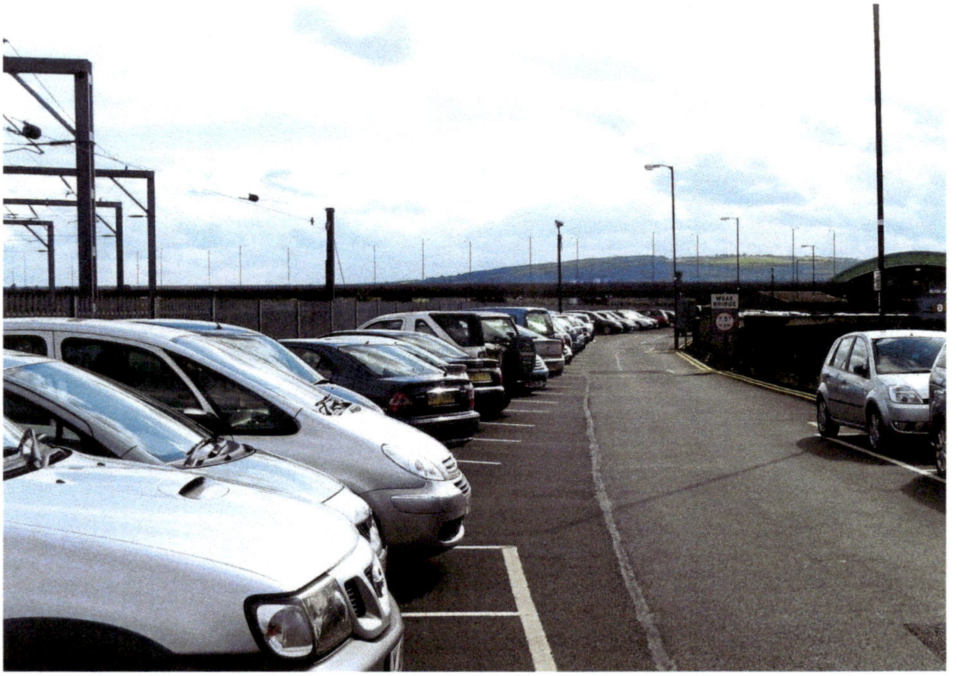

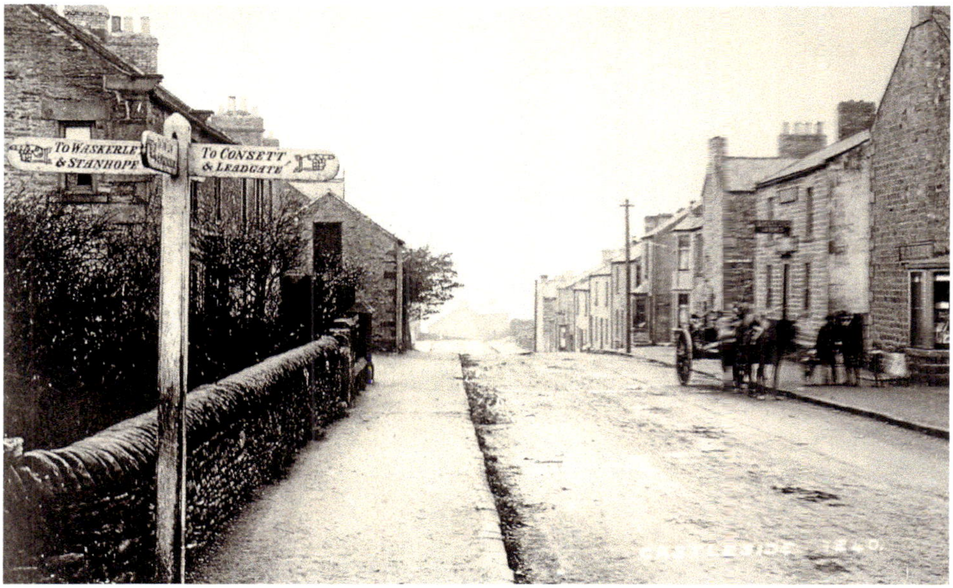

Castleside Cross Roads, near Consett, NZ 078 487

The road ahead leads north into Scotland, a road that was turnpiked in 1792; the delightful finger-post reminds us that turnpike trustees were required to erect guide posts as well as milestones. Castleside stands between lead mining areas to the west, and coal and iron districts to the east. Hence the Smelters Arms on the right may refer to lead or iron smelting. In the distance, standing obliquely to the road, is the Fleece, another inn of long standing. As part of a main route between England and Scotland, Castleside provided a number of hostelries for travellers. Postcard *c.* 1920; photograph 2011.

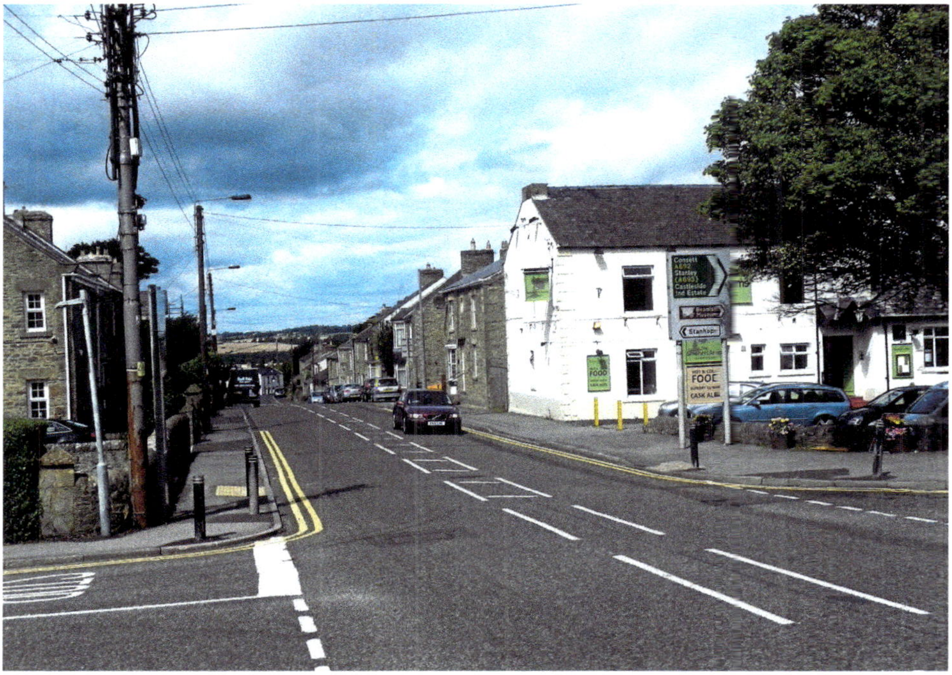

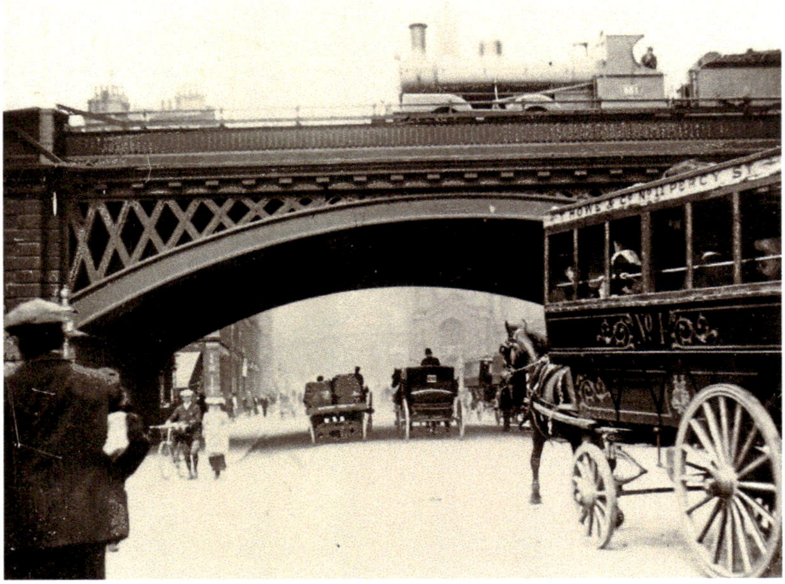

Road and Rail Traffic in Newcastle, NZ 250 639

The railway bridge in the foreground, and the combined road and rail High Level Bridge behind the camera position, both opened in 1849/50 as part of the railway system converging on Newcastle's Central Station. The 'Iron Horse' stands only a few feet away from the flesh-and-blood version, but the technological gulf between the two modes of transport is enormous. Pedestrians were charged one penny to walk across the High Level Bridge, but Howe Brothers introduced a horse bus service over the bridge for a halfpenny fare – hence the name 'The Ha'penny Lop'. The High Level Bridge was extensively reconditioned in 2002–07, and on its re-opening, traffic was restricted to the north-south direction only, except for cyclists and pedestrians. Trains, however, still run over both bridges in both directions. Photographs *c.* 1890 and 2011.

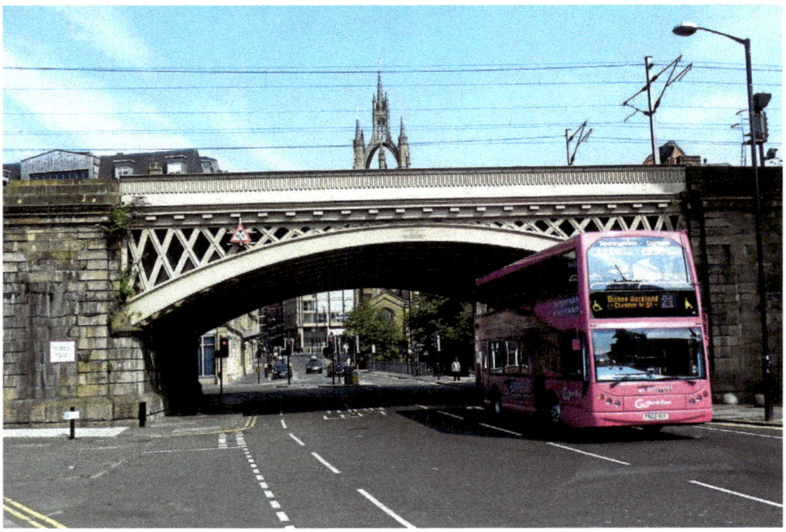

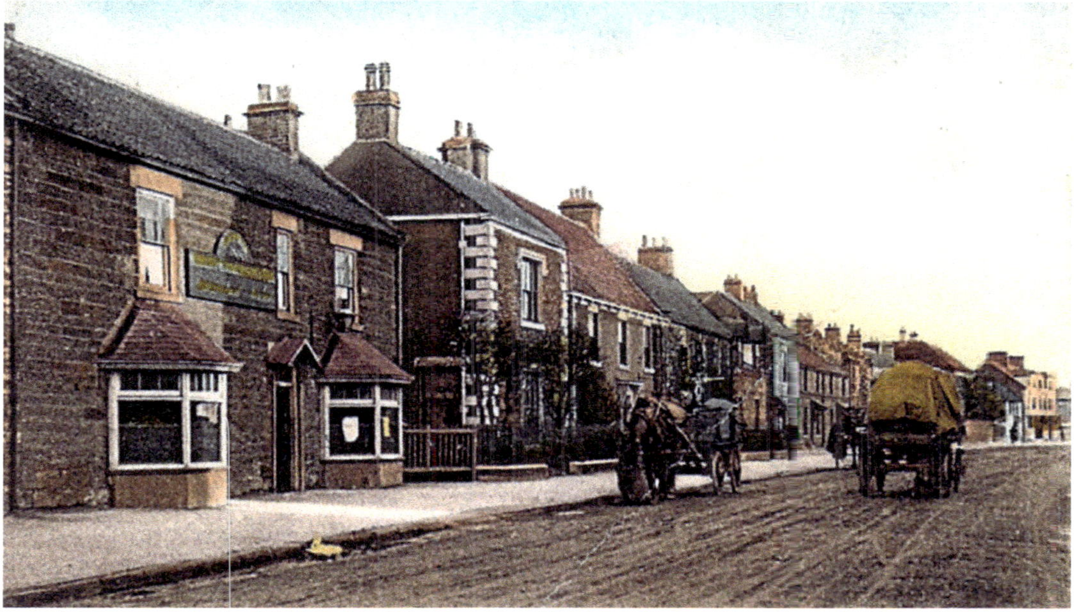

East Boldon, NZ 363 612

Once a village with a very large village green that was infilled many years, if not centuries, ago, with the main Sunderland to Newcastle road running through it. The road surface top dressing was probably beaten earth over gravel, for tarmac roads did not come into widespread use until after 1907. The scene is little changed today, except that cars have replaced horses as a means of transport. The Black Bull Inn is only slightly altered externally. Postcard *c.* 1905; photograph 2009.

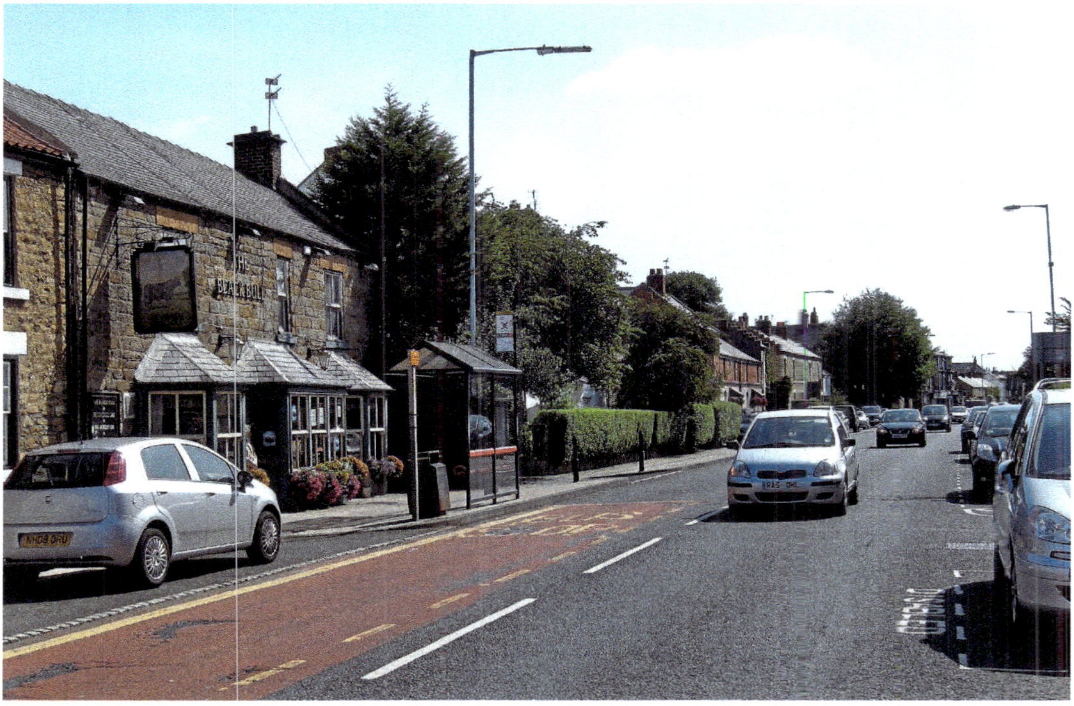

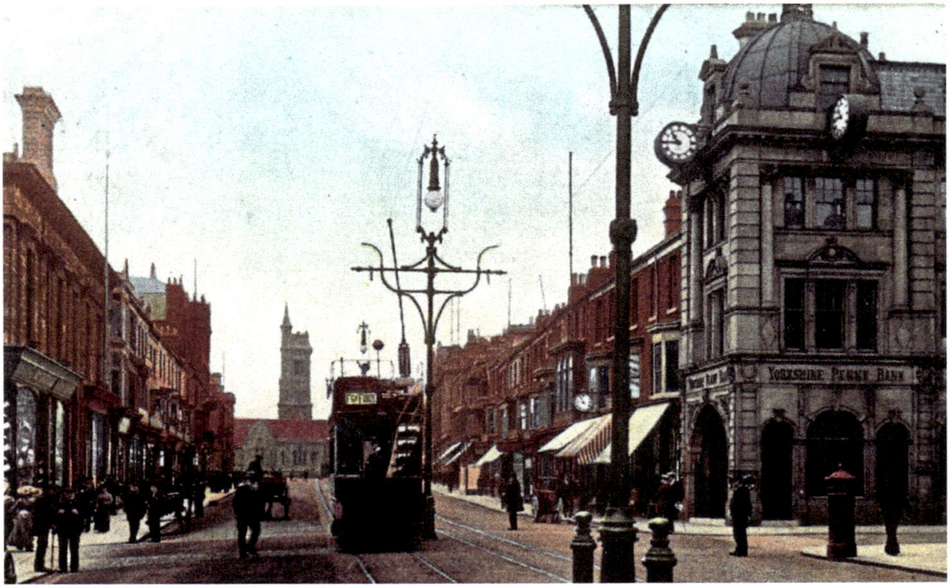

Hartlepool Church Street, NZ 512 326

The first trams in the Hartlepools were steam-powered, but conversion to electric traction came in 1895/96. An extension from Church Street to Seaton Carew opened in 1902, and this postcard may celebrate that extension. The tramway system gave way to trolley and motor buses by 1927, the former continuing until 1953. The Yorkshire Bank building on the right has been closed for some years, apart from its ATM, and the Athenaeum of 1851 built as a Literary and Mechanics' Institute, still stands on the left. Postcard dated 1905; photograph 2011.

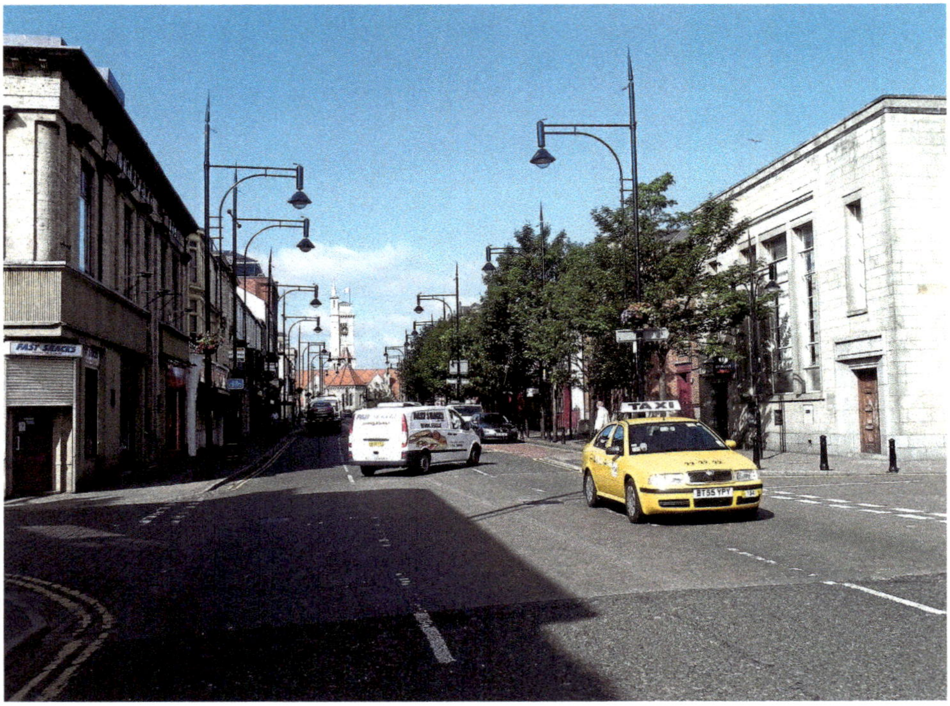

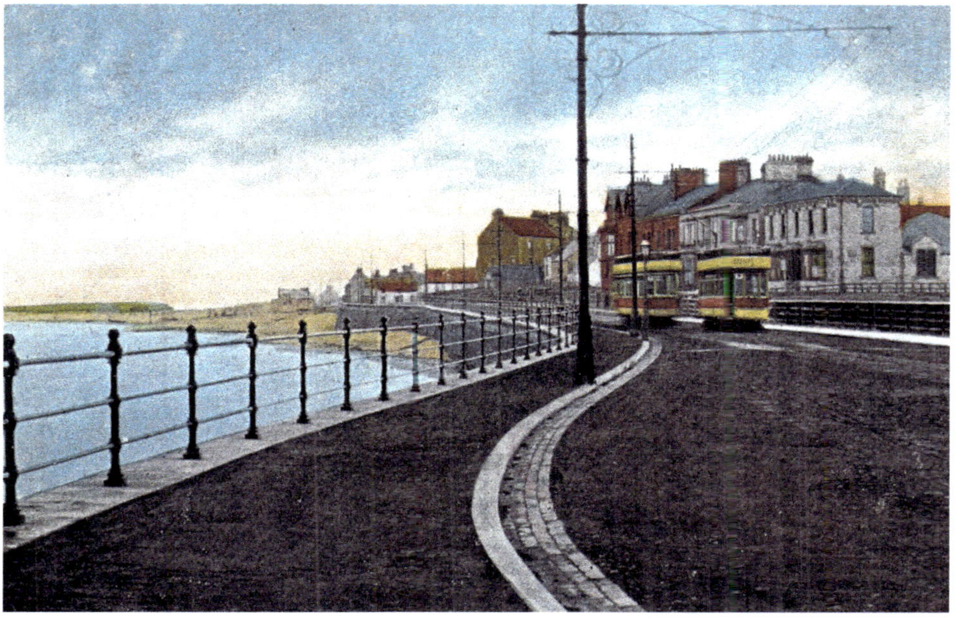

Seaton Carew, NZ 525 301

The small resort of Seaton Carew had its heyday around the time of the postcard, its rows of pretty houses and its extensive sandy beach attracting seekers of simple seaside pleasures. The tramway was opened along a reserved track from Hartlepool in 1902, but it only lasted until 1927 to be followed by trolley buses and then motor buses. The equivalent scene is little changed today, but the splendid Art Deco bus station and beach shelters of the mid-1930s further along the road, emphasise the triumph of the omnibus over the tram. Postcard dated 1906; photograph 2010.

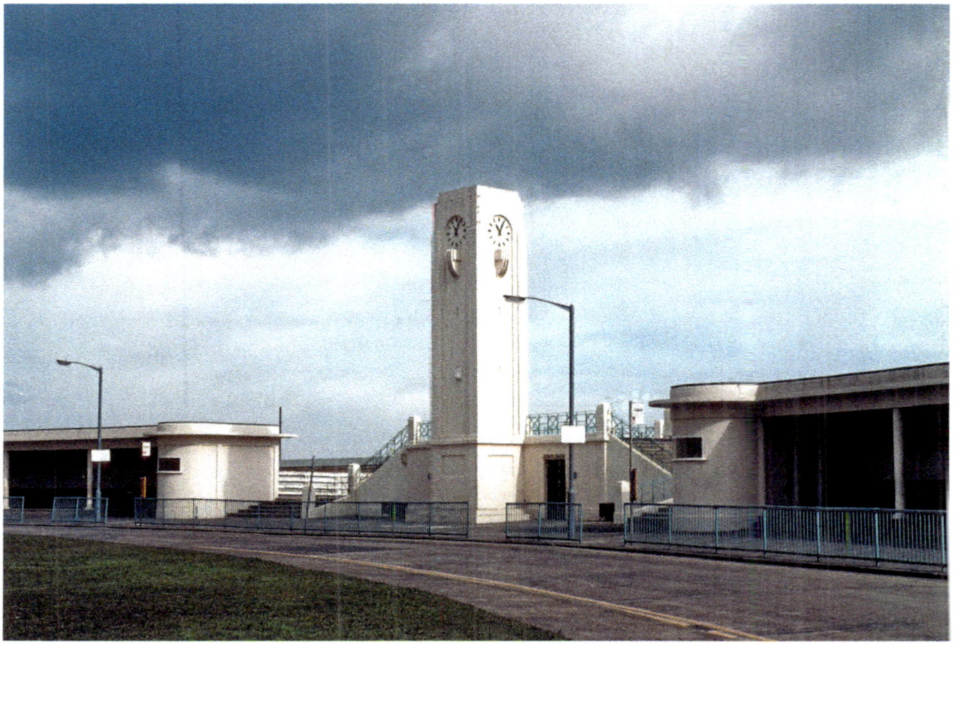

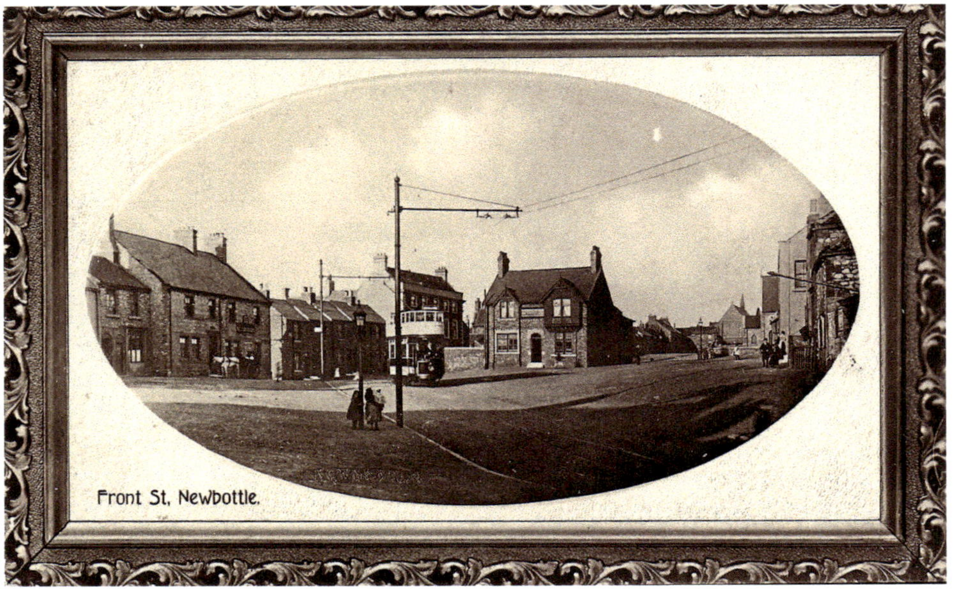

Front Street, Newbottle, NZ 337 513

A pre-industrial 'green village' that nevertheless had the earliest known commercial pottery in north-east England, hence the Jolly Potter's Inn seen prominently on the left of the postcard image. The brick-built cottages of Edith Terrace abut the fine Georgian Newbottle House of around 1720, (partly obscured by the tramcar), while St Matthews Church of 1886 can be seen in the distance. The tramway opened in 1905 and the postcard image may date from that year, but it had lost out to omnibuses by 1925 when road widening may have required the demolition of the house on the green. The Jolly Potter remains, as does St Matthews, while Newbottle House is now a working men's club. Postcard dated 1910; photograph 2009.

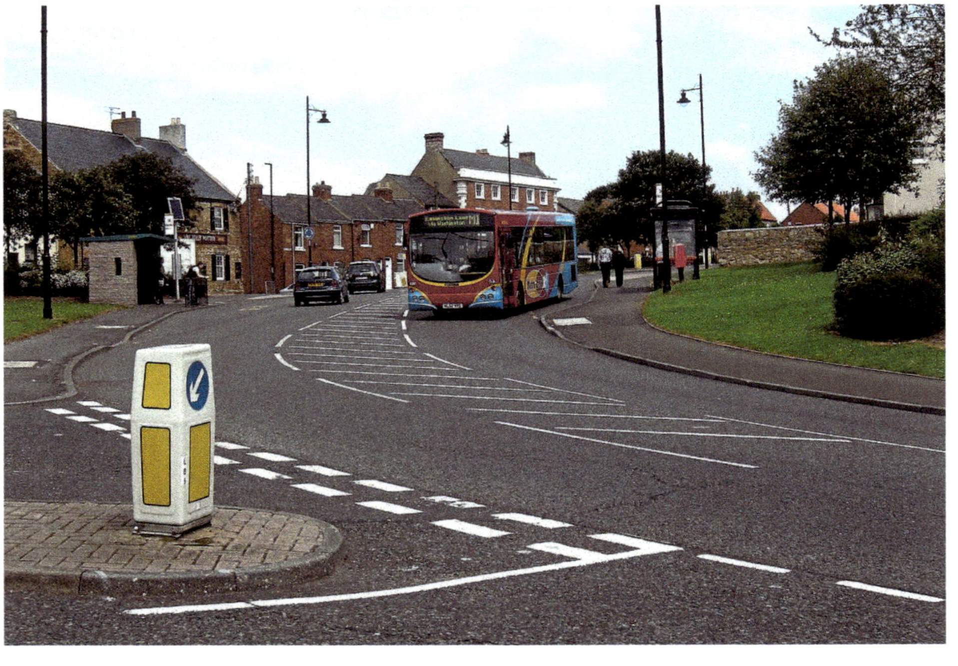

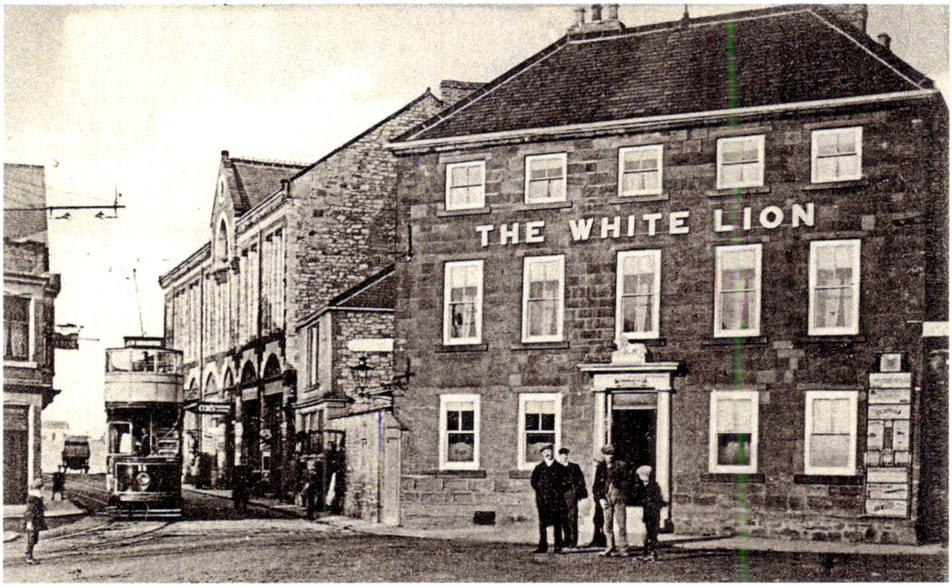

Houghton le Spring Tramcar, NZ 341 499

The tramway opened between Sunderland and Houghton in 1905 and the postcard shows a car just leaving its Houghton terminus, passing the White Lion and some splendid shops on the right, and the Britannia on the left, on its way down Newbottle Street. Quite a different scene today, and one not improved by fairly brutal architecture. The Britannia remains unharmed, however, apart from the blocking up of its corner door. Postcard dated 1910, photograph 2009.

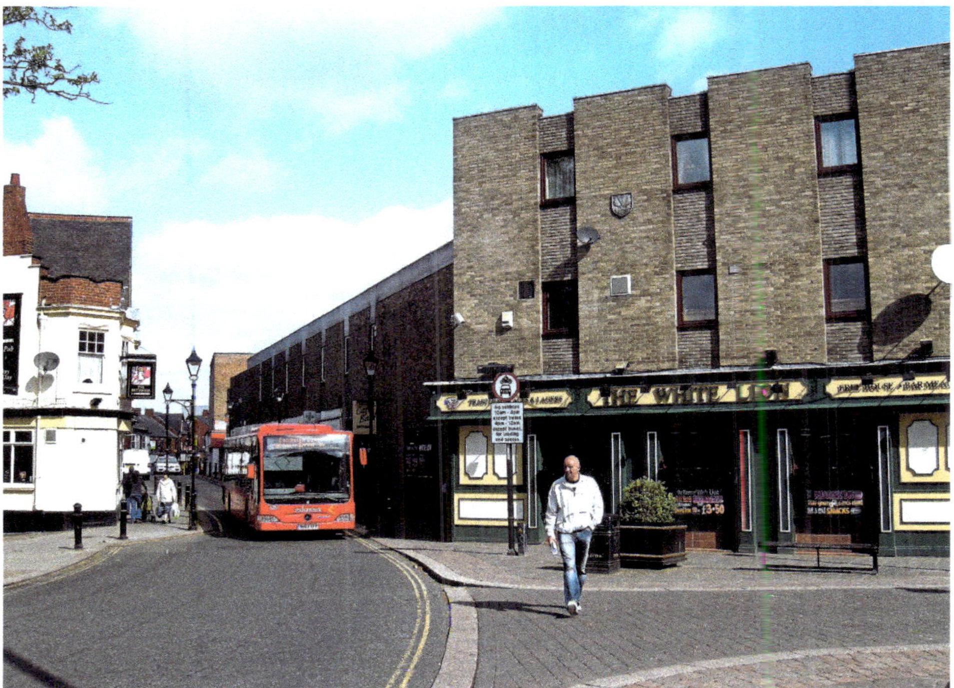

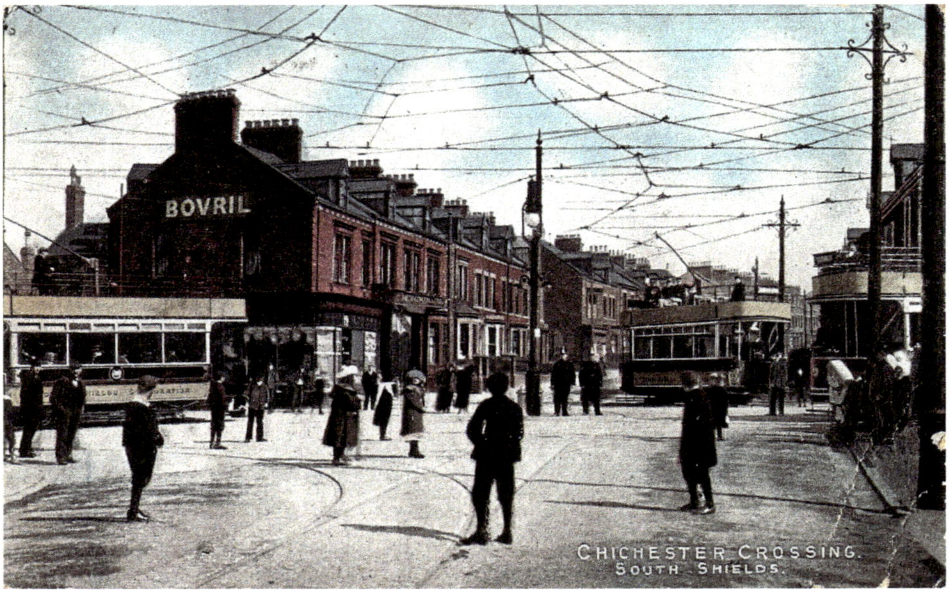

Chichester Crossing, South Shields, NZ 365 659

Open-topped tramcars negotiate a tricky crossroads with tramlines in every direction beneath a veritable cobweb of overhead lines, while observers look on under the watchful gaze of two bobbies; perhaps all were witnessing the opening of the South Shields electrified tramway system in March 1906. Subsequently trolley buses came and went as motor buses came to reign supreme for urban public transport and it is now almost impossible to stand casually in the middle of the crossing. Yet history maybe repeating itself, for directly behind the camera position stands the Chichester station of the Tyneside Metro, sometimes called the 'Supertram'. Postcard dated 1907; photograph 2009.

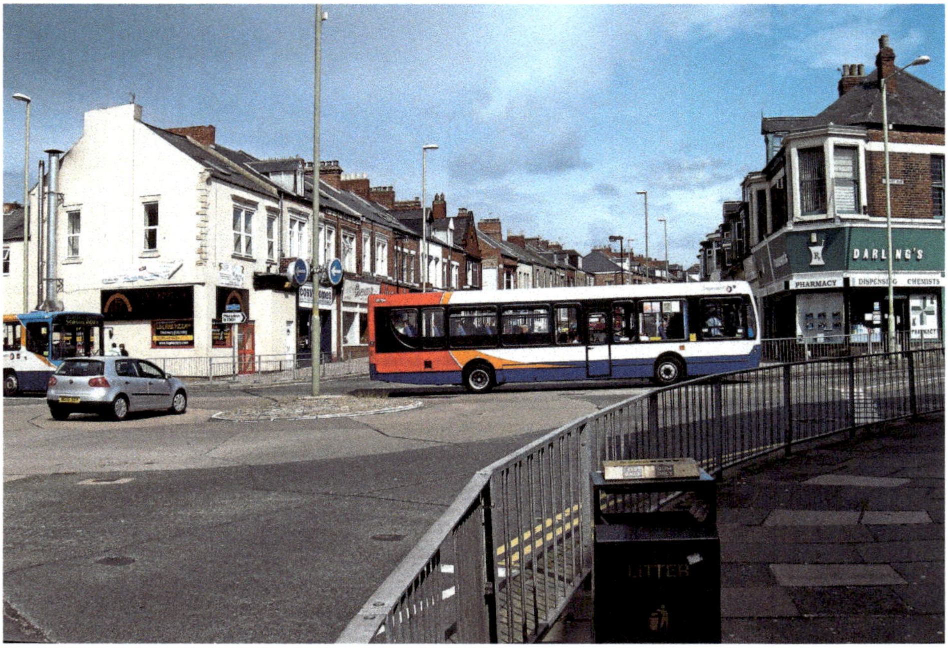

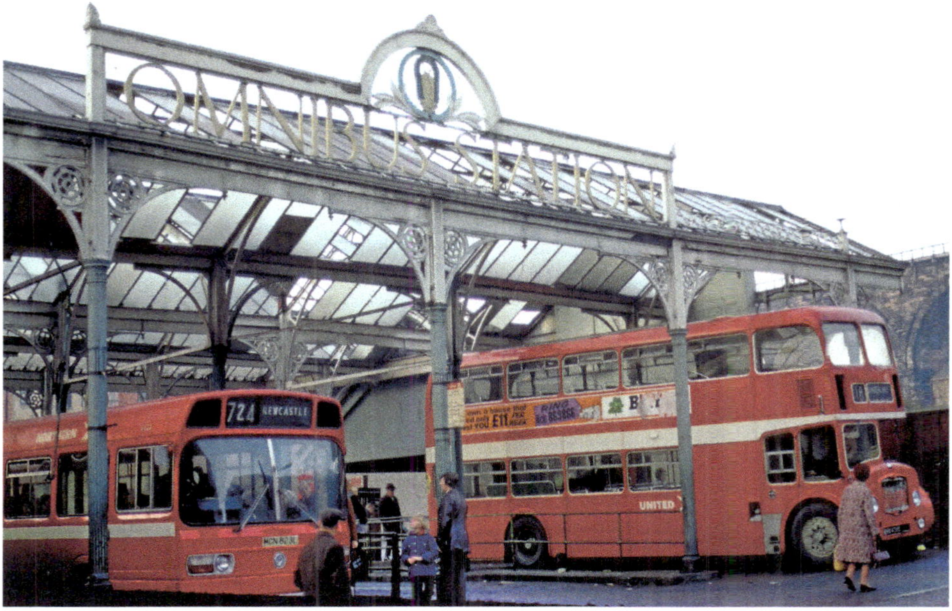

Durham Omnibus Station, NZ 270 425

The old bus station proudly proclaimed itself in glass and iron with the British Electric Traction symbol as its centrepiece, and was framed by Durham's splendid railway viaduct to the side. Although BET began as a tramway operating company, it was not slow to adapt to motor buses as they gradually took over from the trams. The old station was demolished in 1976 and its present-day equivalent hides itself away behind a bland brick façade. Photographs 1975 and 2011.

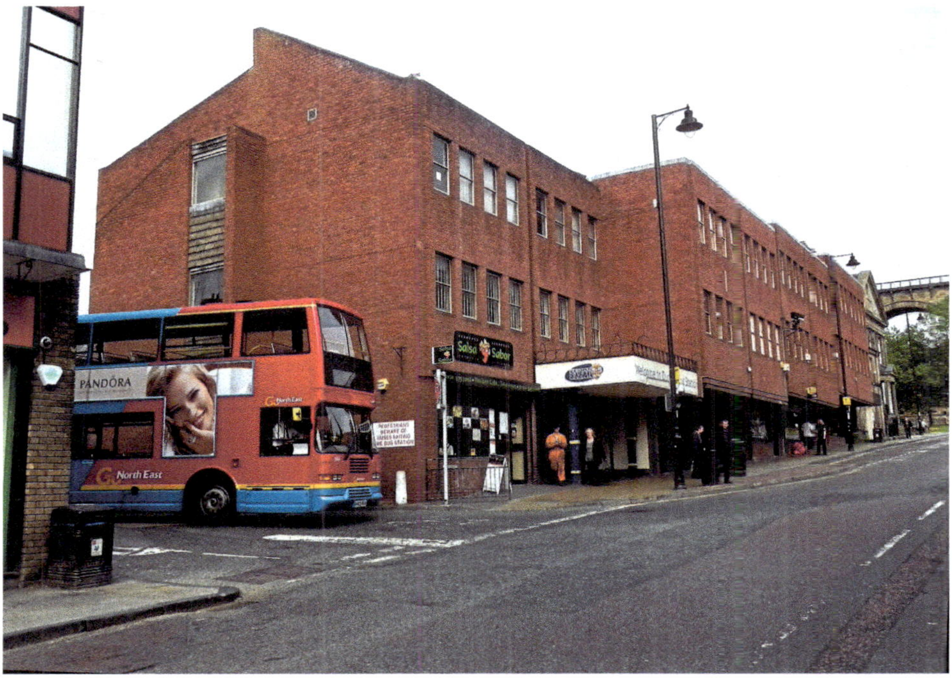

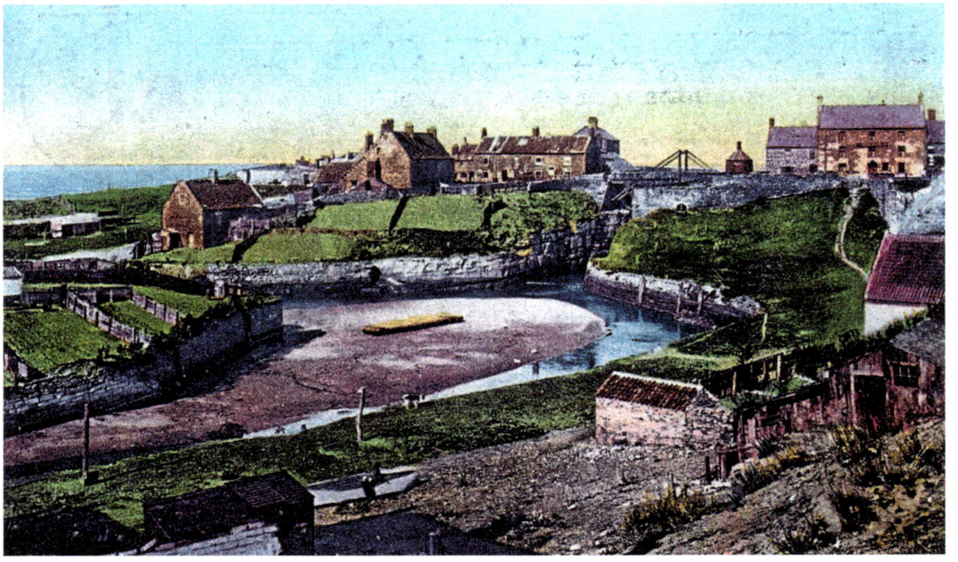

Seaton Sluice Harbour, NZ 338 767

To overcome the problem of silting in the small Hartley harbour, in the seventeenth century Sir Ralph Delaval arranged for it to be scoured by releases of river and high-tide water, dammed behind a sluice; the harbour was thenceforth known as Seaton Sluice. As trade expanded, the harbour was improved in 1761–64 by driving an easterly cut through the headland to the sea, as can be seen towards the right in both images. The supporting industries had finished by 1872 and the harbour works either rotted away or were dismantled. Some occasional tidying-up work has been carried out in recent years. Postcard dated July 1912; photograph 2009.

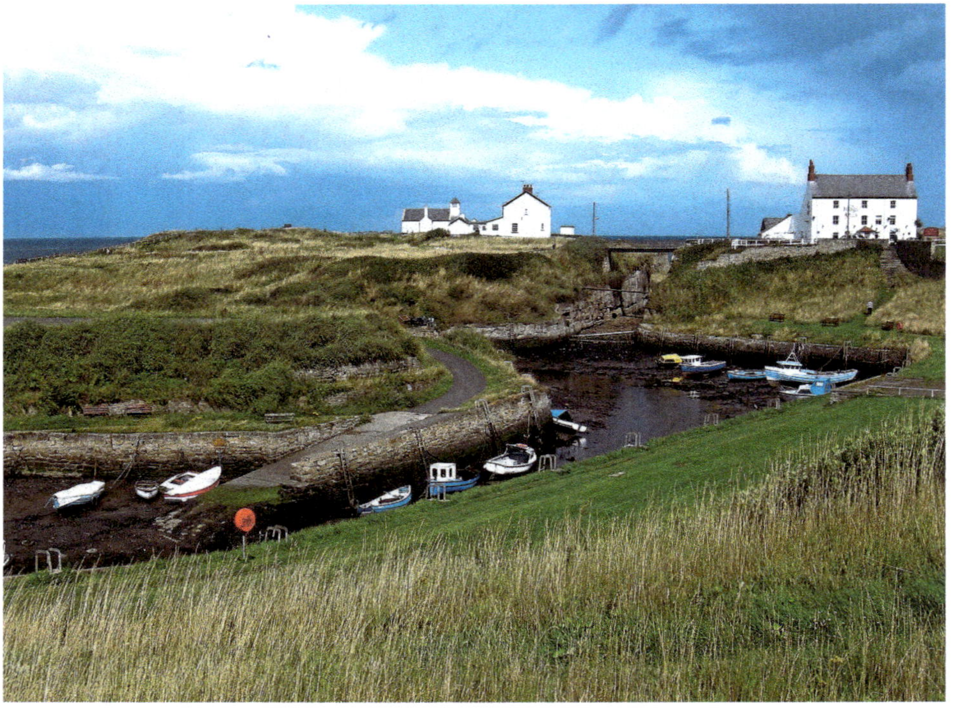

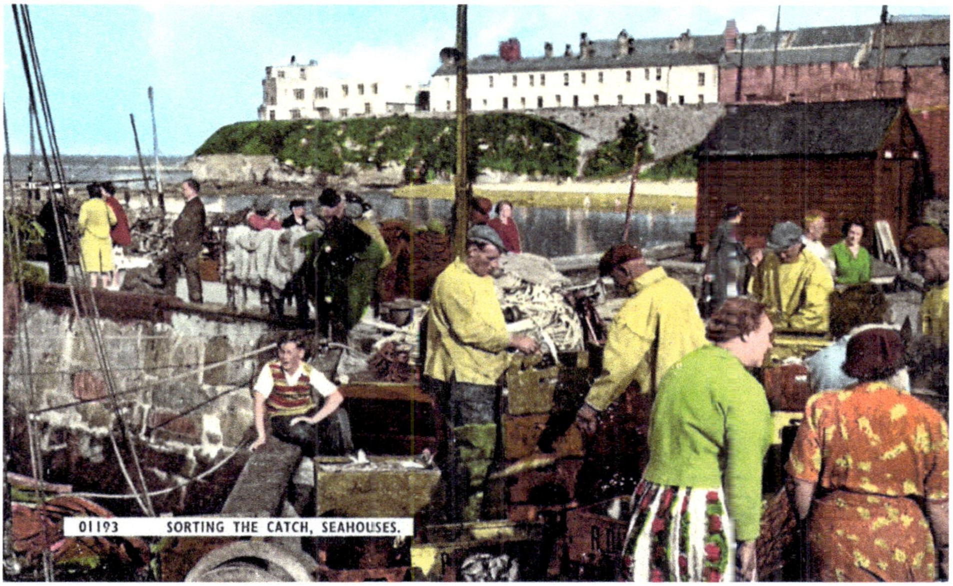

Seahouses Harbour, NU 220 321

Originally called North Sunderland Sea Houses, the harbour was developed from a small haven firstly in around 1786, but with later modifications and new piers in 1886–89. Fishing, boatbuilding and lime burning were then the main harbour activities. Lime burning ceased around 1860, while fishing operations are much reduced, but tourism is now the economic mainstay of Seahouses. The all-pervading and always enticing aroma of fish and chips has long replaced the acrid smoke of the limekilns. Postcard *c.* 1930; photograph 2011.

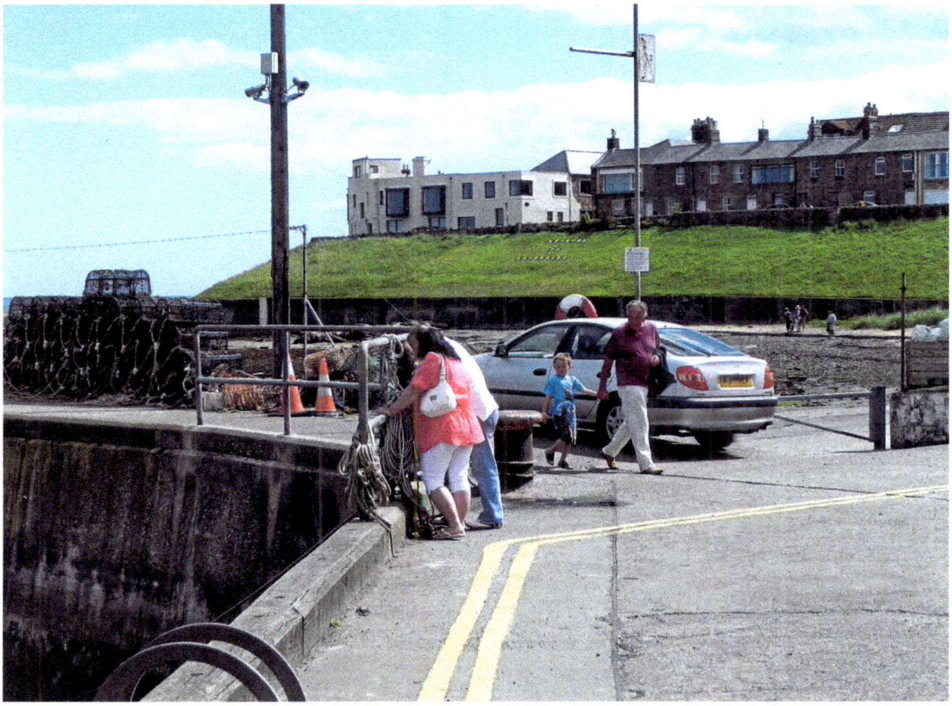

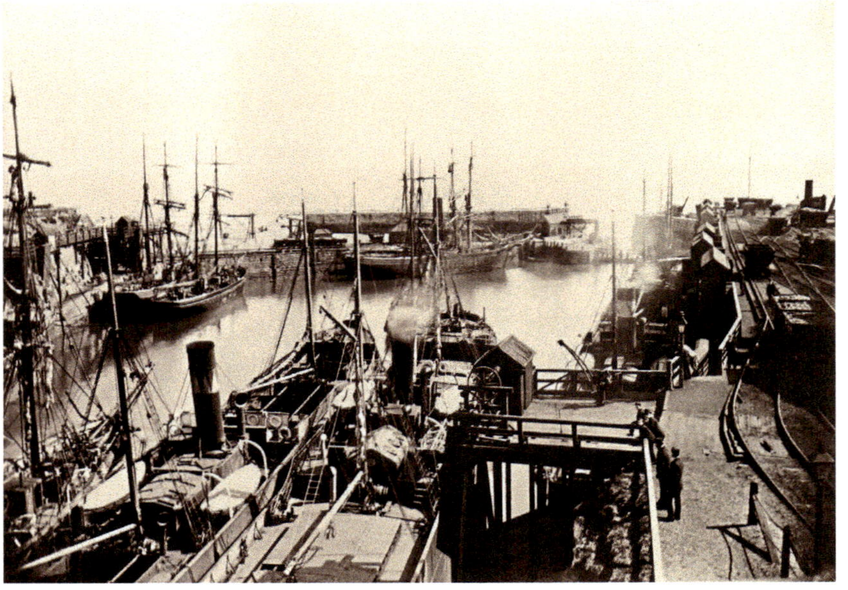

Seaham Harbour I, NZ 435 492

Seaham north dock, gouged out of the magnesian limestone as part of a much larger artificial harbour creation, was opened in 1831. It was used primarily for the export of coal. Here in 1903, a sizeable fleet of sailing and steam colliers are being loaded from the staiths, perhaps more than would usually be present in the dock, for the south dock was being extensively remodelled at the time. The north dock is now undergoing change in a £3 million regeneration scheme, to include a marina for seventy-eight vessels, new automatic lock gates, and a utility building to provide offices, workshops, café, public toilets etc. Photographs 1903 (David Angus) and 2011.

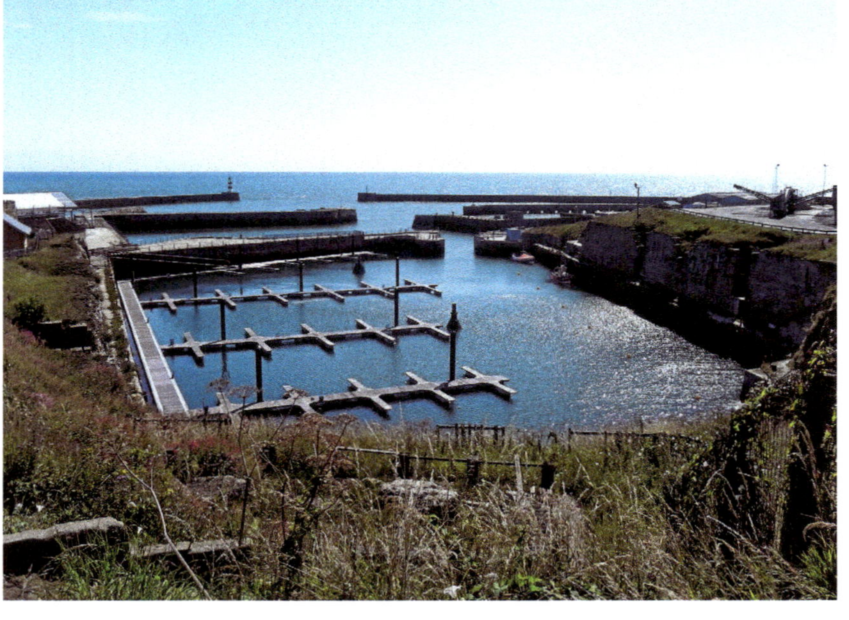

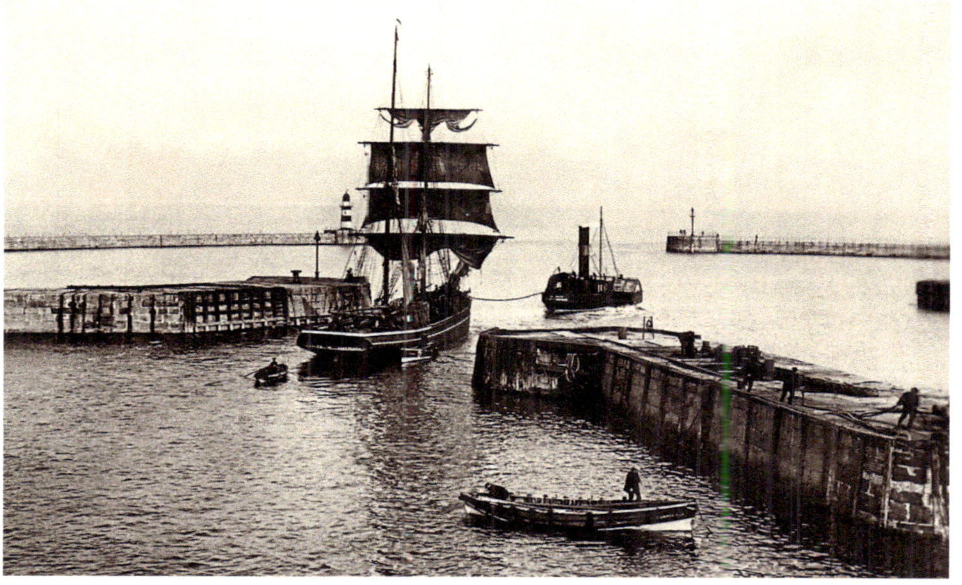

Seaham Harbour II, NZ 435 492

A collier brig leaves Seaham's north dock under tow in 1905, although it seems unlikely that much coal was shipped from that dock after the south dock was remodelled and extended in 1898–1905. As late as 1973 coal was still being shipped coastwise from the south dock to places as far apart as Poole in Dorset, and Shetland, but the coaling staiths were demolished soon after that date and the switch was made to general cargo handling; in such trades the south dock remains quite active. Photographs 1903 (David Angus) and 2006.

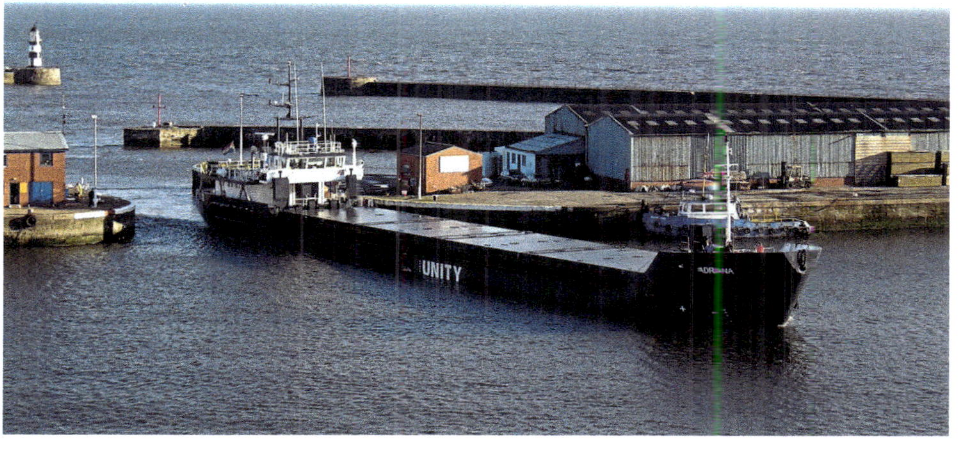

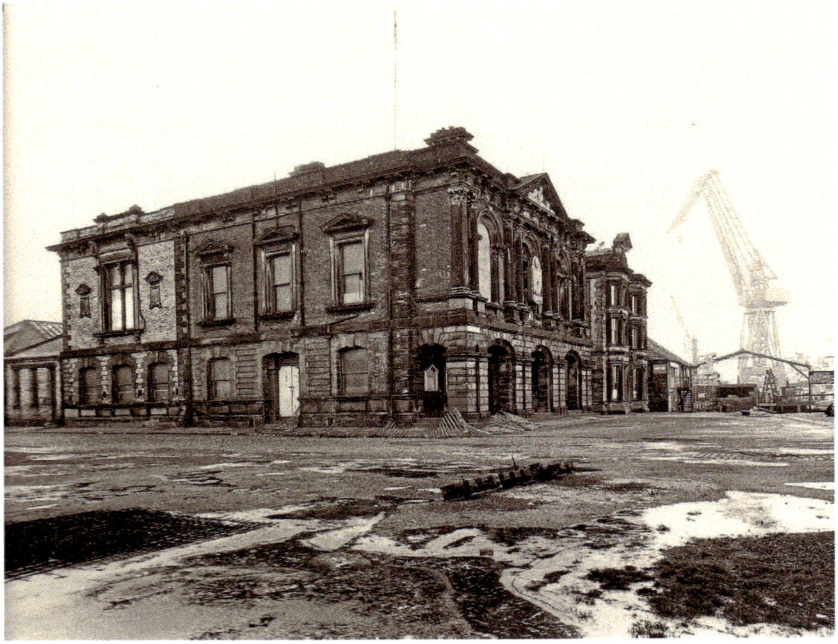

Custom House, Mill Dam, South Shields, NZ 359 659

Two significant river-related buildings – the former Customs Office of 1863/64, and the River Police Offices of 1886 – were in a semi-derelict state in 1978. Demolition was imminent until they were listed as buildings of historic interest, providing opportunity for adaptive reuse. Eventually they were transformed into a cultural centre for arts, drama, and live music. The 1990 statue in the foreground is dedicated to those merchant seamen who lost their lives in the Second World War. Photographs 1978 (Graham Smith) and 2011.

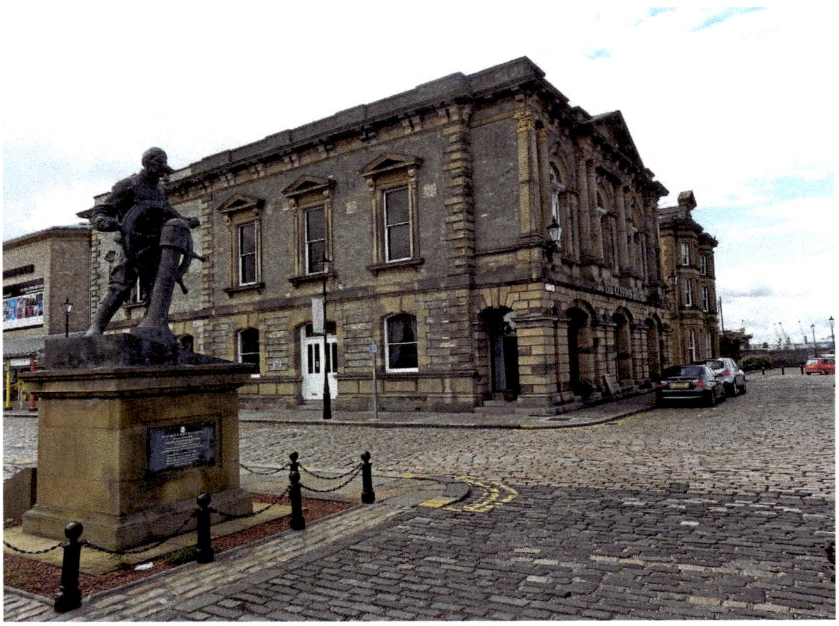

Seaton High Light Beacon, Hartlepool, NZ 514 305 and 515 331

An attractive simple Tuscan column, its doorway dated 1839, leading to a spiral stairway that could be ascended only with difficulty to access the lantern platform above. It was surrounded by ironworks buildings in the 1970s but was dismantled and re-erected almost two miles to the north within the Hartlepool docks and marina complex. Photographs 1974 and 2010.

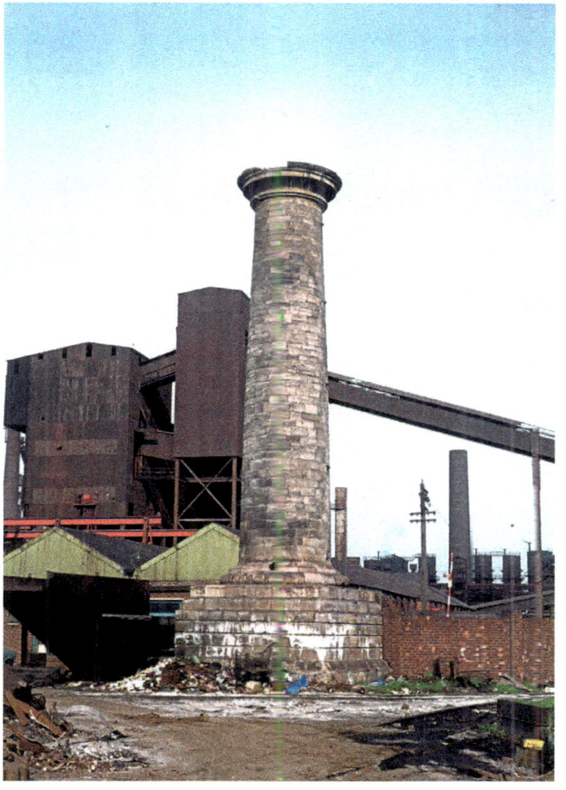

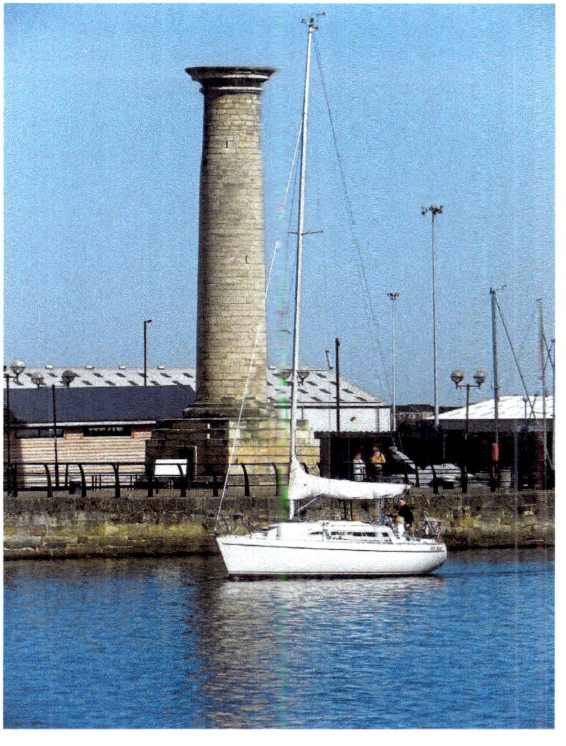

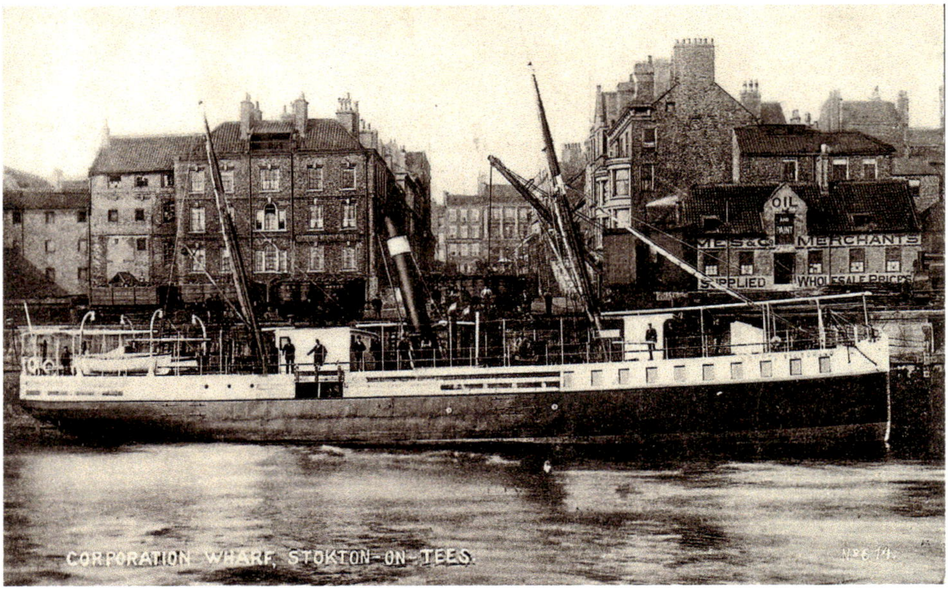

Stockton Corporation Quay, NZ 448 192

Stockton-on-Tees effectively became the head-port of the River Tees in 1771, a position formerly occupied by Yarm, some 7½ miles further upriver. The 1825 Stockton & Darlington Railway initially emphasised Stockton's role as the chief port of the Tees, but the extension of that railway to the new town and port of Middlesbrough, from 1830 onwards, was to bring about its slow demise. Stockton's Corporation Quay continued to serve the town into the 1960s but was closed down in that decade. Recently the river frontages at Stockton and neighbouring Thornaby have been transformed by extensive new developments, the prominent building in the modern photograph being the Stockton Baptist tabernacle. Postcard dated 1905, photograph 2011.

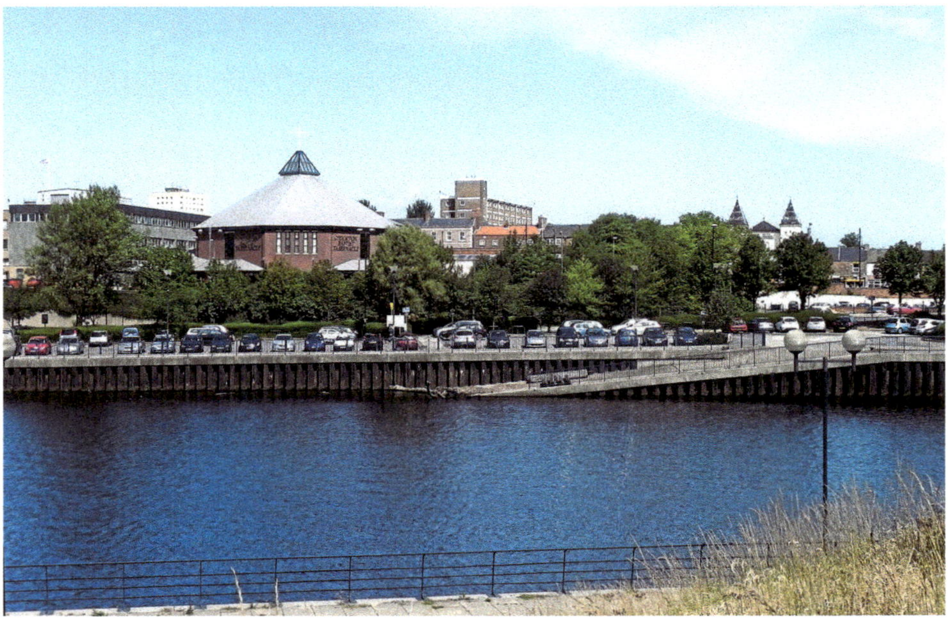

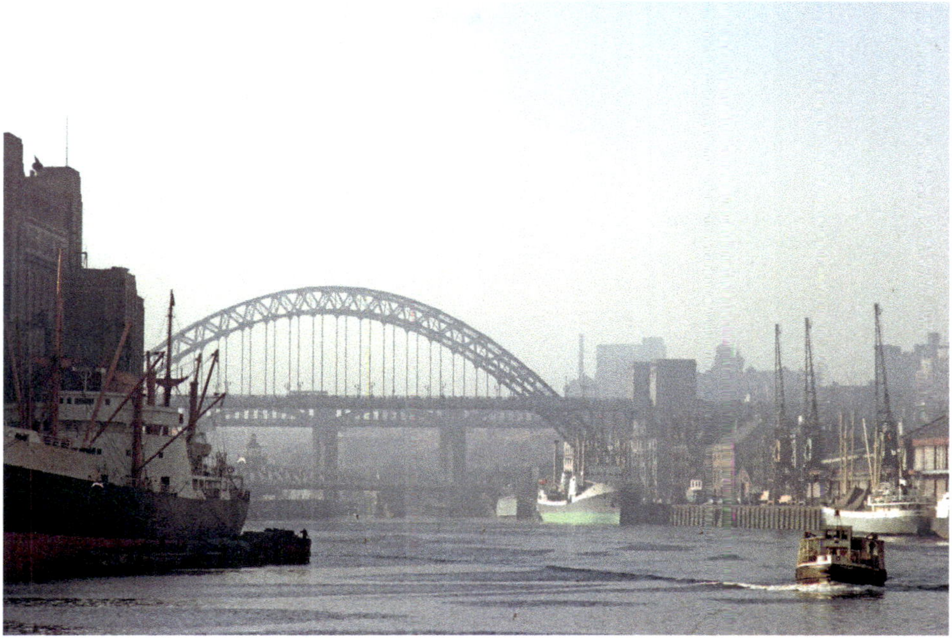

Port of Tyne, NZ 255 638

The middle reaches of the Port of Tyne were still quite busy in the 1960s. The Baltic flour mill on the left was still active, and shipping still berthed at Newcastle's Corporation Quay. But by 2011, the flour mill had become an art gallery, a new pedestrian bridge had been built, and both the Newcastle and Gateshead quaysides largely given over to educational, artistic and leisure pursuits. Photographs 1967 (Bob Rennison) and 2011.

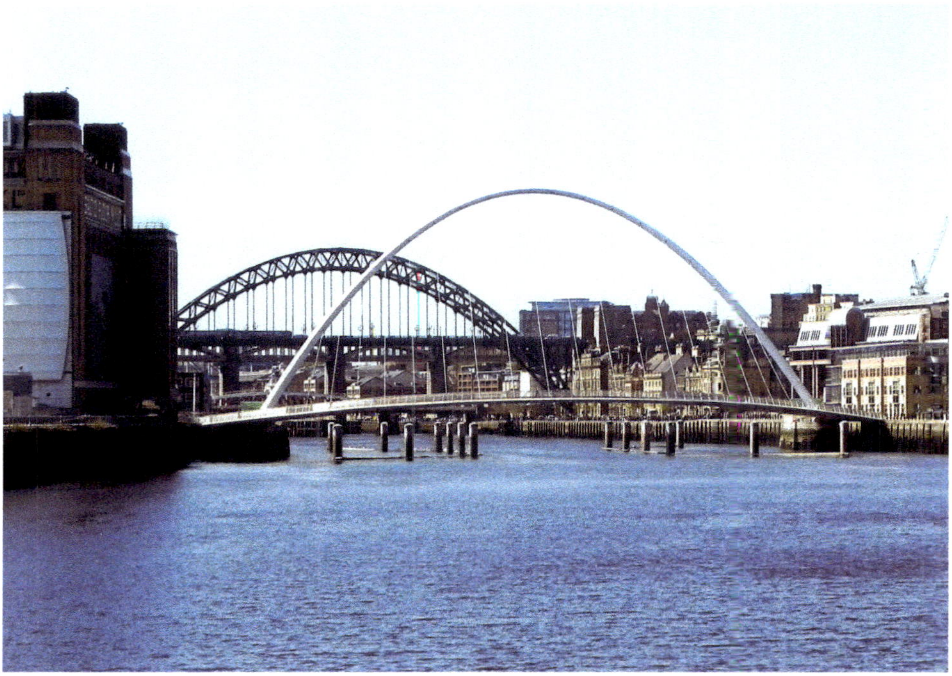

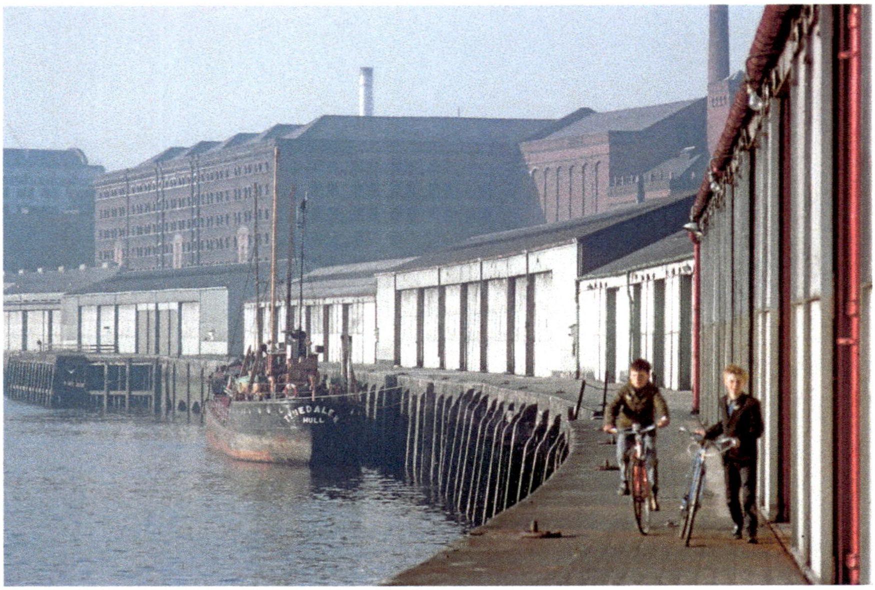

Newcastle Quayside I, NZ 255 640

The Newcastle Quayside was, historically, the heart of the town, and was of particular importance when the Newcastle Corporation acted as conservators for the entire Port of Tyne, a position that they only lost in 1850 with the formation of the Tyne Improvement Commission; even so the Corporation retained control of this section of the river. The earlier image, looking upriver, the scene dominated by a CWS grain warehouse overlooking some quayside sheds. As can be seen, this part of the riverside has been transformed in recent years although, happily, cyclists can still use it. Photographs 1967 and 2011.

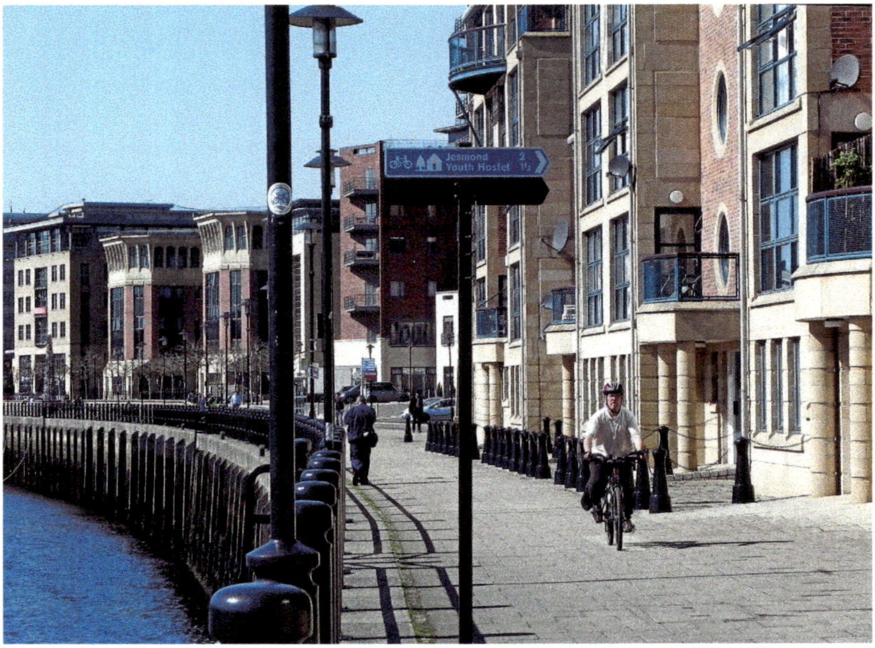

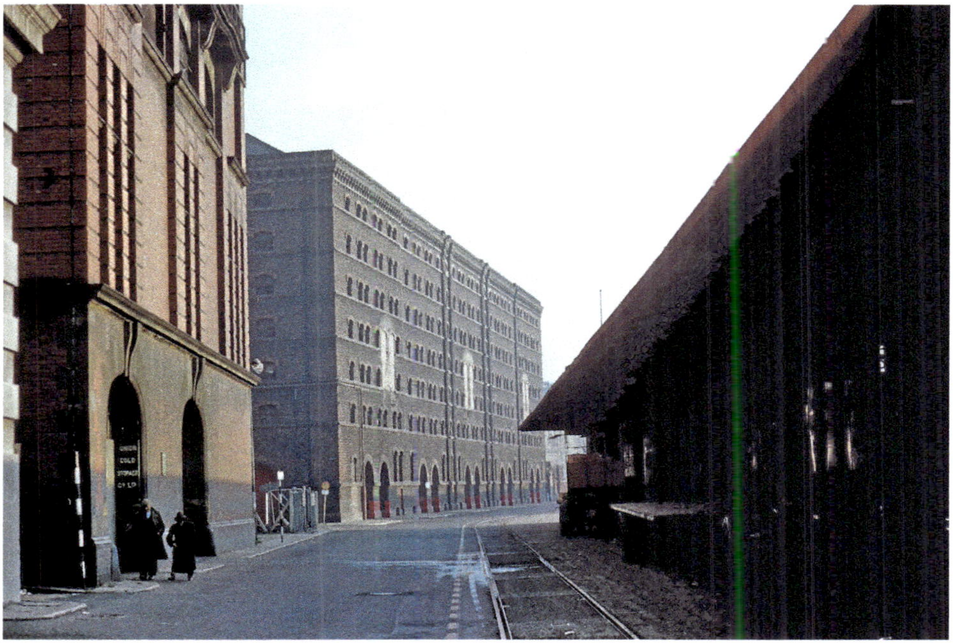

Newcastle Quayside II, NZ 259 642

The CWS grain warehouse again features strongly in this photograph looking downriver. It was, after all, reputed to be the largest individual brick-built building in Europe, and it easily dominated the trading part of the Newcastle quayside. Few people wandered around this part of the quayside for fun in the 1960s, but the modern photograph shows how much that has changed. Photographs 1965 (Bob Rennison) and 2011.

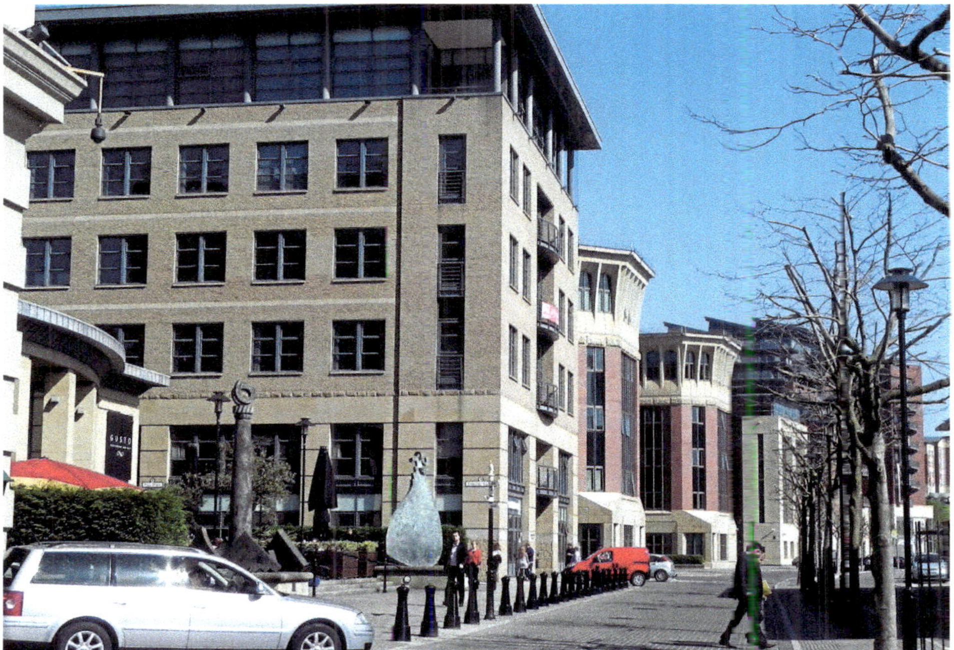

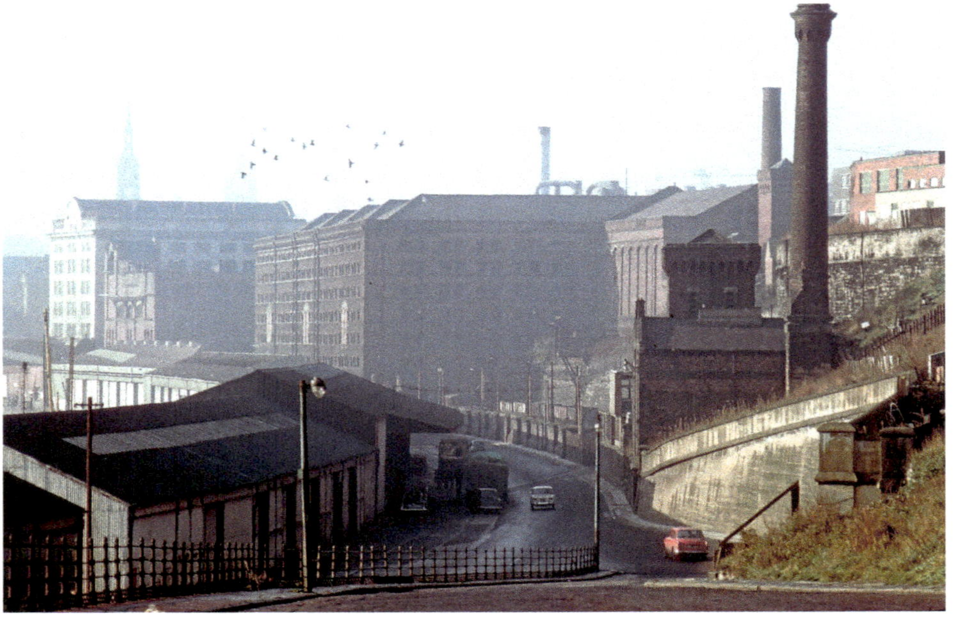

Newcastle Quayside III, the Hydraulic Power Station, NZ 262 641

One of the most attractive industrial buildings on the Newcastle Quayside was the hydraulic power station seen on the right. It ought to have been preserved but was demolished without obvious reason in 1976. In the middle distance is the grain warehouse and beyond that another important CWS warehouse, which is probably the oldest surviving large-scale ferro-concrete building in the country. Constructed between 1897 and 1900, it had stood largely unused from the 1950s. Fortunately it found a new use in the revamping of the quayside of the 1990s. Photographs 1967 (Bob Rennison) and 2011.

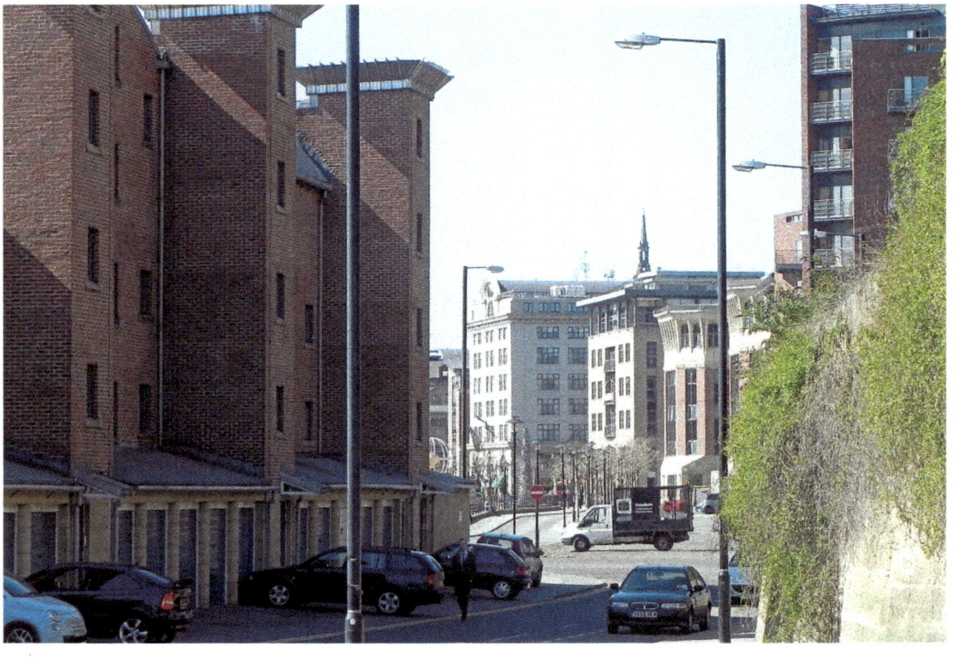

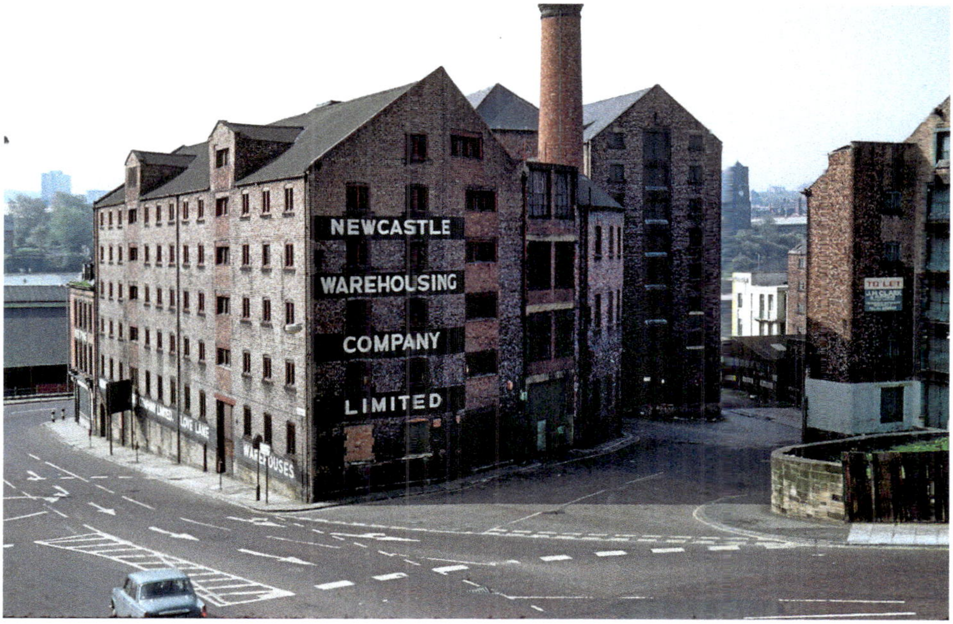

Love Lane Warehouses, Milk Market, Newcastle, NZ 256 642

A series of large warehouse buildings were built from Broad Chare to the Milk Market in Newcastle from the beginning of the nineteenth century, some of which were particularly fine, and most of them intact into the 1970s. Most were subsequently demolished but the Love Lane warehouses built from the 1830s were converted to residential accommodation, while new but fairly sympathetic developments were created alongside. Unfortunately the view down the lane and across the Tyne to St Mary's in Gateshead was lost. Photographs 1967 (Bob Rennison) and 2011.

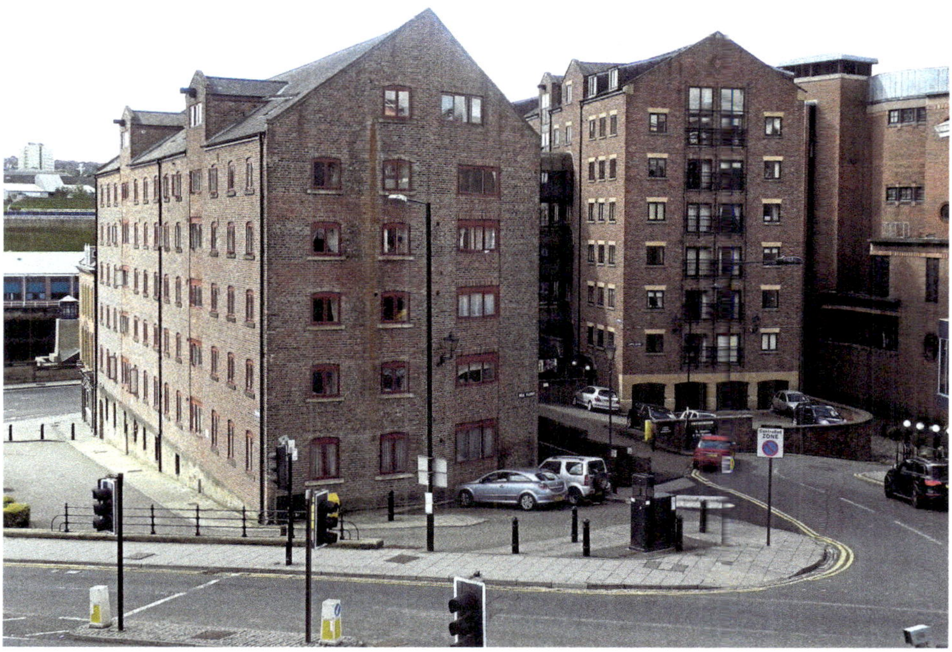

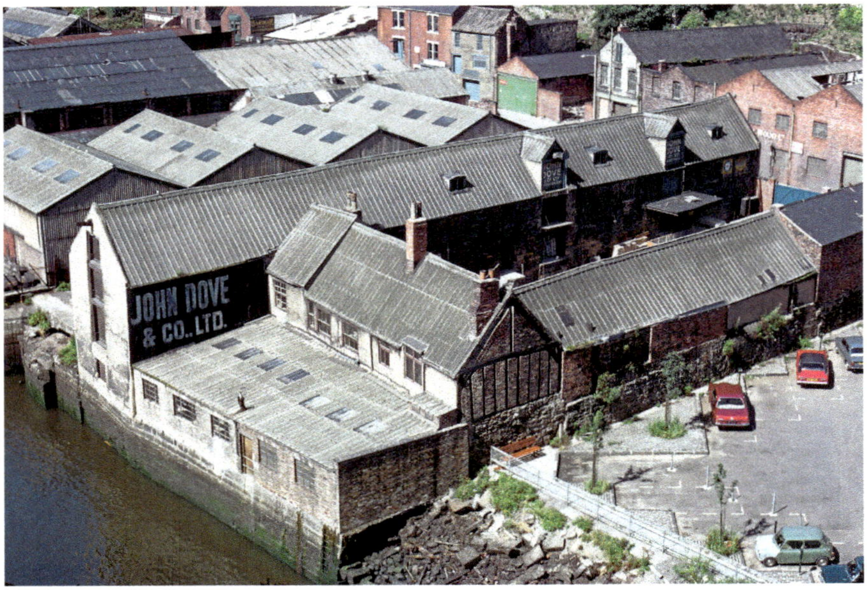

Doves Warehouse, Newcastle, NZ 250 637

J. T. Dove, builders' merchants, occupied a riverside site on the Newcastle quayside for many years, its own wharf giving direct access to river-borne traffic for both import and export. The warehouse probably originated as a late sixteenth-century merchant's house. After the site was abandoned by Doves, a promenade was created along the river frontage and the buildings converted into a pub and restaurant in around 1989. This was one of the earliest leisure developments in the Newcastle quayside area but it was soon followed by many more. Photographs 1973 and 2011.

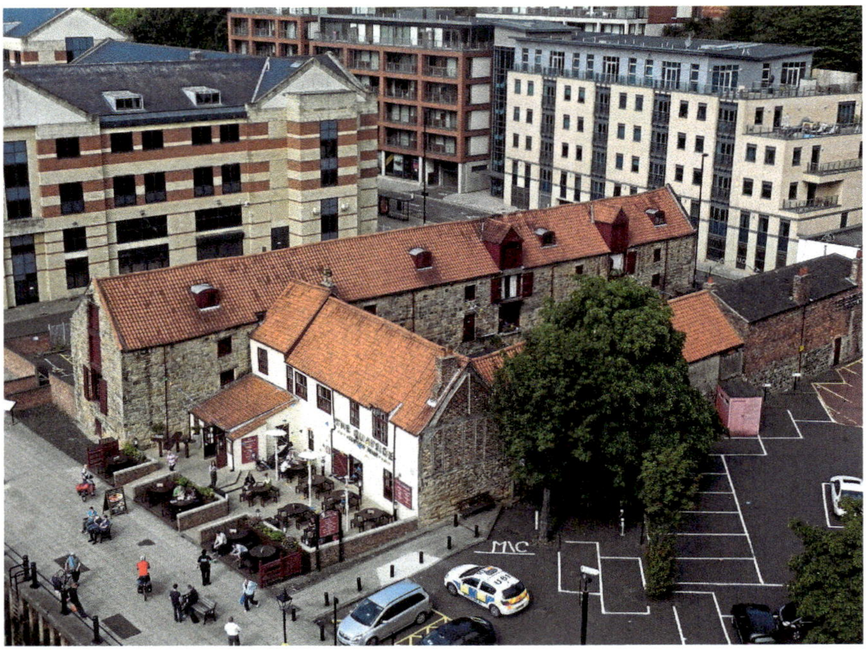

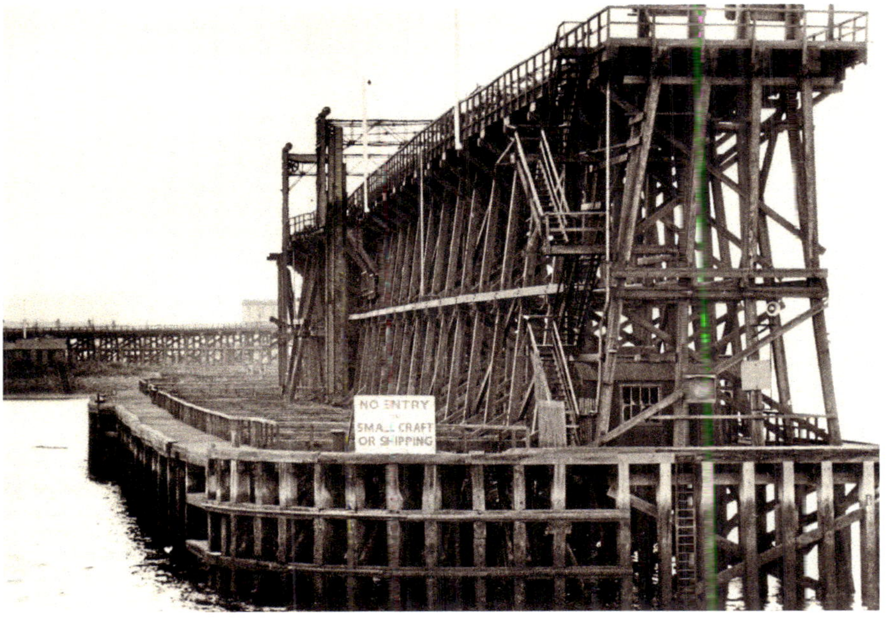

Dunston Staiths, NZ 236 626

Dunston Staiths, built in stages by the North Eastern Railway in 1893 and 1903 for the loading of colliers, was severely damaged by fire in the 1970s, but continued working until about 1980, after which some sections were dismantled. However, much of the structure had survived intact and was featured as part of the Gateshead International Garden Festival in 1990. Another fire in November 2003 destroyed part of the staith, but it remains a visual focal point for a new housing development adjacent to the river. Photographs 1980 and 2009.

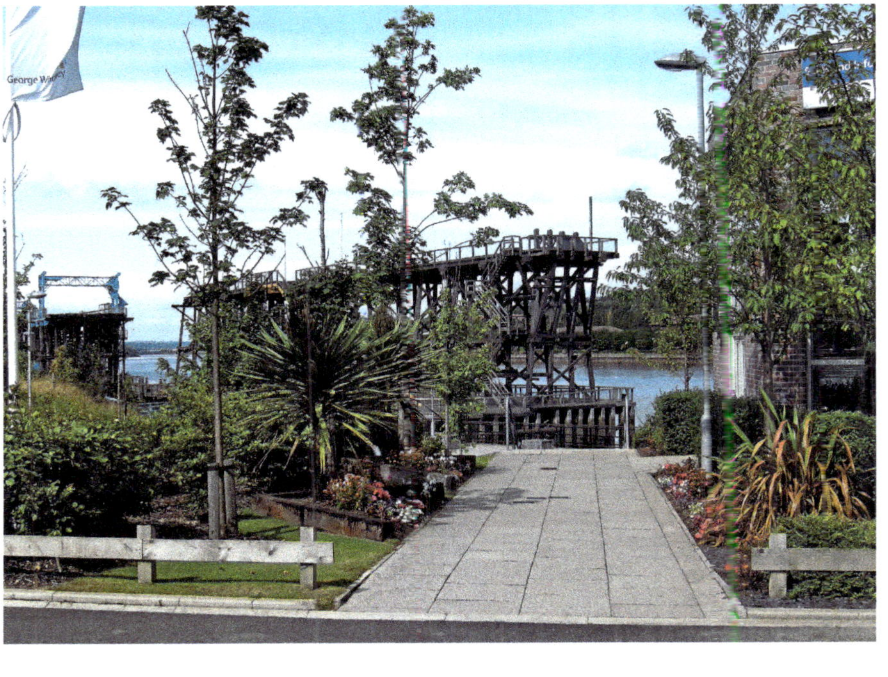

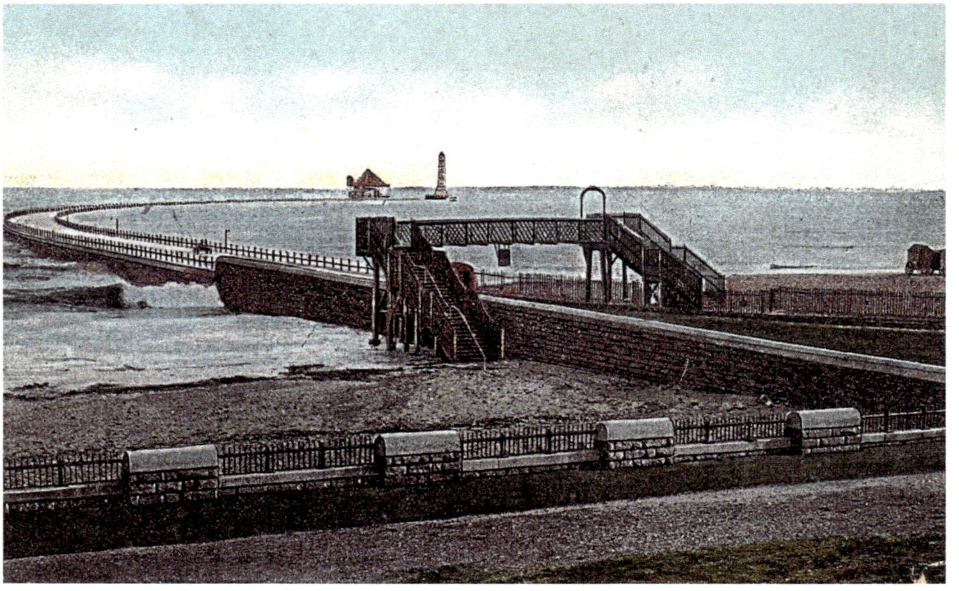

Roker Pier, Sunderland, NZ 413 586

It is now difficult to imagine that entering the River Wear from the sea was once a treacherous business. Rocks, sandbars and sandbanks made the narrow navigation channels particularly difficult. Extensive dredging and the construction of the massive outer piers were just some of the improvements carried out by the harbour commissioners. The northern Roker Pier, shown to the left, and built between 1885 and 1903, was some 2,880 feet long – considered to be the longest breakwater in England. The new South Pier, on the right of the modern photograph, was some 2,700 feet long and constructed in 1893–1914. Postcard *c.* 1905, photograph 2011.

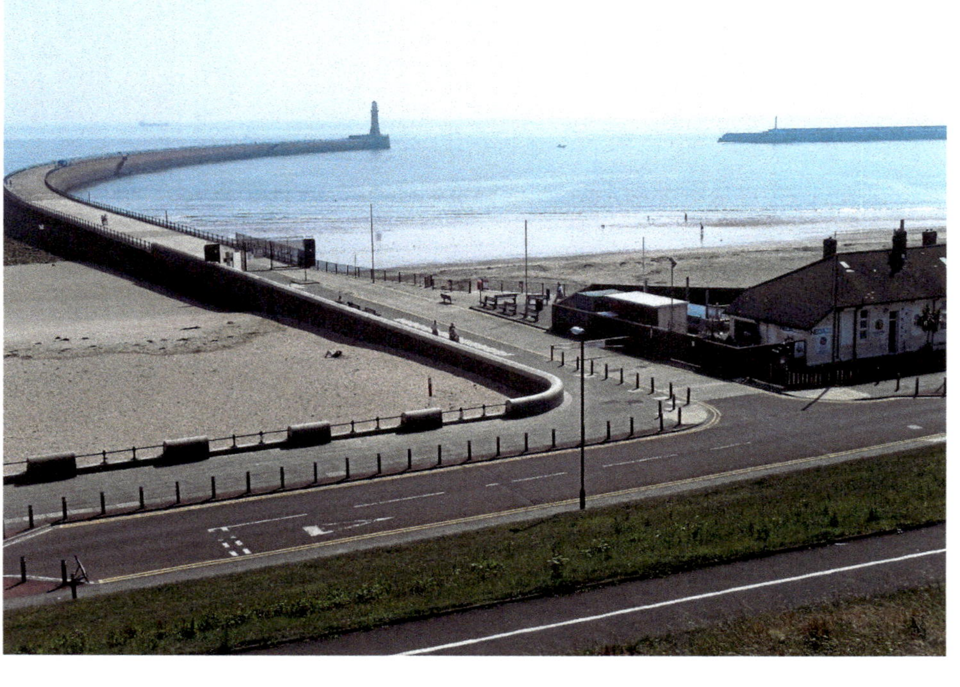

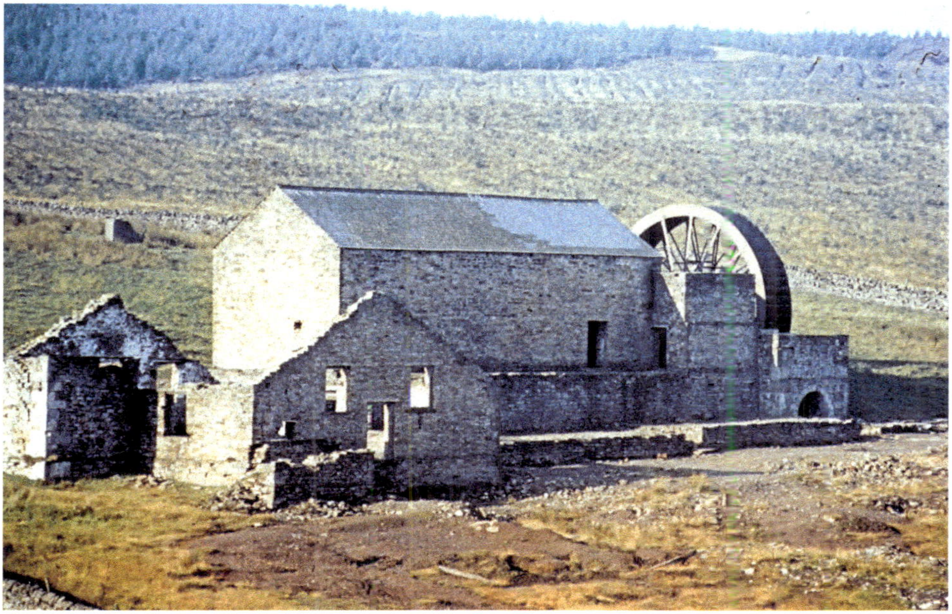

Killhope Park Level Mill, NY 827 429

Killhope lead mine and its dressing floors are dramatically located near the head of Weardale. The mine was effectively closed in 1910, and its site stood unused and decaying until about 1970 when Durham County Council began its restoration. The concomitant provision of visitor facilities has resulted in Killhope's emergence as an important leadmining museum. Photographs 1970 and 2011.

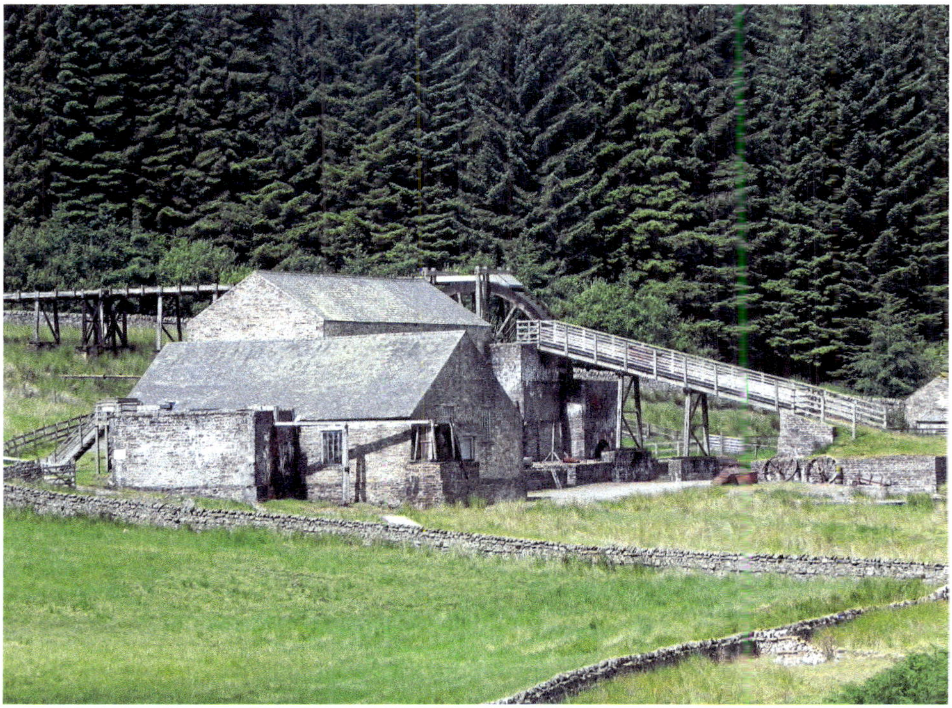

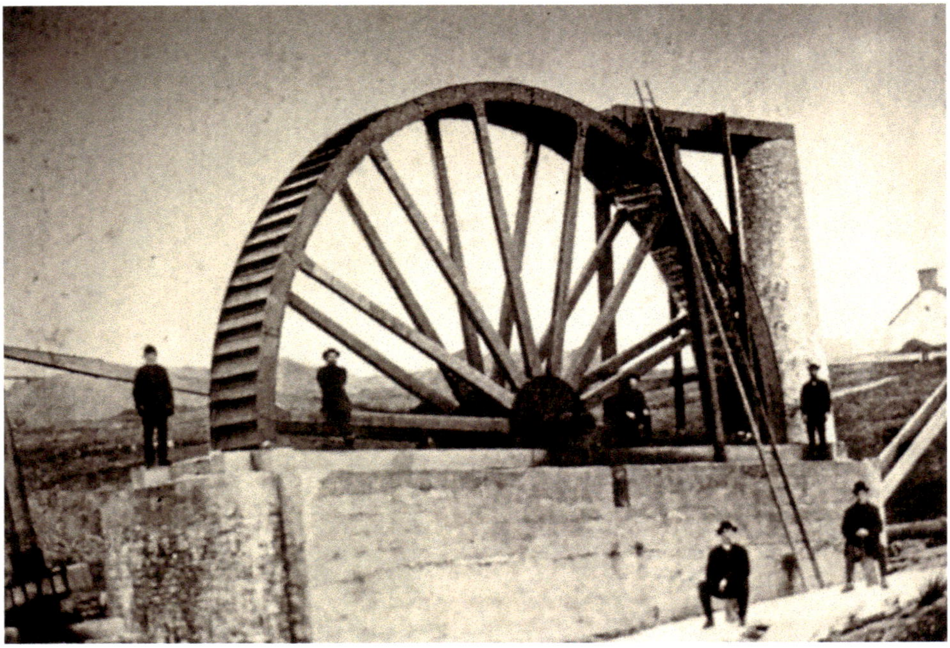

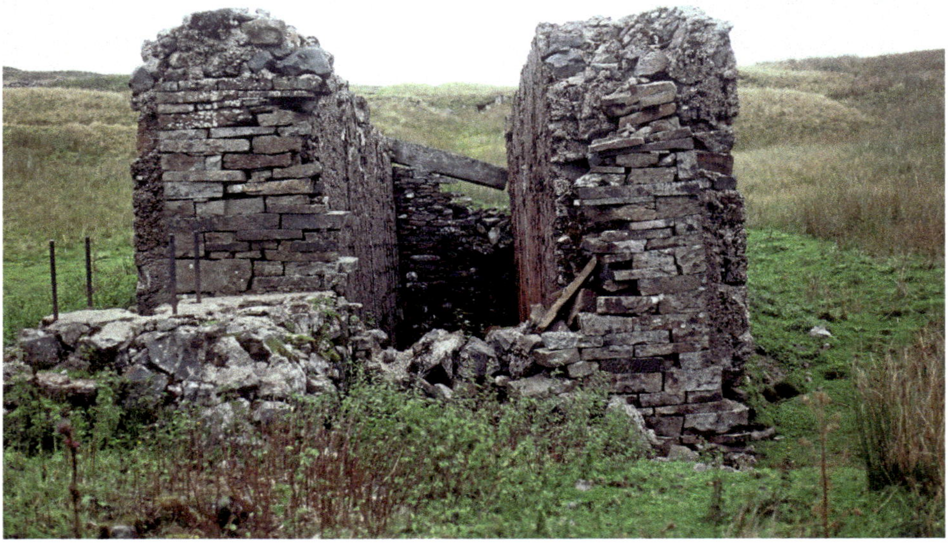

Greenhurth Lead Mine, NY 783 327

This silver-rich lead mine, situated at 1,900 feet AOD and a couple of miles across the fells from the nearest road, was worked by the Greenhurth Mining Company between 1868 and 1902. The large waterwheel, here perhaps newly installed, was used for pumping, hoisting, ore washing and dressing. It may have been moved elsewhere on closure, and only fragmentary remains of its wheel pit are now evident, although other remains make this site one of the best surviving dressing-floor complexes in the region. Photographs *c.* 1890 and 1994.

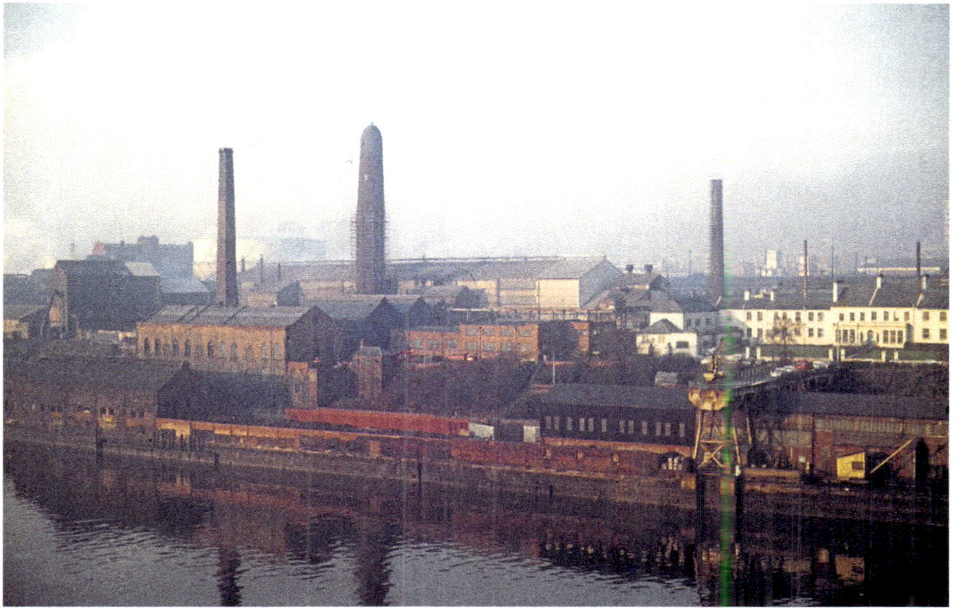

Elswick Leadworks, Newcastle, NZ 242 633

The first north-eastern leadworks was that formed at Elswick in 1778, and the Elswick shot tower was in operation by 1797. Shot production ceased in 1951 and although the tower was listed as an Historic Building, it was demolished in 1968/69. The works seems to have closed in the 1990s and the site was subsequently entirely cleared. The scene is now dominated by The Metro Radio Arena, a concert and exhibition venue built on former railway sidings to the rear of the leadworks. Photographs 1969 and 2009.

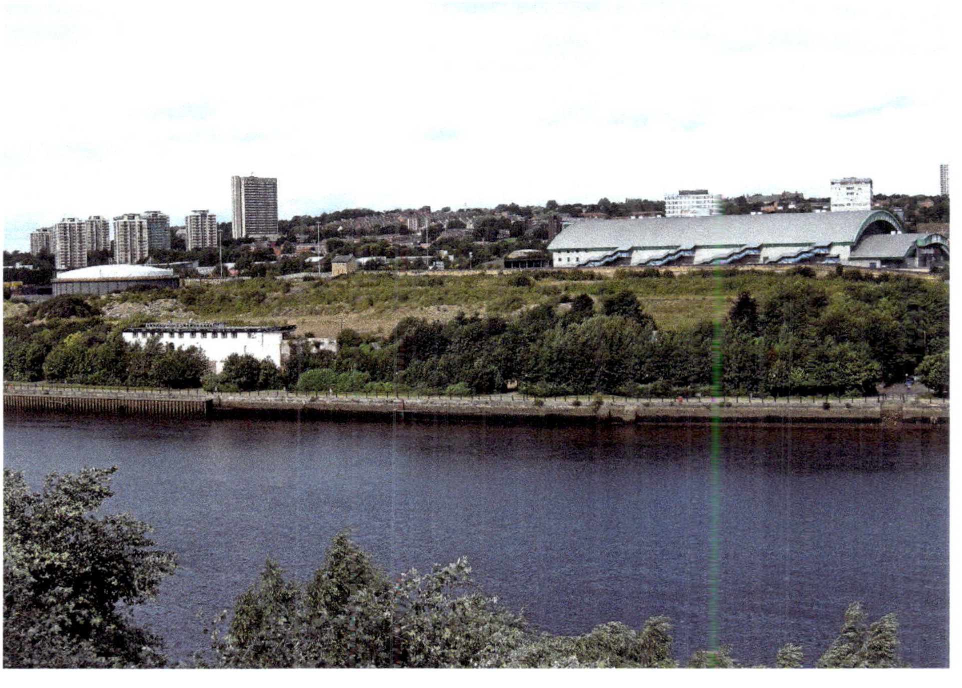

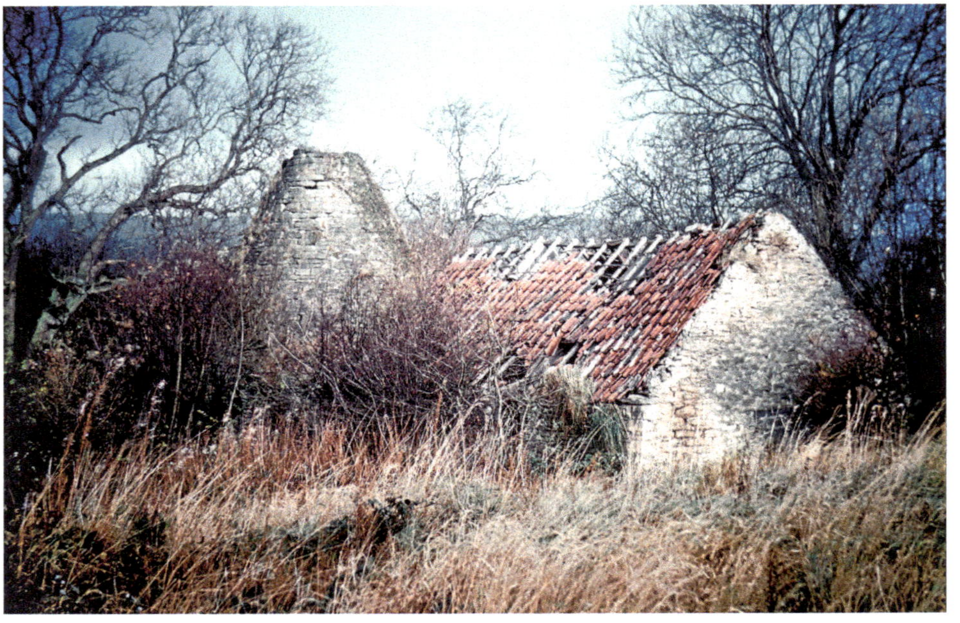

Derwentcote Cementation Furnace, NZ 127 566

The Derwentcote cementation steel furnace is one of the most important historical metallurgical sites in the Country, if not in Europe. Seemingly in a state of terminal decay in 1971, the site was made a Scheduled Ancient Monument, and after excavations and survey work, followed by a programme of consolidation and restoration, the furnace has been opened to the public. Photographs 1971 and 2011.

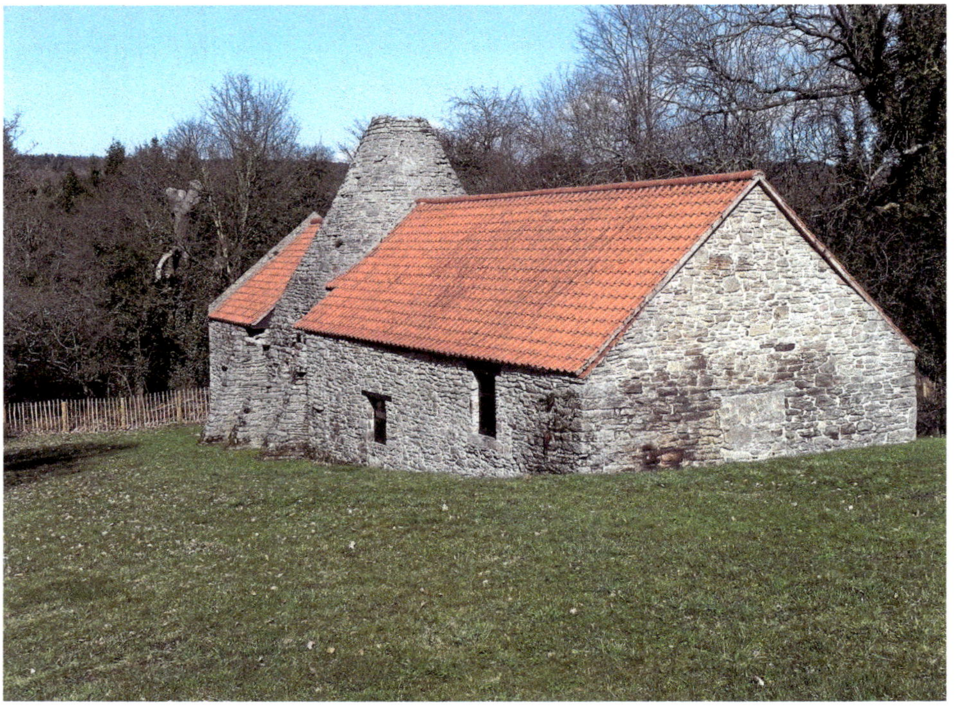

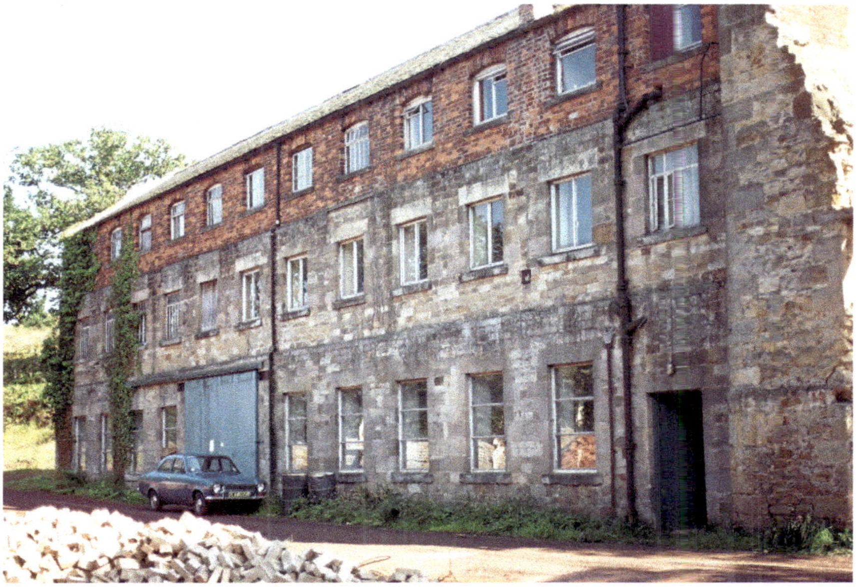

Acklington Park Tin and Iron Foundry, NU 207 029

In around 1776, a group of speculators opened a water-powered factory by the River Coquet, designed by the great John Smeaton, but the enterprise soon failed, only to become a successful woollen mill, the main building being extended upwards; later it became a dye and bleach mill. After lying semi-derelict for a number of years the buildings were converted into 'luxury accommodation' in around 1980. Smeaton's dam, probably the finest eighteenth-century dam in the country, remains largely unaltered, and were it in North Wales, we would probably have to pay good money to see it. Photographs 1973 and 2011.

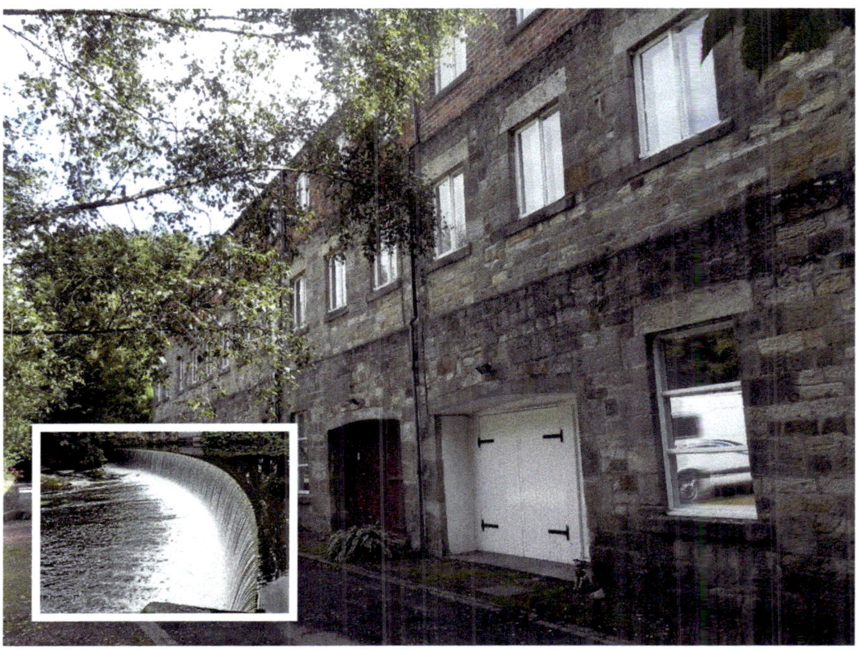

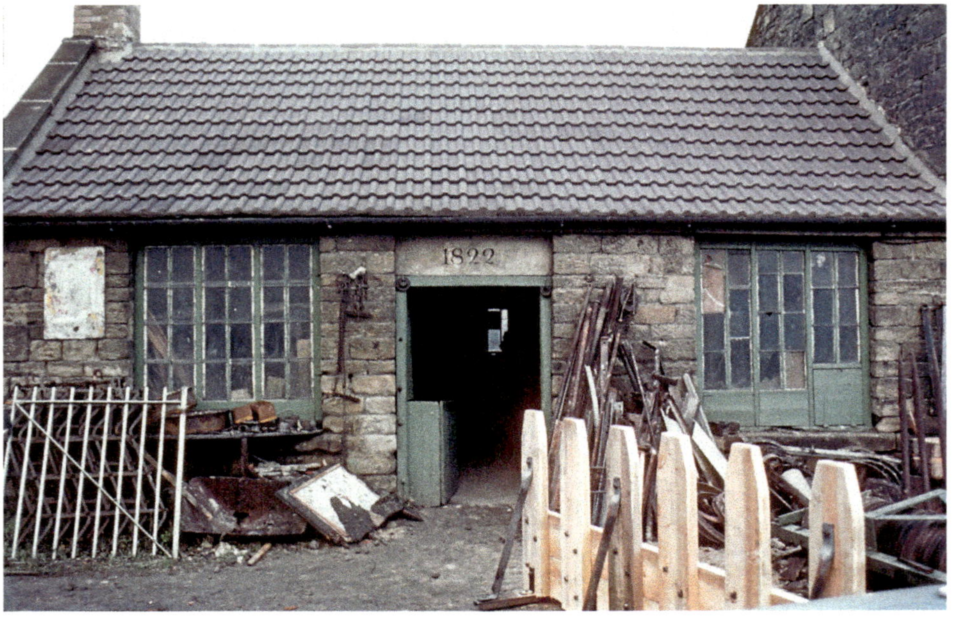

Ponteland Smithy 1, NZ 167 728

In the middle of the nineteenth century there were around 200 working smithies in Northumberland, but few of these survived beyond the middle of the twentieth century. One that did, however, was that built in Ponteland in 1822, fully working in 1969, although the then blacksmith was approaching retirement. After its closure the Smithy was converted to an eating place – the Smithy Bistro – now the New Rendezvous Chinese restaurant. Photographs 1969 and 2011.

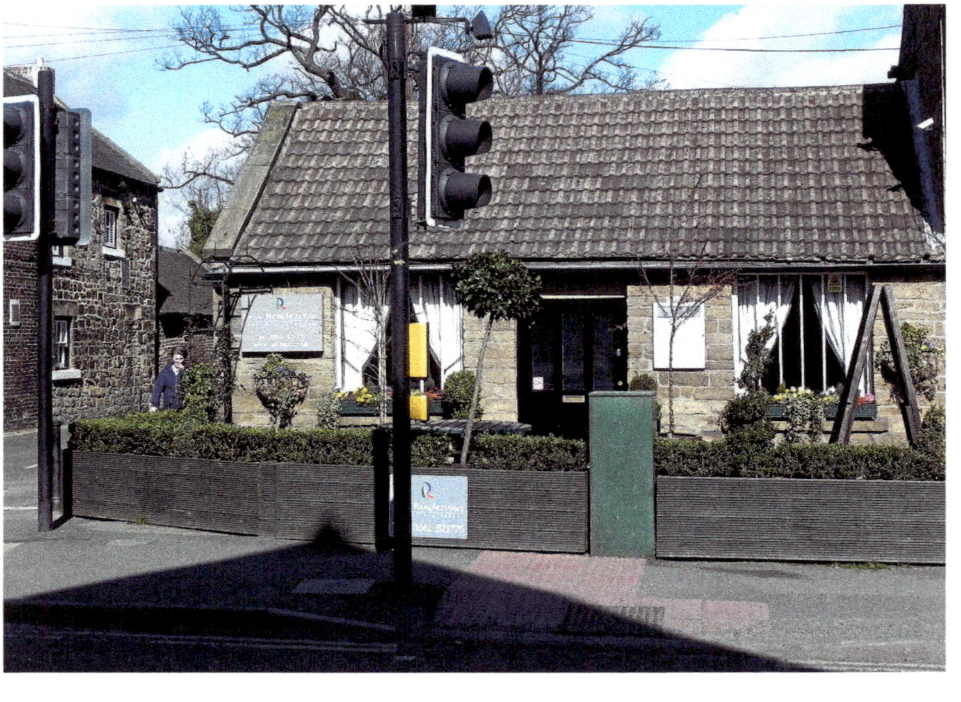

Ponteland Smithy 2, NZ 167 728

The last blacksmith at Ponteland was not your stereotypical blacksmith – no shirt open to the waist, no heavy leather apron, no rippling biceps – just a white shirt, waistcoat and tie, and a steady eye; in some ways not too dissimilar to today's waitress, although not so pretty. Photographs 1969 and 2011.

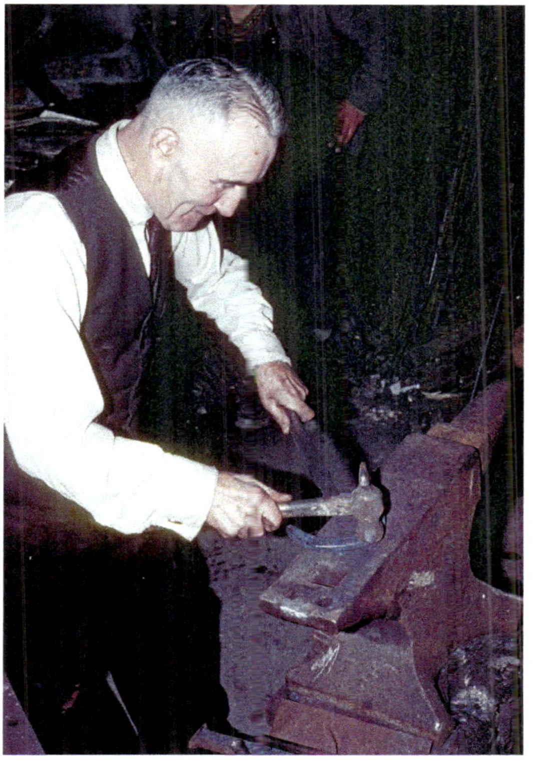

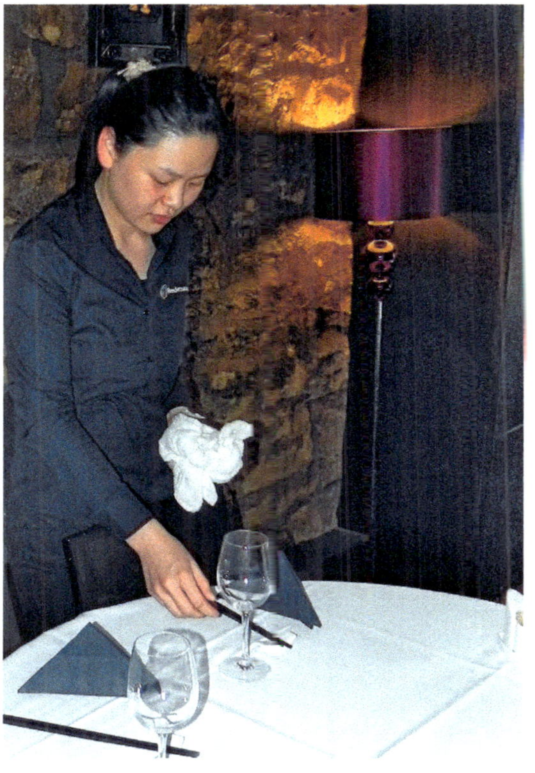

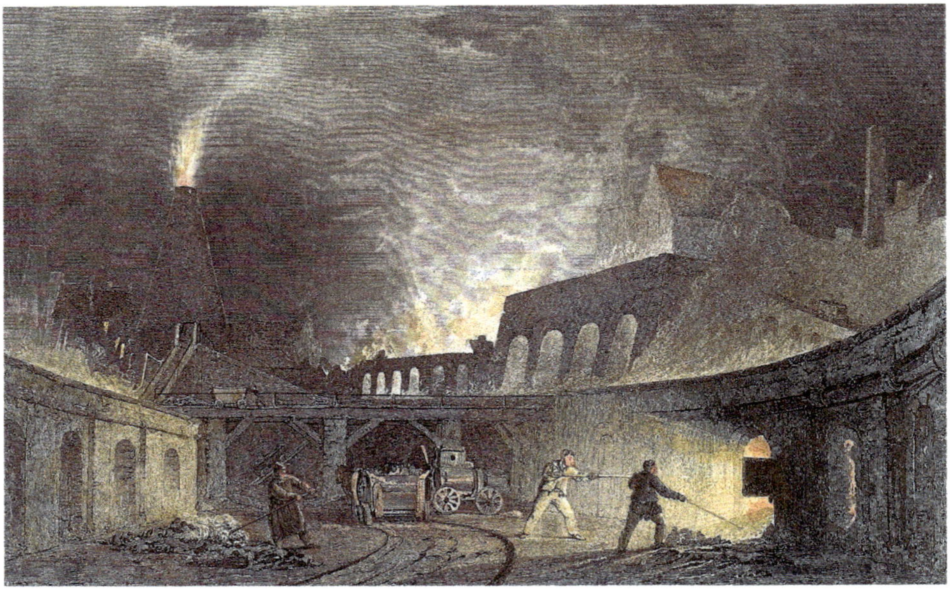

Lemington Glassworks and Ironworks, NZ 182 643

The glassworks, one of whose cones is seen to the left of the engraving, with improbable flames emerging from the top, was commenced in 1787. Immediately east of the glassworks stood the first fully integrated ironworks in the North East, established in 1797. The artist has compressed the scene considerably, and it is quite impossible to replicate it. But the surviving glass cone is one of the most important industrial monuments in the region. The ironworks closed in around 1890 and was largely demolished, while the glassworks closed in around 1997; almost all the glassworks buildings except the cone were demolished to make way for a car showroom and other buildings. Engraving *c.* 1820; photograph 2009.

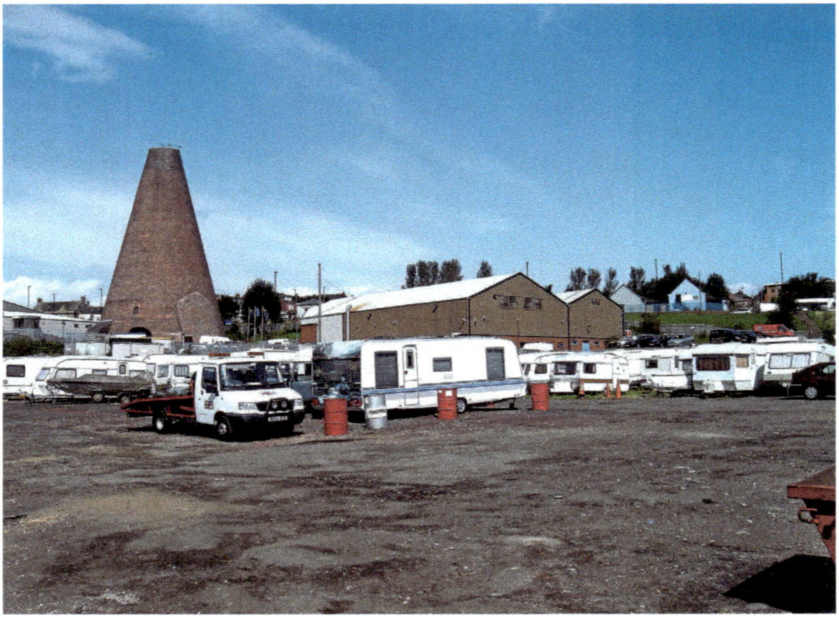

Portrack Lane Ironworks, Stockton, NZ 450 197

Three cupola furnaces stand adjacent to the casting shed of this small-town foundry, overshadowed by a large gasholder. The ironworks, originating in 1800 on a different site in Stockton, moved here sometime around the mid-nineteenth century. It was a veritable museum even when it was working and so it is no surprise that some of its equipment found its way to the nearby Preston Park Museum. It closed in 1978 and its site was subsequently cleared, but the gasholder remains, and small service industries occupy part of the ironworks site. Photographs 1979 and 2011.

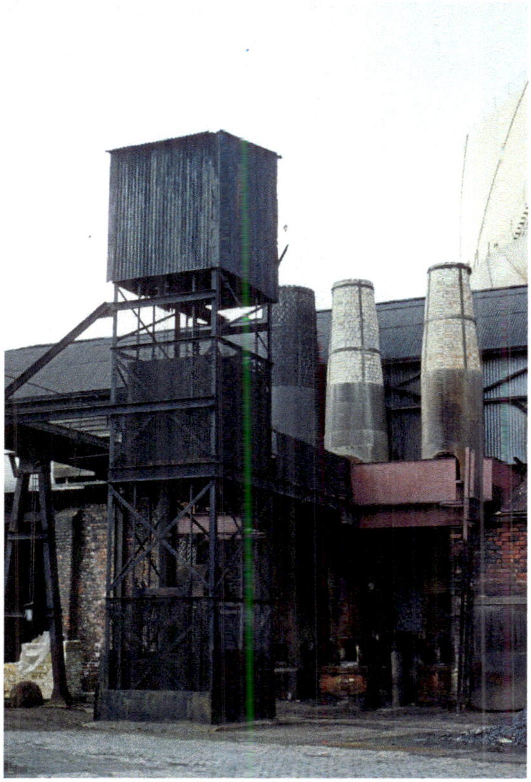

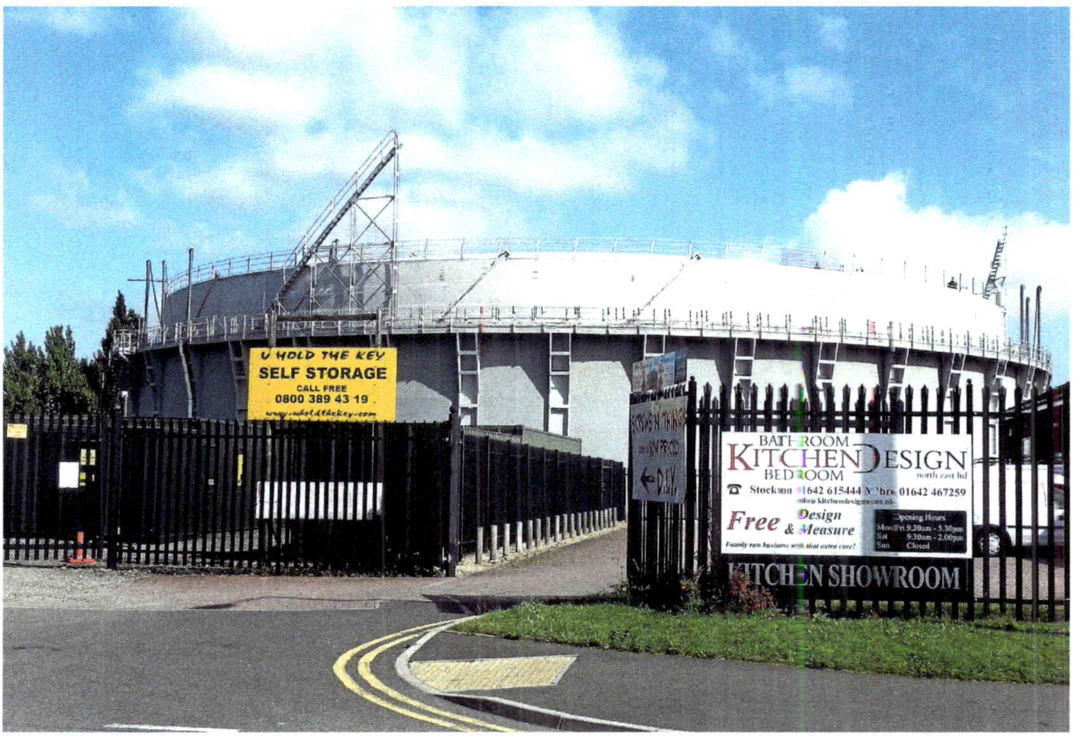

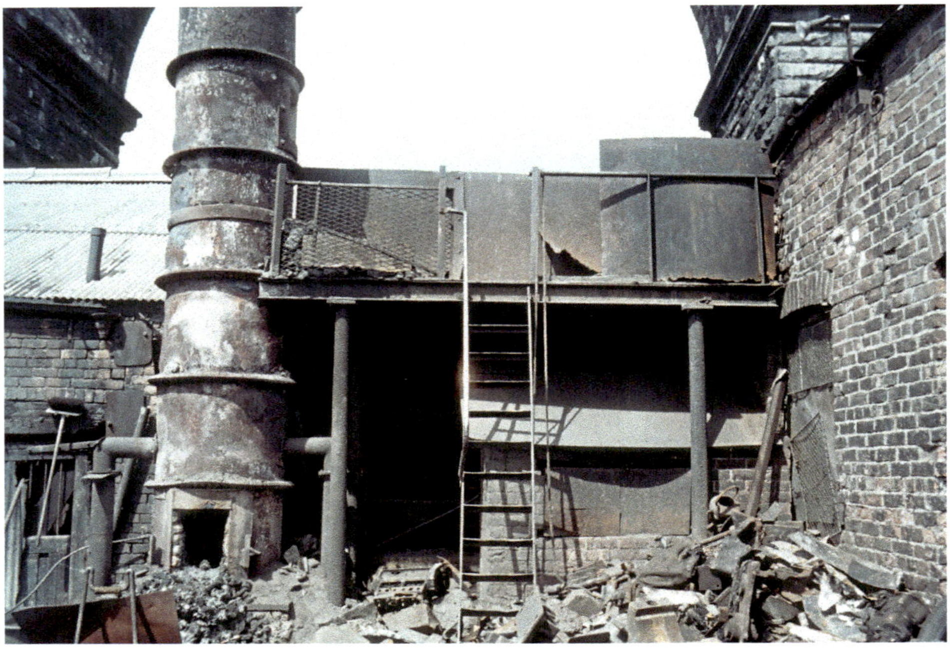

Hauxwell's Iron Foundry, Durham City, NZ 268 425

This small iron foundry, which stood in the shadow of the railway viaduct in Durham city, closed in 1970 and was soon thereafter swept away in favour of a new road scheme. The viaduct, of course, remains, and beneath it a Hauxwell manhole cover. Photographs 1969 and 2011; inset 2011.

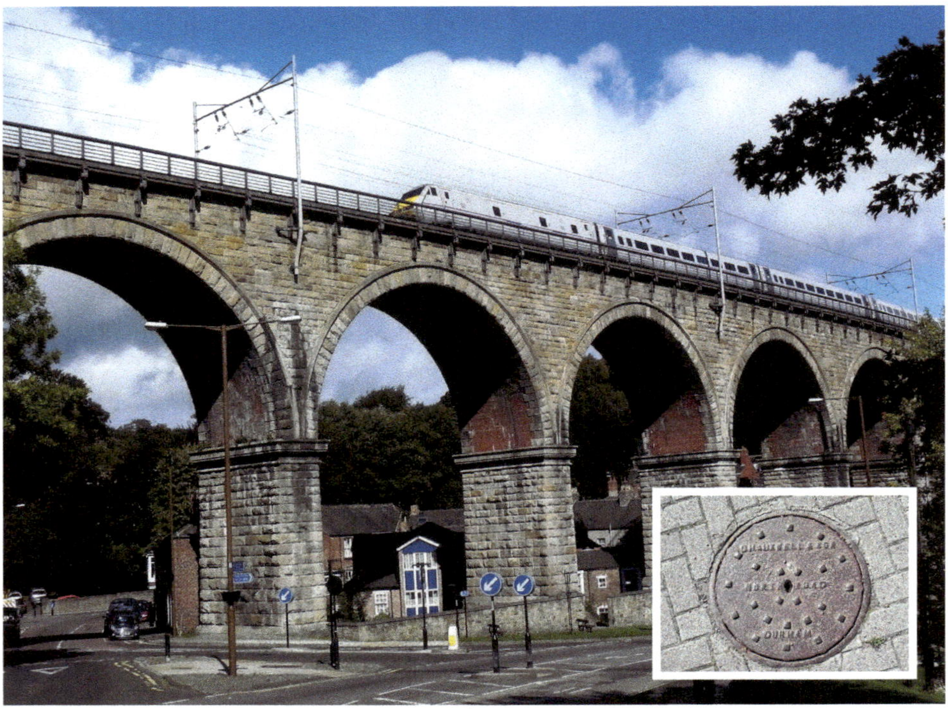

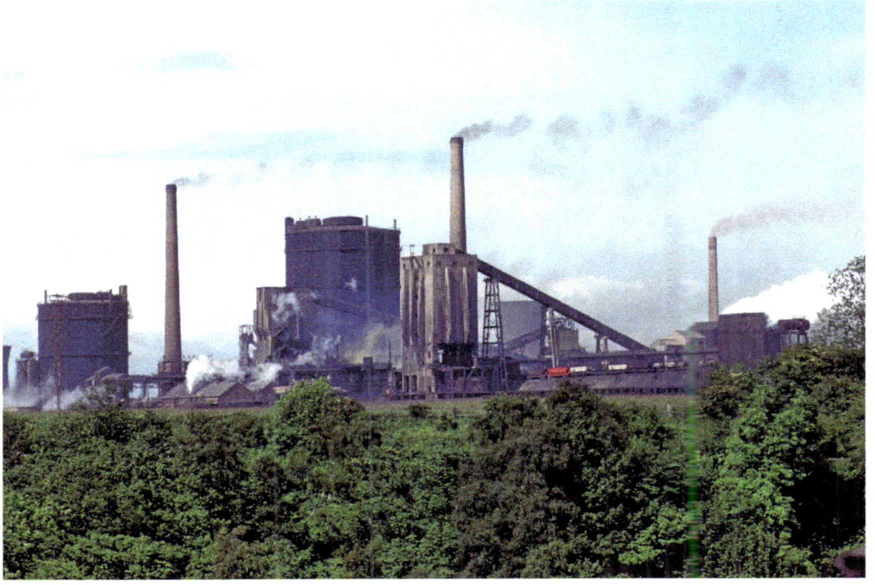

Consett Ironworks, NZ 100 504 and NZ 099 493

The Consett Ironworks was formed in 1841 and the concern soon became second in size only to the Dowlais works in Wales. Although it came to be described as being 'famous only for its size and for its inability to make a profit', the company went on to become one of the country's most successful ironworks. Its geographic isolation, however, was starkly demonstrated with the depletion of the local ore reserves, and the works closed in 1980. Little now remains of the ironworks, but a rescued slag tippler stands alongside the former Stanhope & Tyne Railway, which served the works until their coincident closure. Photographs 1972 and 2011, both taken from the same position near the Hownes Gill Viaduct.

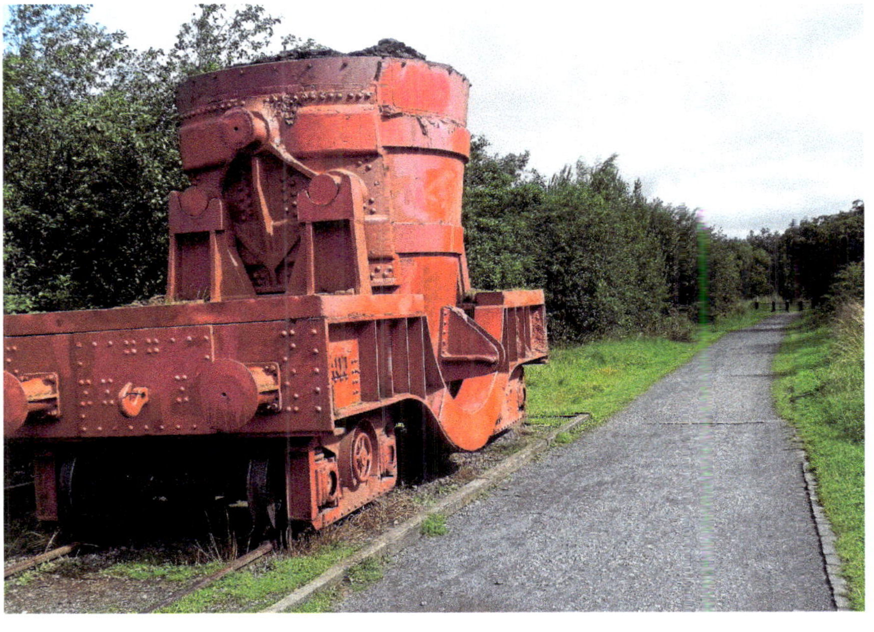

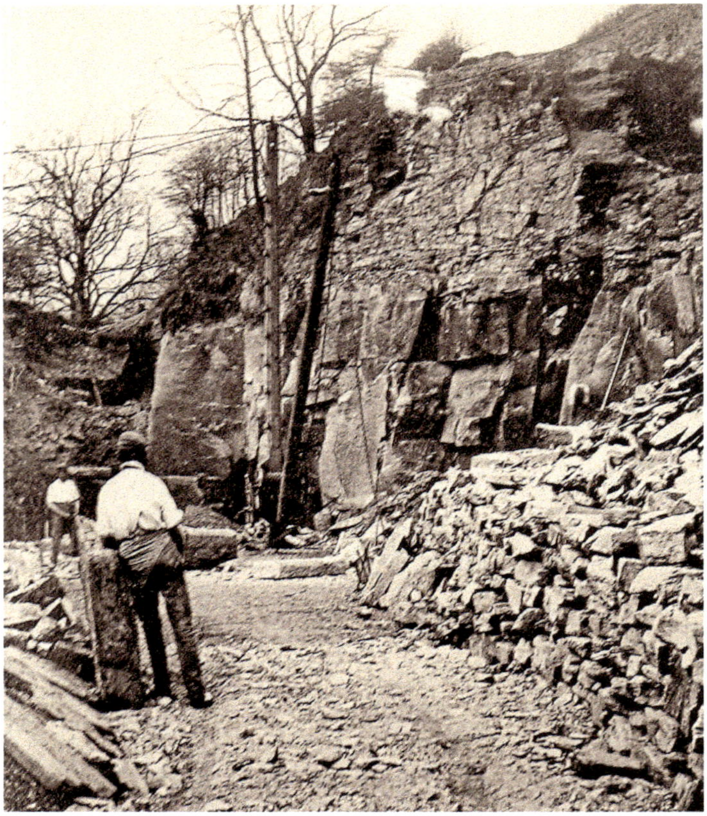

Jesmond Sandstone Quarry, Newcastle, NZ 260 670
The North East was blessed with freestones (sandstones) ideally suited to building purposes. Although quarrying is regarded by many as an eyesore, an abandoned quarry is often considered picturesque and quite suitable for a picnic area. This old quarry has long been a feature of the public park in Jesmond Dene, and happily it remains so. Photographs 1930s and 2009 (both Tom Yellowley).

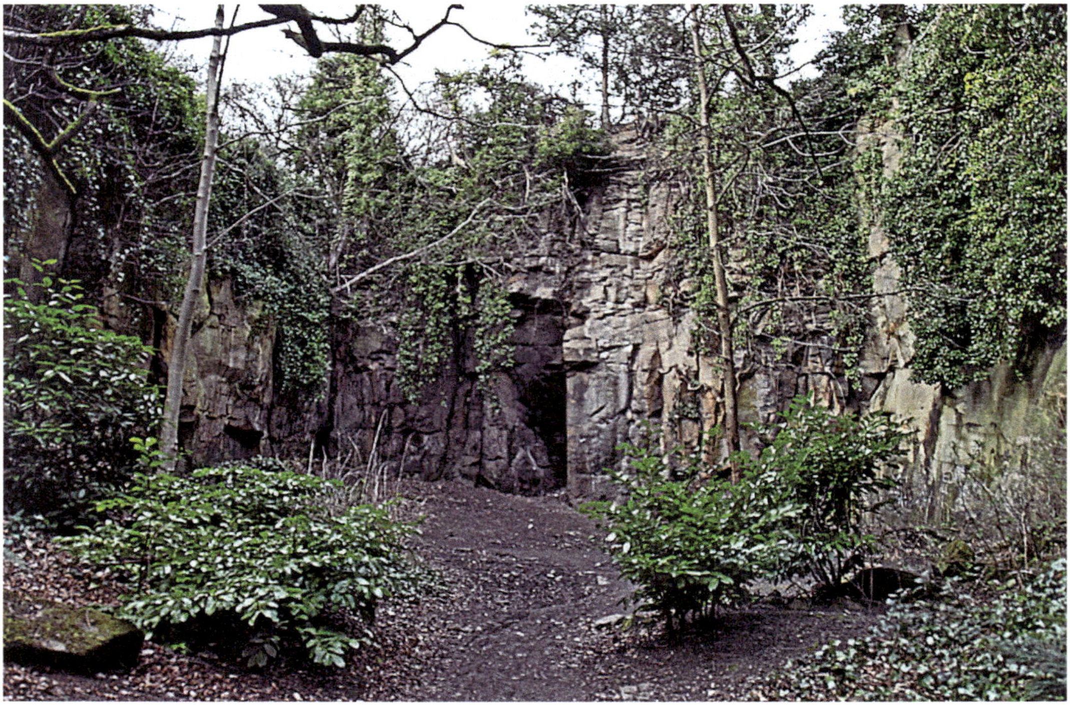

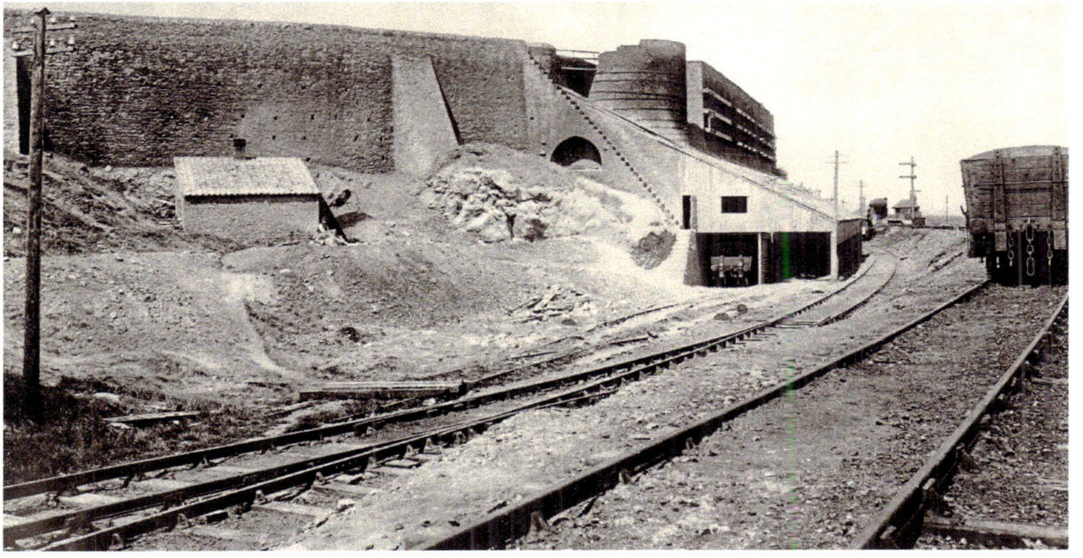

Marsden Lime Kilns, NZ 405 641

These kilns, built in two stages in the 1870s and around 1895, obtained their limestone from quarries behind them, while coal came from the nearby Whitburn Colliery. The 1870s colliery railway in front of the kilns carried passengers from 1888 and was known locally as the 'Marsden Rattler'. The kilns seem to have closed in the 1950s but were scheduled as an Ancient Monument, the only other similarly designated structures in South Tyneside being Arbeia Roman Fort and the monastery at Jarrow. Photographs 1901 (Harry Beamish, National Trust) and 2011.

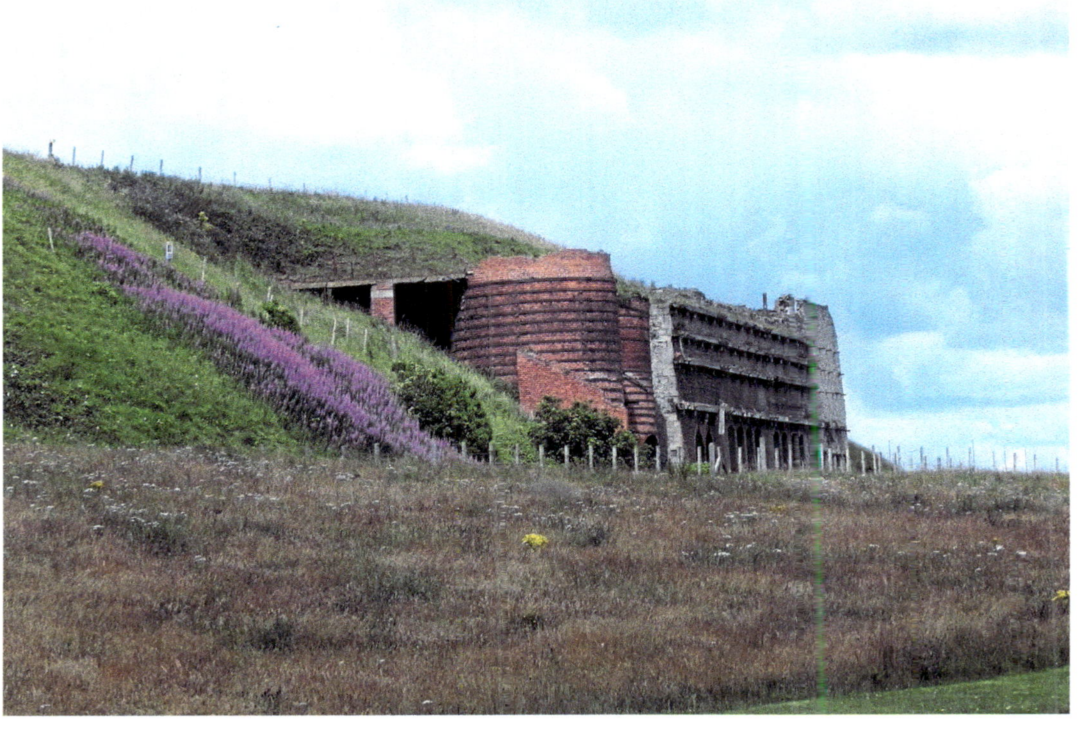

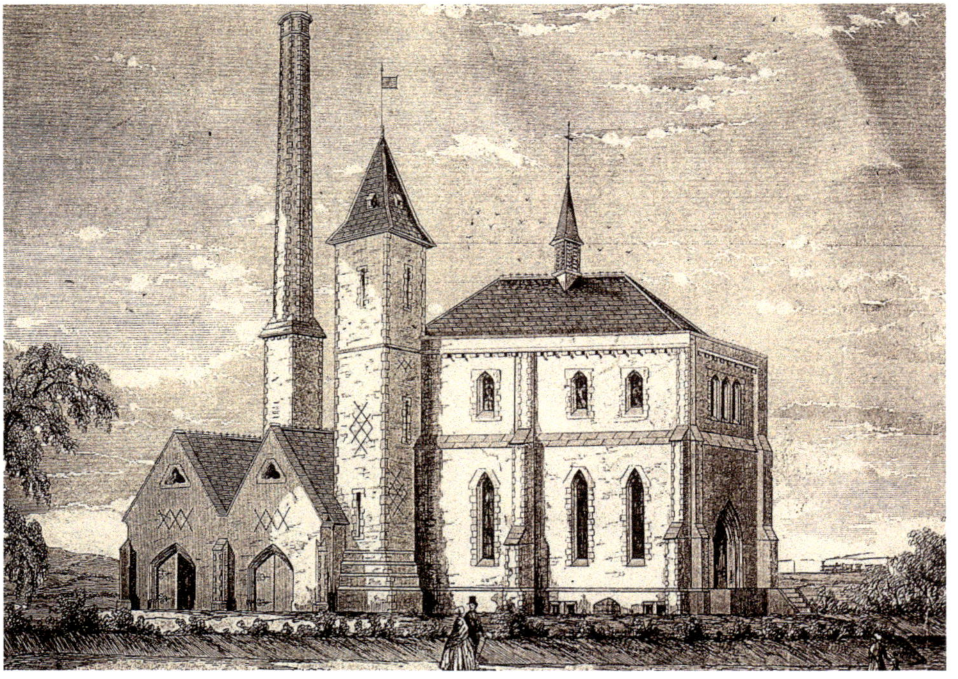

Fulwell Water Pumping Station, NZ 389 606

Constructed for the Sunderland & South Shields Water Company to the design of their consulting engineer, Thomas Hawksley, the station was in operation by 1856 with steam-powered pumping engines. Was it just artistic licence, or did ladies in crinolines regularly perambulate around the grounds? The station was electrified before 1975. Somewhat depleted and largely unused, it is clearly recognisable today. Engraving *c.* 1860; photograph 2011.

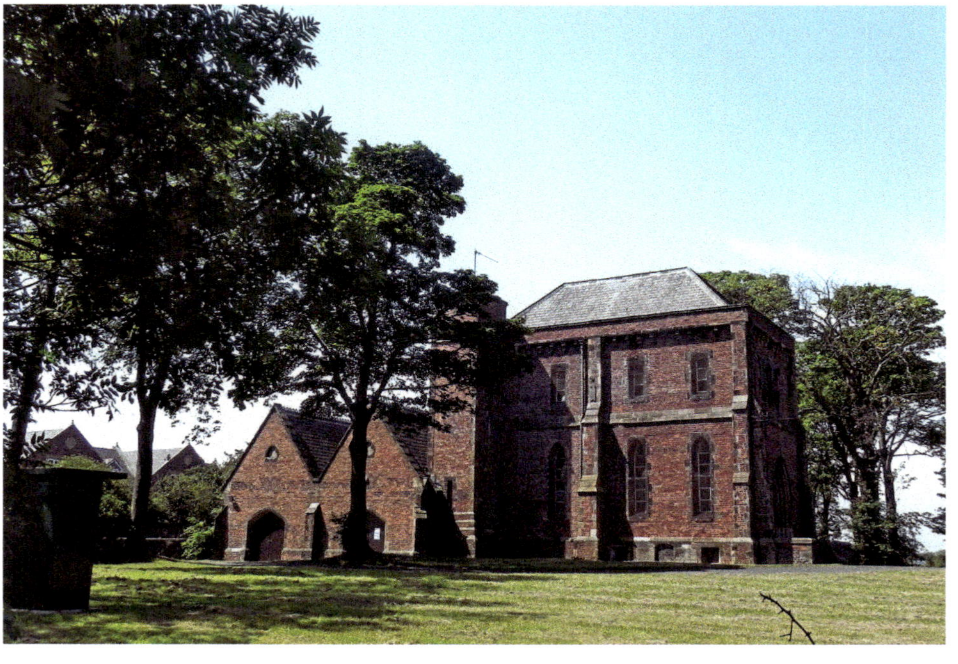

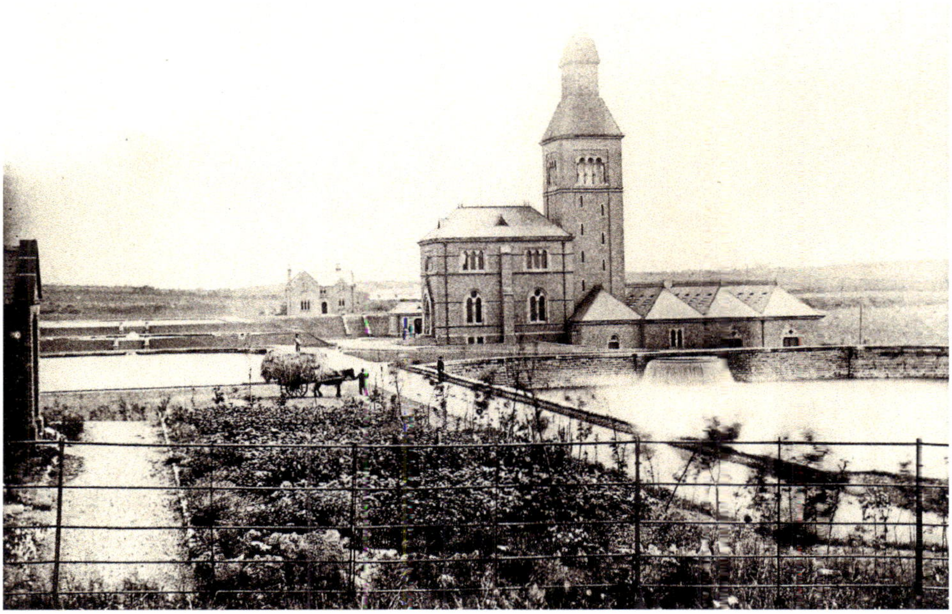

Cold Hesledon ('Big Dalton') Water Pumping Station, NZ 411 47c
This steam-powered pumping station was built between 1872 and 1881. As can be seen, such works were far from utilitarian, for cleanliness was 'next to godliness'. It was closed down in 1941, and subsequently much of its chimney tower was removed but two Cornish (non-rotative) steam-powered beam pumping engines remain. A recent plan to turn the former boilerhouse into a restaurant and public house seems also to have run out of steam. Photographs *c.* 1890 and 2011.

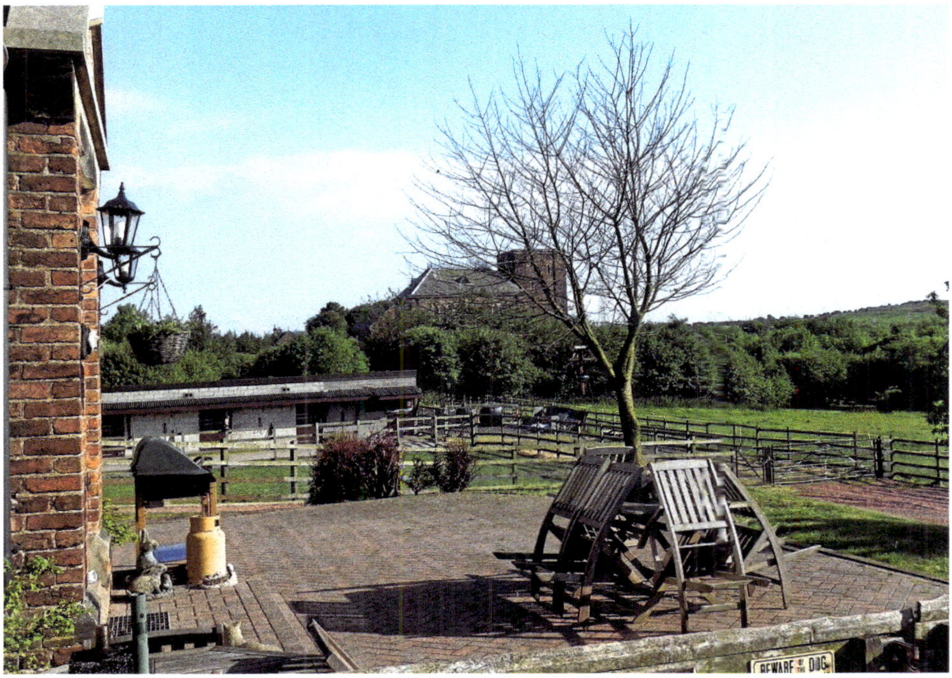

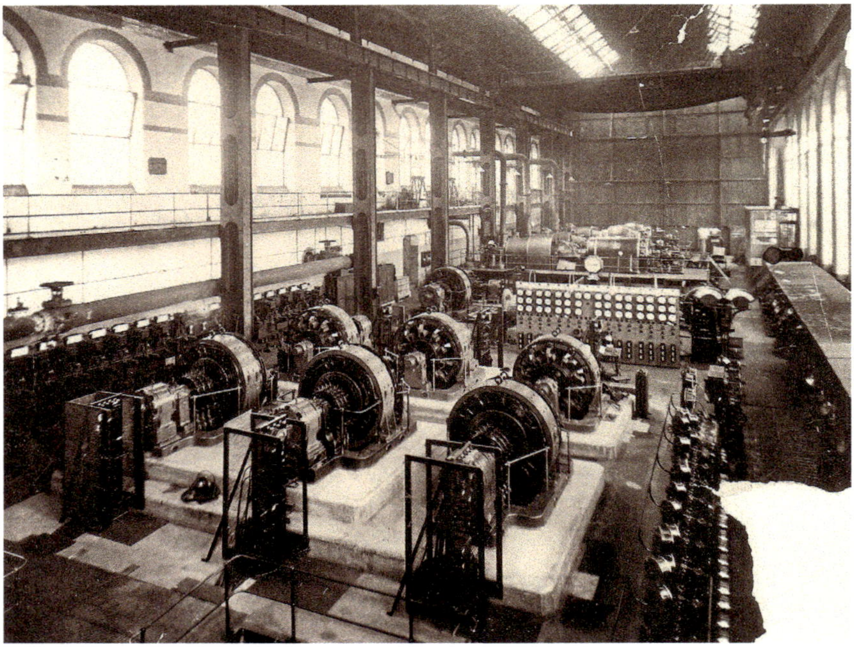

Tramways Offices and Power Station, Melbourne Street (Manors), NZ 254 643

The Newcastle Corporation Tramways Offices and Power Station was opened in 1901, but the station ceased generating in 1936 and the former generator hall, seen here, was eventually gutted to become an indoor car park. The underused building was by acquired by the city church in 1997. The main auditorium of the church, a space capable of holding 550 people, was created within the former generator hall, which retains its massive 50-tonne overhead crane; clearly its users possess a very considerable faith. Photographs 1936, 2011 and 1975 (inset).

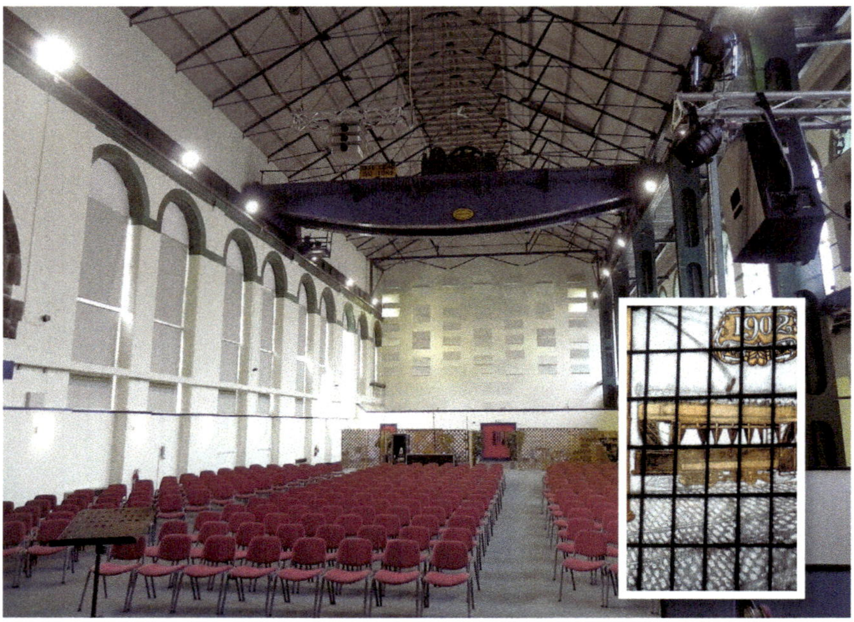

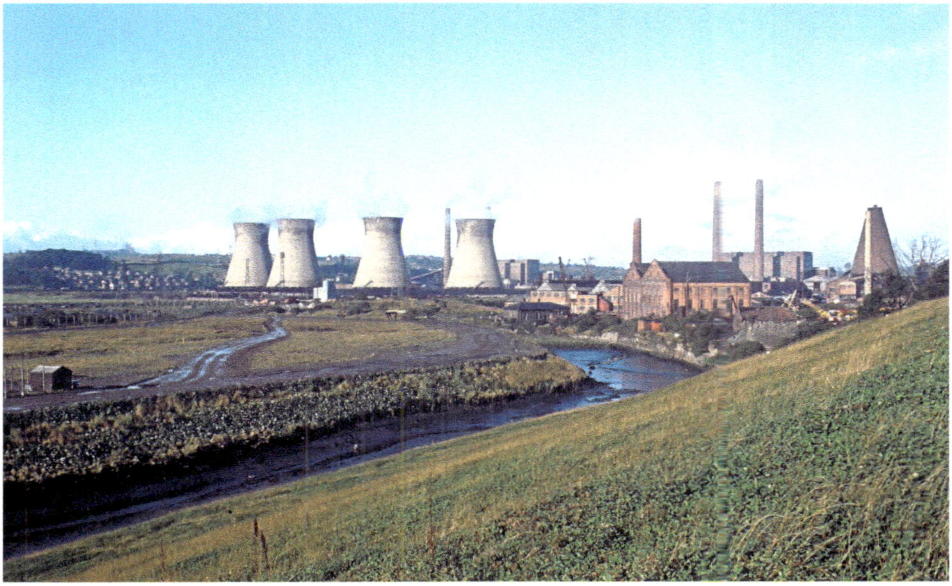

Stella North and South Power Stations, NZ 176 646 and 173 643

A once typical Tyneside industrial scene, here in the 1970s, with two functioning power stations and one former power station (the double-fronted red-brick building of 1903/4), with the Lemington glassworks behind it, and a bypassed section of the river Tyne. The two operating power stations were closed in the early 1990s and demolished soon after, while the glassworks closed around 1997. Trees now clothe the scene but the glassworks' cone still stands proud. Photographs *c.* 1972 and 2011.

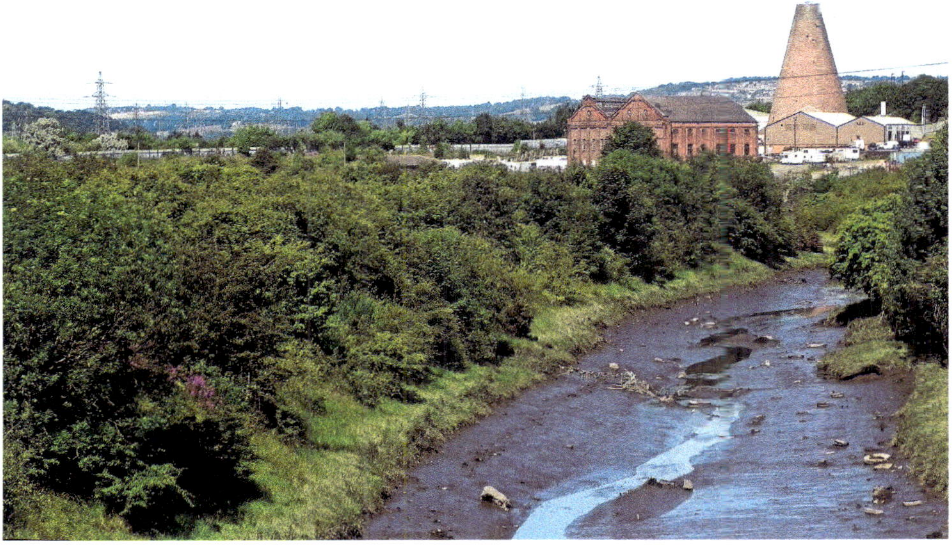

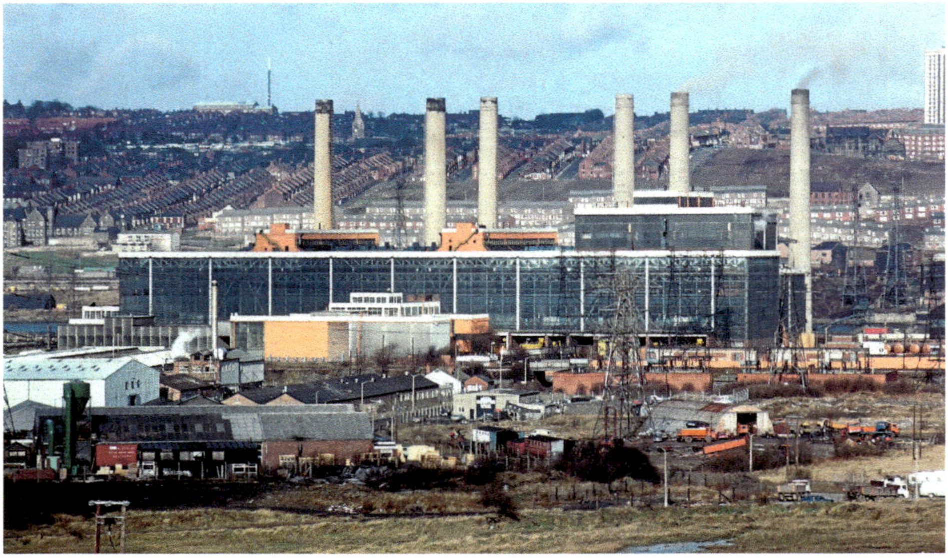

Dunston B Power Station, NZ 220 630

Dunston B Station was commissioned in January 1933, and was regarded as an important example of power station architecture, with its simple structural frame and glass curtain wall. Even so it was demolished around 1982, and much of its site remained a vacant lot in around 2008. The Gateshead Metro Centre shopping complex now dominates the scene, while farming in the foreground field continues on its ageless cycles of activity. Photographs 1976 and 2011.

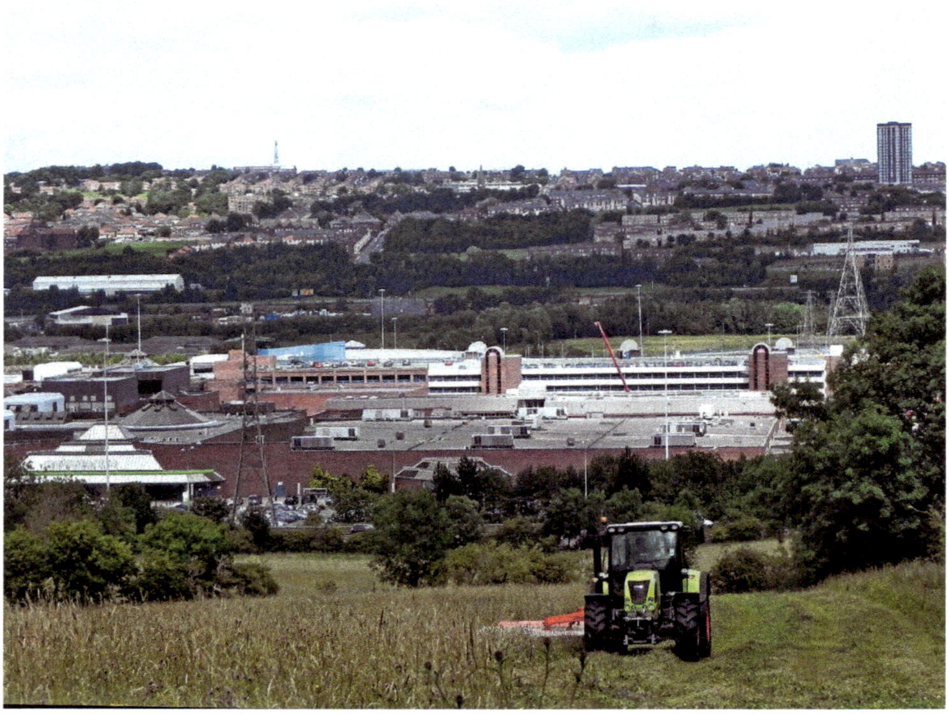

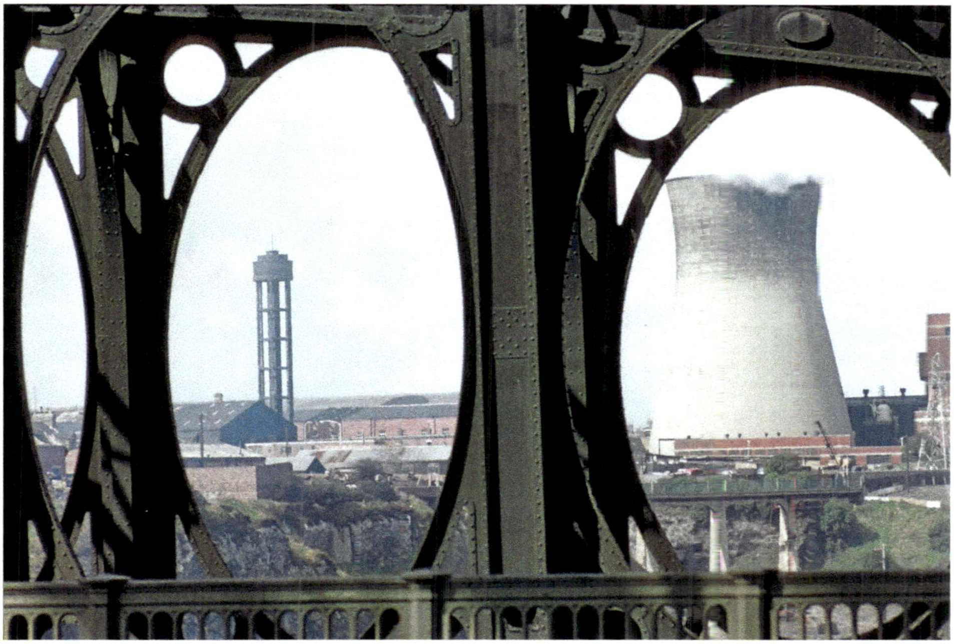

View Through Wearmouth Railway Bridge, Sunderland, NZ 397 574

Sometimes said to be the largest wrought-iron hog-back girder bridge in the world, this bridge of 1879 is best seen from a moving bus on the adjacent road bridge. But the once dramatic views through its oval openwork stiffening webs, of a power station and a water tower, are no more, for both have been demolished. Photographs 1973 and 2011.

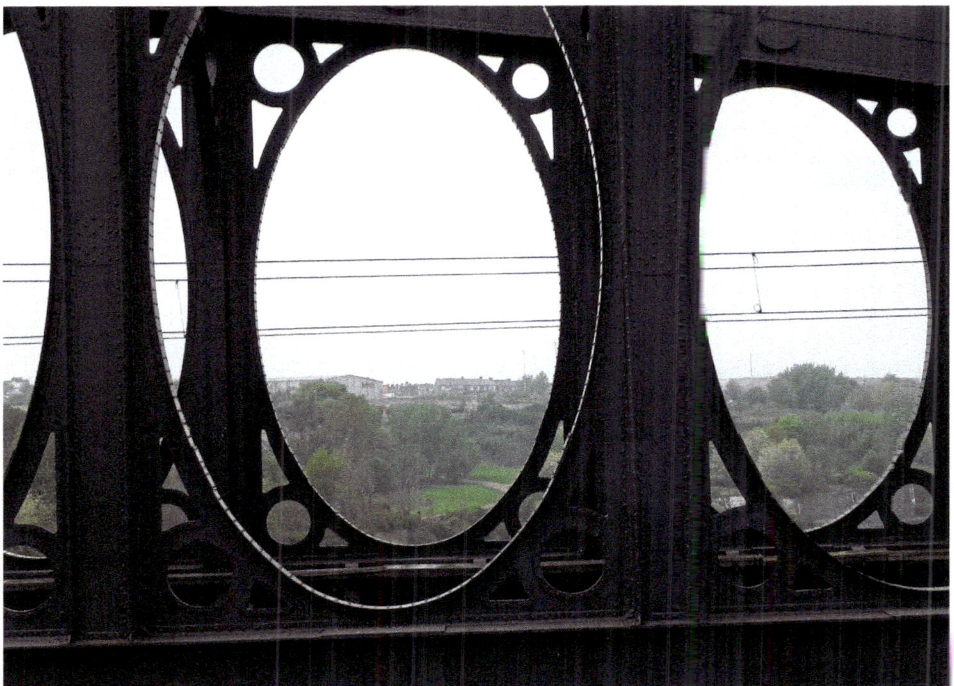

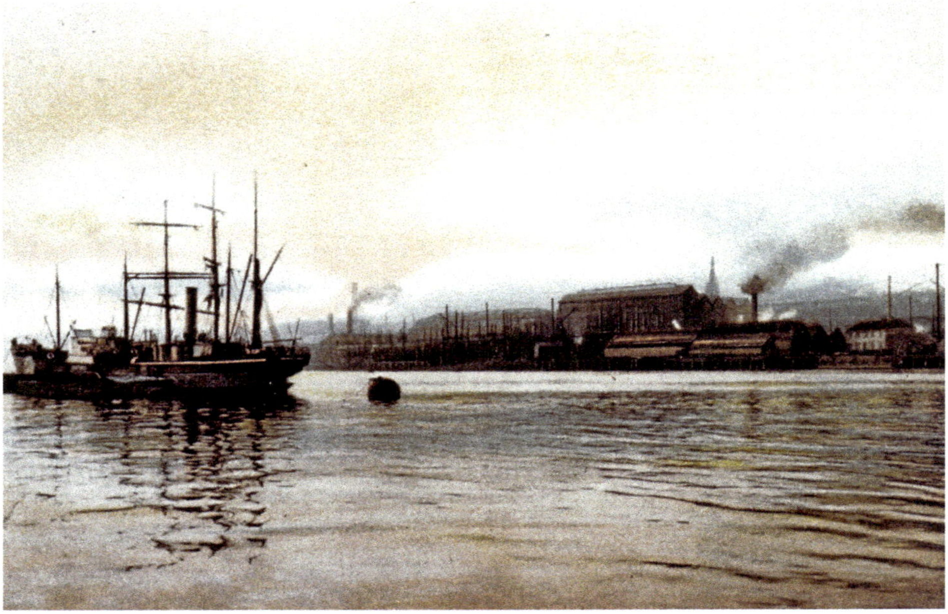

The Armstrong Elswick Works, Scotswood Road, Newcastle, NZ 326 629

The Armstrong Works was established in 1847, initially to construct hydraulic equipment, employing some twenty or thirty men. By 1852 about thirty-five workers were employed at the works, rising to about 13,000 by 1892. The works was then also building ships, producing armaments, and operating its own blast furnaces. The firm continued strongly into the twentieth century, but the 1950s saw the beginning of a struggle for survival. That fight was ultimately lost, and the works was closed in the early 1980s, a business park being built on its site. Postcard *c.* 1910; photograph 1990.

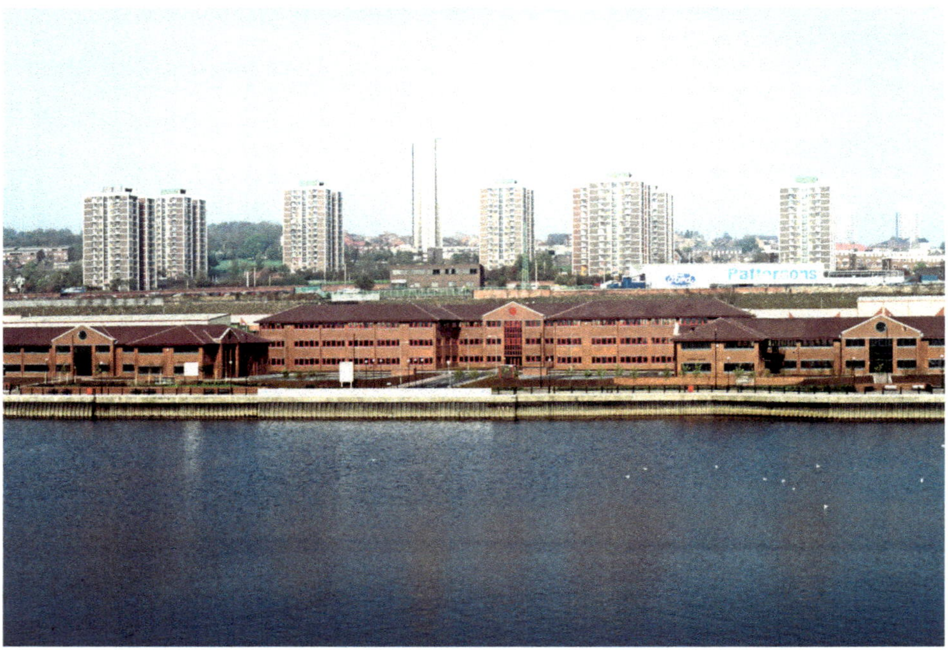

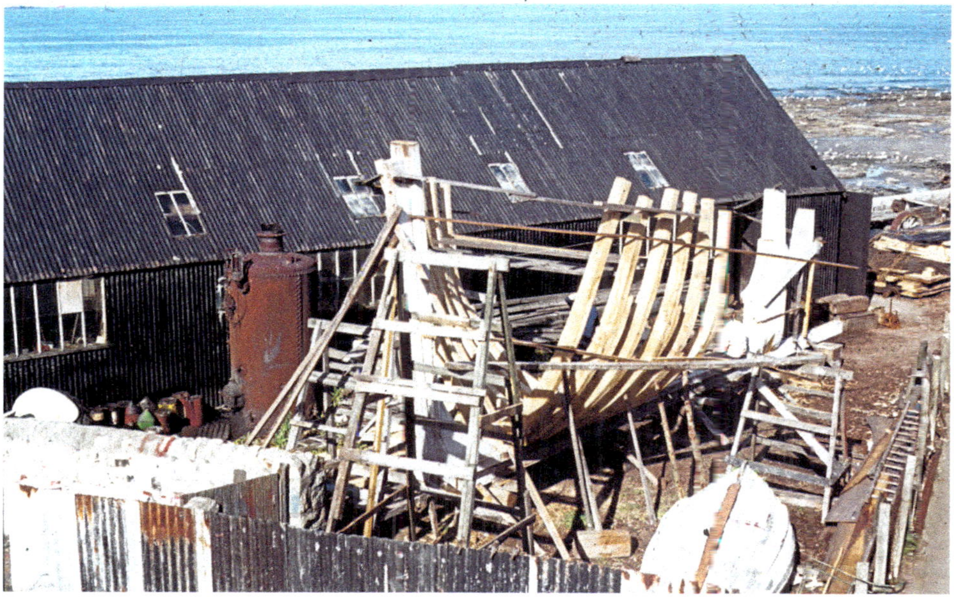

Seahouses Boatyard, NU 220 321

R. Dawson & Sons ran a traditional boatyard at Seahouses. By the 1970s it was the only such yard left in the North East of England. The boats were constructed in the open air, using techniques that any eighteenth-century shipwright would have recognised - a keel fashioned from a single piece of oak, oak framing and larch skin. This method of boatbuilding was a dying craft, and unfortunately Dawson's closed in the 1990s. The site of the yard is now a largely vacant lot, alongside the lifeboat house, just another car and boat park. Photographs 1974 and 2011.

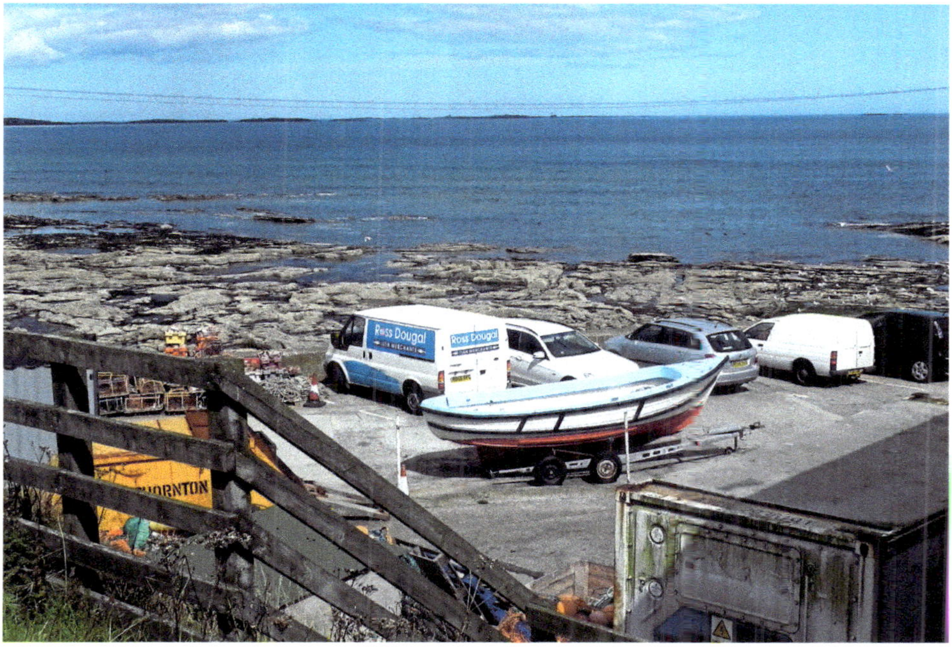

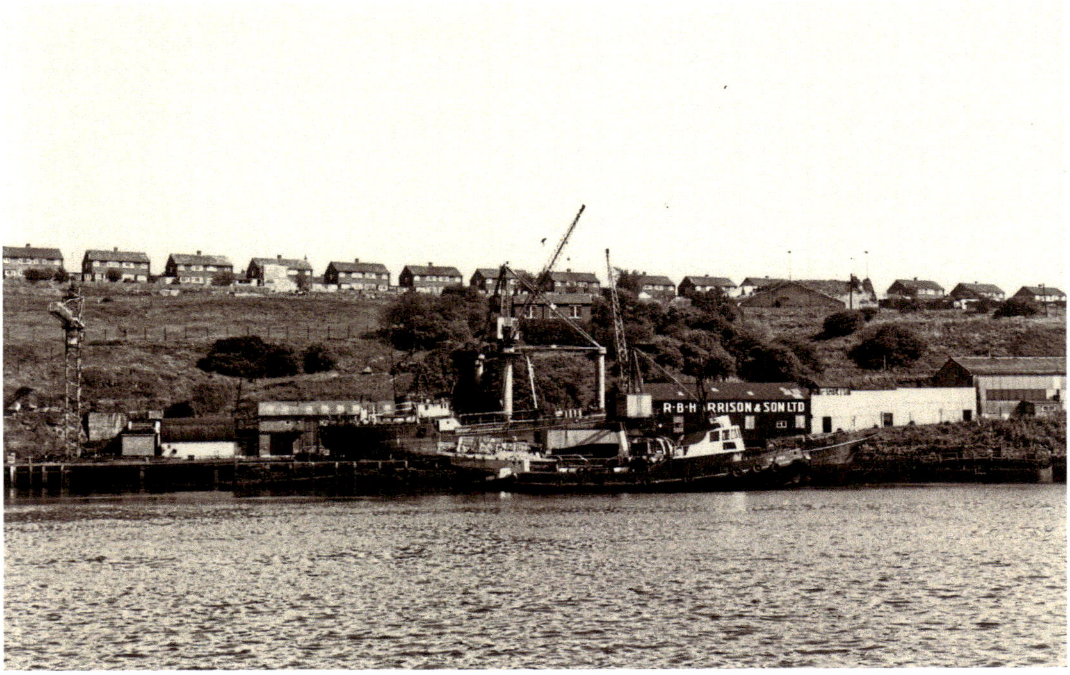

Harrison's Boatyard, Bill Quay, NZ 295 629

This small shipyard, one of the last operating on the Tyne by 1986, had long specialised in the building and repairing of small boats. In 1969, the yard restored the paddle tug *Eppleton Hall*, which was then paddled 11,000 miles from the Tyne to the San Francisco Maritime Museum (see inset). The yard closed in 1990 and the site is now quite derelict, only the concrete pillars of the derrick cranes remain standing. Photographs *c.* 1976, 1992 (Tom Yellowley) 2002 (inset, Tessa Gray).

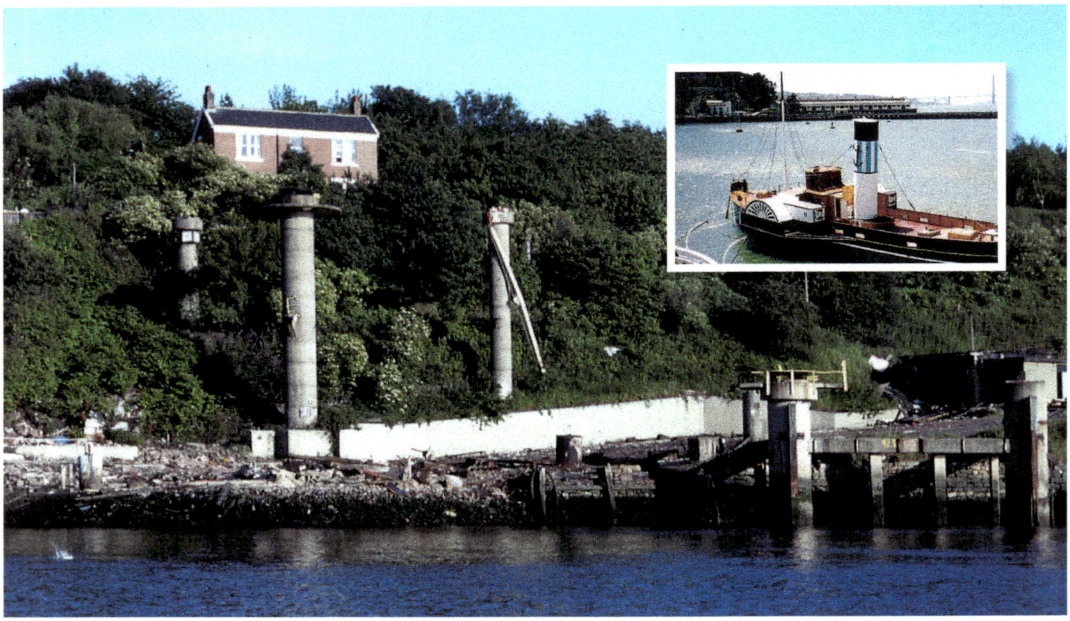

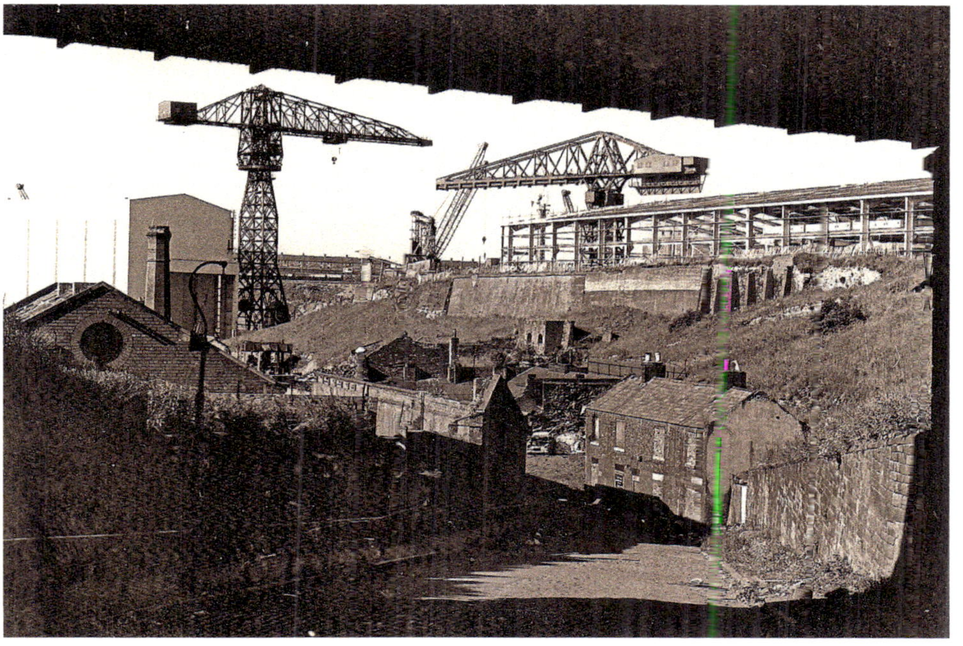

Down Wellington Lane, Deptford, Sunderland, NZ 393 573

Under a railway bridge of a former mineral line in Sunderland, the immediate scene is mainly one of industrial decay and dereliction, apart from the still-active Laing's shipbuilding yard and a new bus depot under construction. Since this 1975 photograph was taken, nature has asserted its domain. Photographs 1975 and 2011.

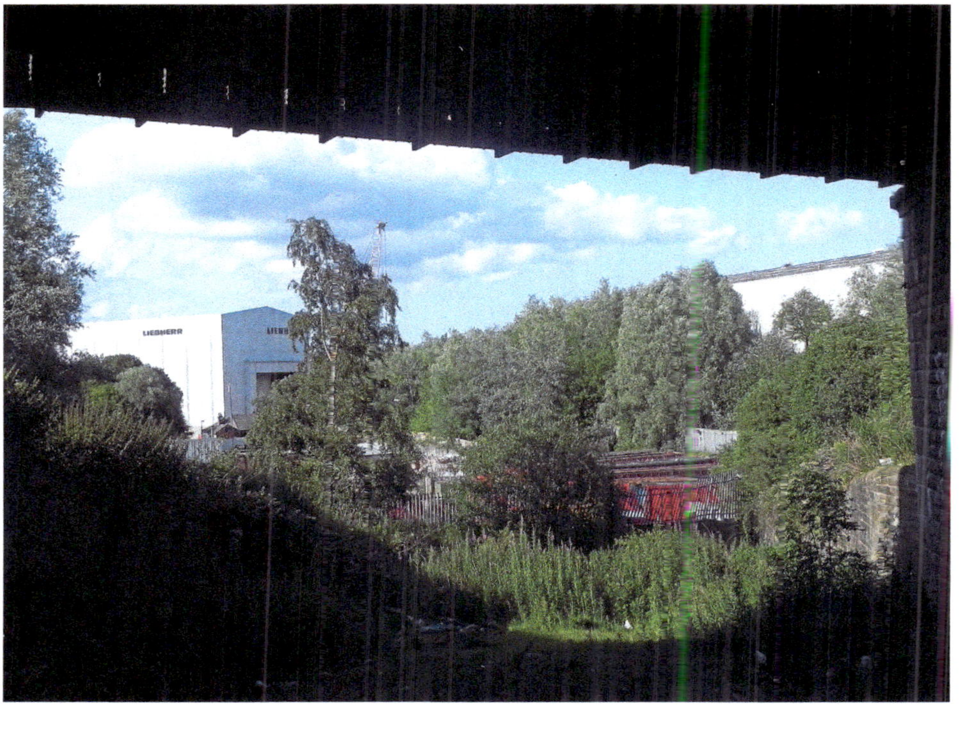

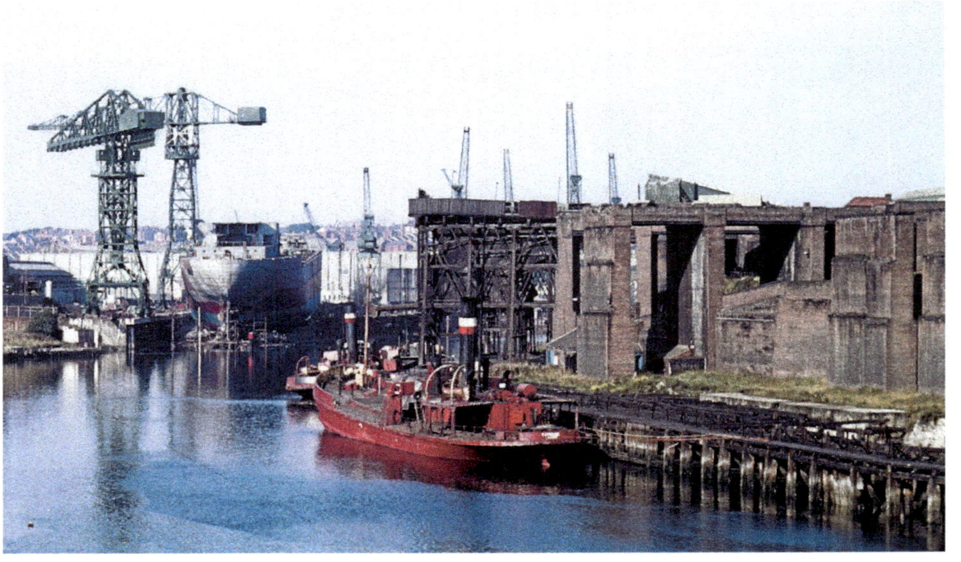

Laing's Shipyard, Sunderland, NZ 388 579

Laing's shipyard, with a vessel on the stocks, faces the Monkwearmouth coal staiths across the Wear. Laing had begun shipbuilding on the Wear in the 1790s, and by 1804 it had the largest yard on the river. Its most famous ship was the *Torrens,* a composite (wood and iron) full-rigged passenger clipper of 1875, the last such ship ever built. Joseph Conrad who served as second mate on the *Torrens,* wrote 'The way that ship had of letting big sea slip under her did one's heart good to watch. It resembled ... an exhibition of intelligent grace and unerring skill'; she was broken up in Genoa in 1910. The yard closed in 1975 and the site was taken over by the German company Liebherr for the manufacture of maritime cranes; they are now the sole representative of heavy industry on the banks of the Wear. Photographs 1971 and 2011.

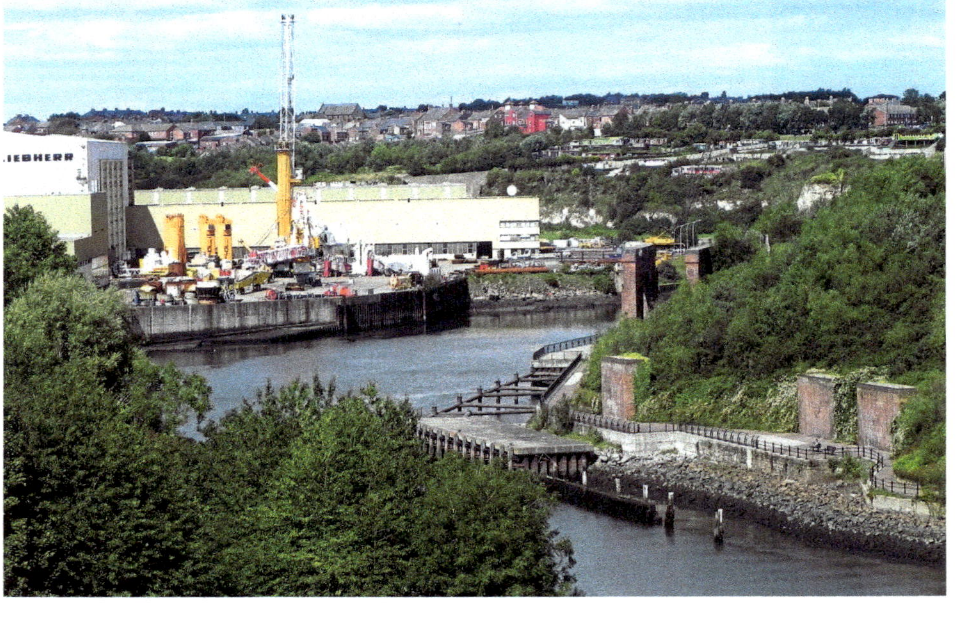

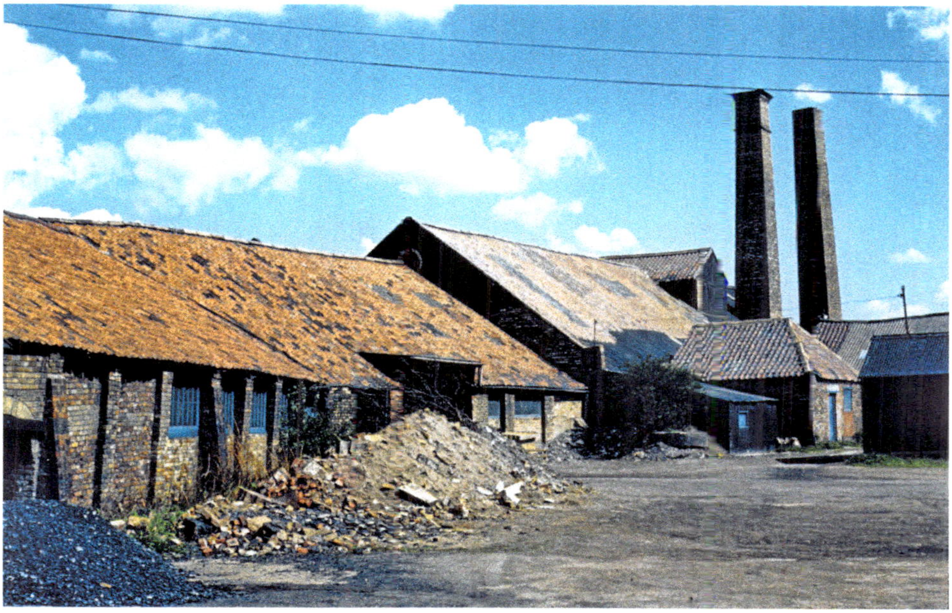

Adams Pict Firebrick Works, Swalwell, NZ 203 627

Numerous local fireclay works, especially those concerned with salt-glazed sanitaryware, closed down from the 1960s, largely due to the widespread introduction of plastic pipes, but this works was different in specialising in high-grade furnace bricks. Even so, its antiquated plant (one building dated from 1858) and absence of mechanisation were probably responsible for its liquidation in 1975. The site has been subsumed within developments around the Gateshead Metro Centre, but it stood somewhere close to the Holiday Inn. Photographs 1973 and 2009.

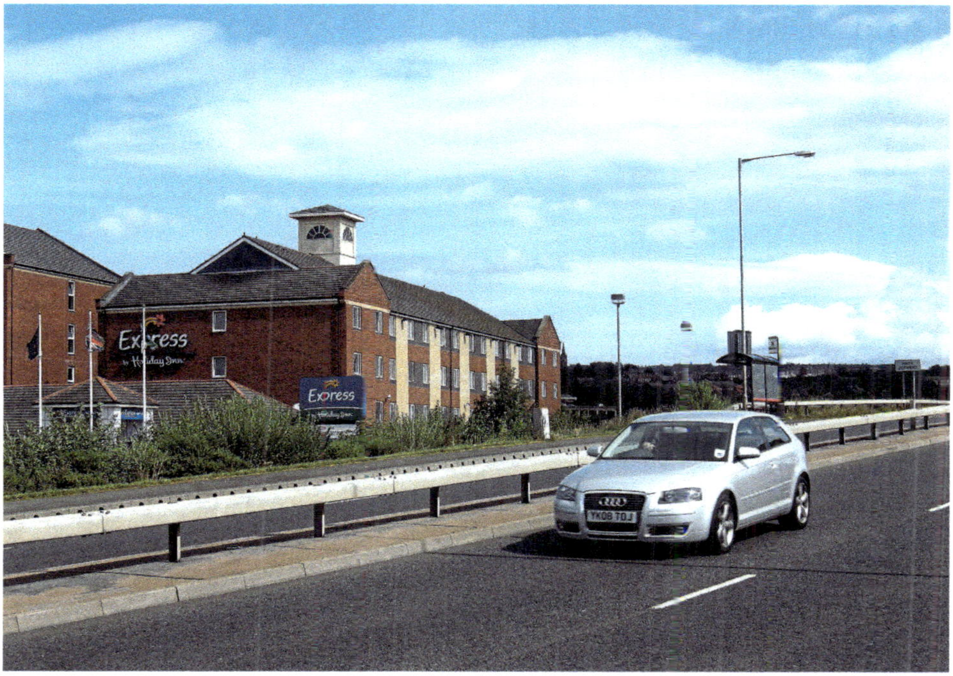

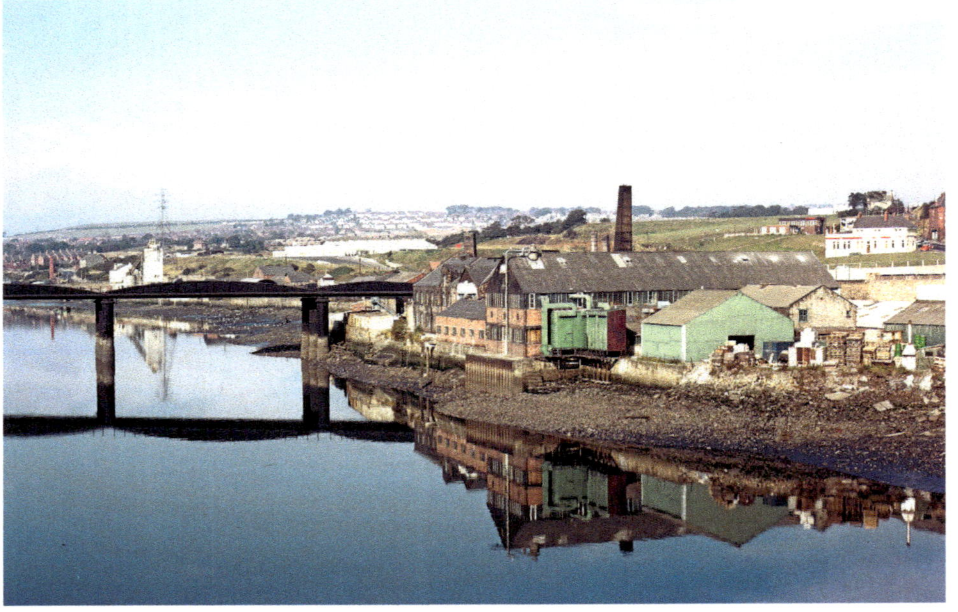

Adamsez Pottery from Scotswood Bridge, Newcastle, NZ 200 636

The Adamsez Company took over a brick and tile works at Scotswood on Tyne in 1903, which part-occupied a former paper mill. Almost from the beginning they produced 'art pottery', but their staple product was more prosaic, and could be found in toilets throughout the world. The works was closed down in around 1975, and many of the buildings were demolished, although others were reused as a pie factory, a tile superstore, and a car and van sale room. The disused railway bridge dates from 1871. Photographs 1972 and 2011.

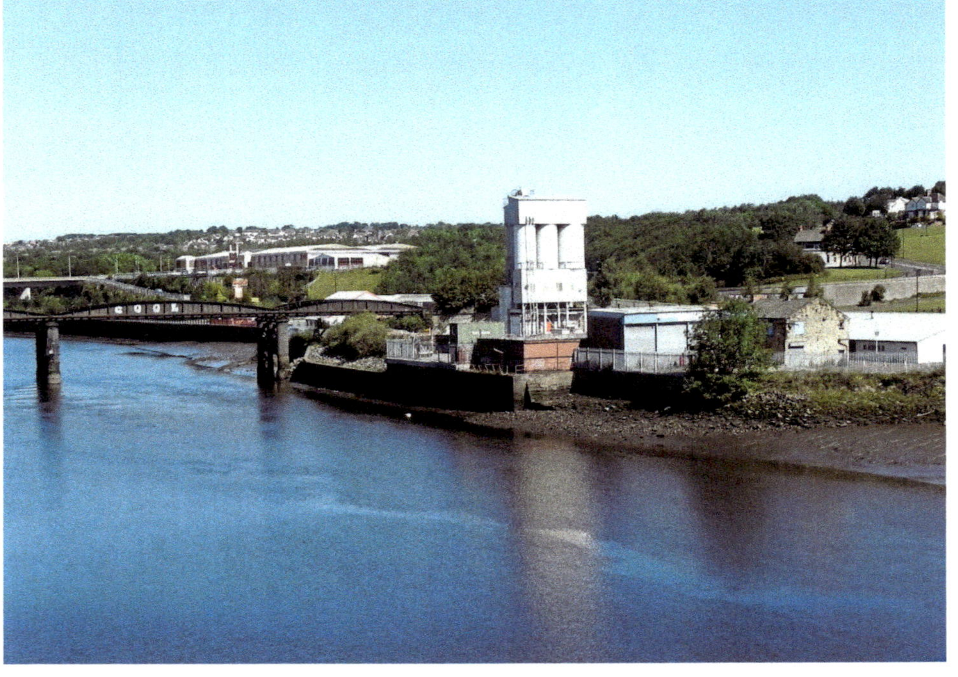

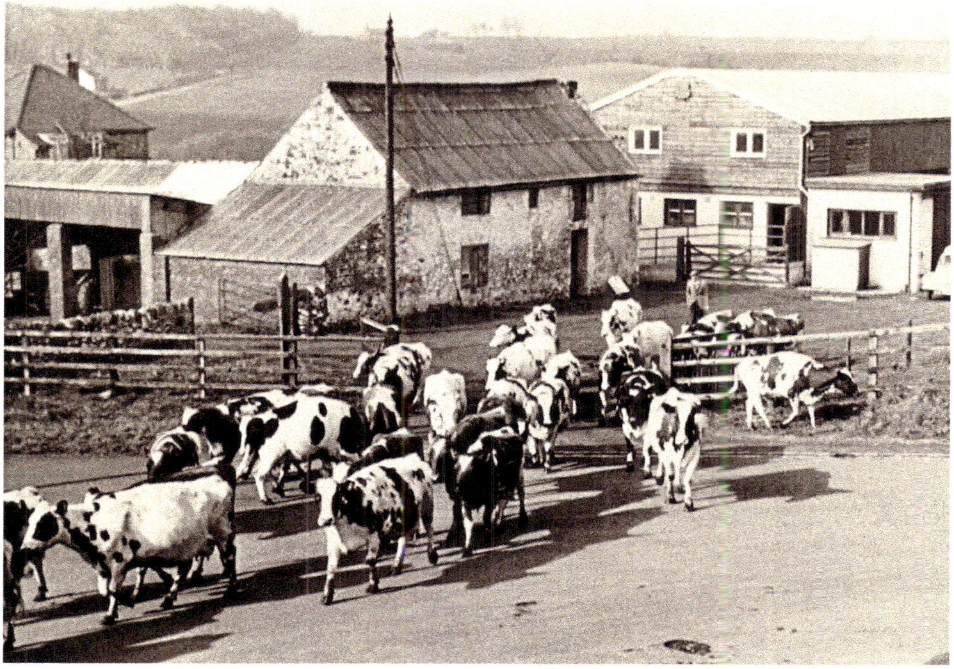

Seaton West Farm, NZ 397 499

Seaton is a pre-industrial village on the outskirts of Seaham, the town and harbour that was created almost from nothing after 1828. Until quite recently there were three working farms in the village, and here cattle from West Farm are being driven up past the village green around 1970. The old farmhouse at centre was thought to date from around 1600, but it had been demolished before 1991. Now flocks of a different sort are escorted up the village. Photographs *c.* 1970 (David Angus) and 2011.

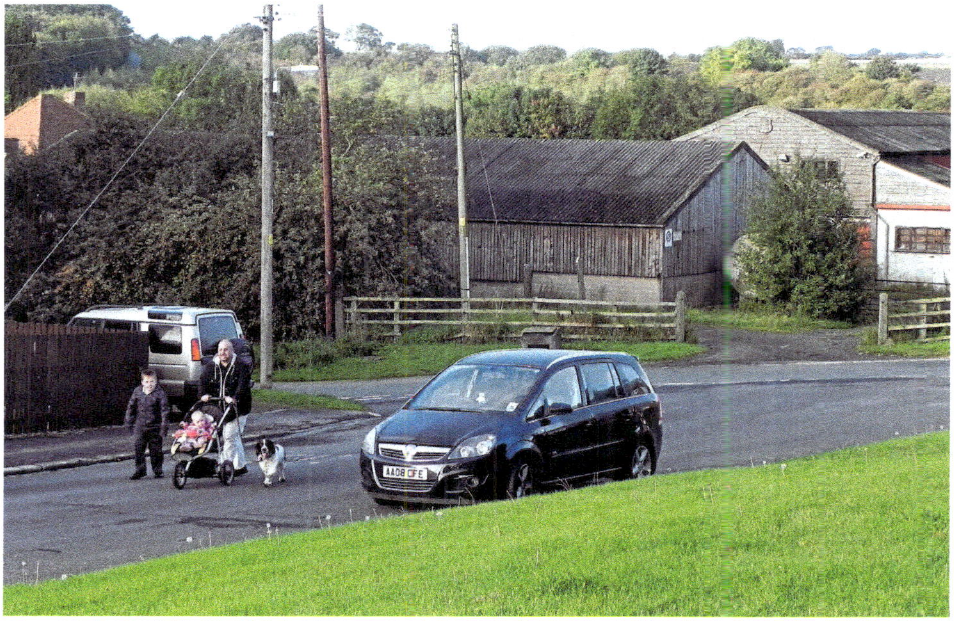

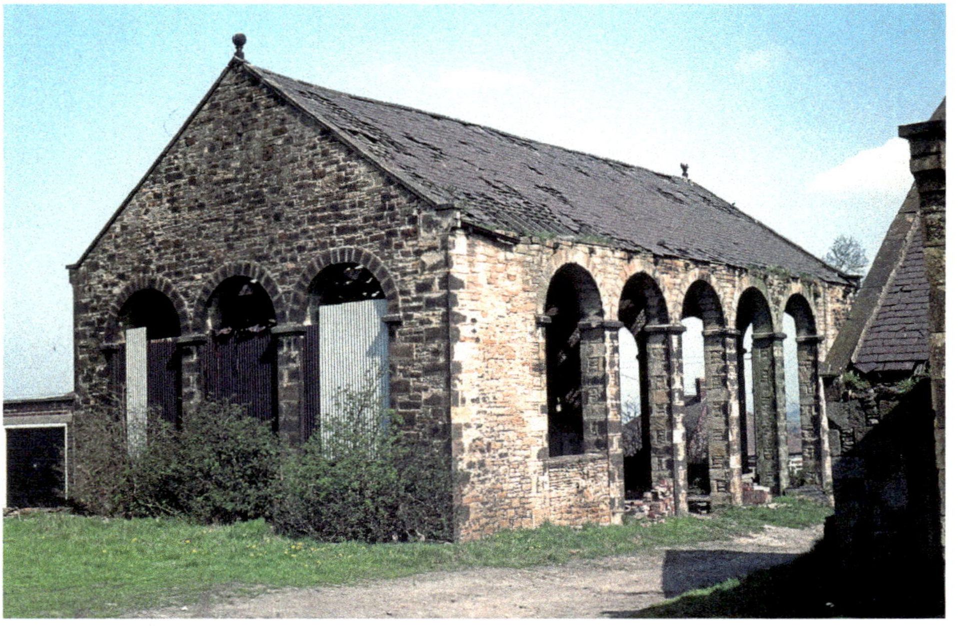

Bridgehill Farm/Barley Mill, Blackhill near Consett, NZ 093 517
Agriculture was always one of the North East's major industries, and most of the region remains predominantly rural today. As in all other forms of industry, radical changes have not been infrequent. Some farms found themselves swamped by urban expansion, their lands being given over to new housing, or their buildings converted for domestic purposes. The stone-built hay barn might have made a fine pergola for a new house built on the site of this farm, but clearly that option was not pursued. Photographs 1974 and 2011.

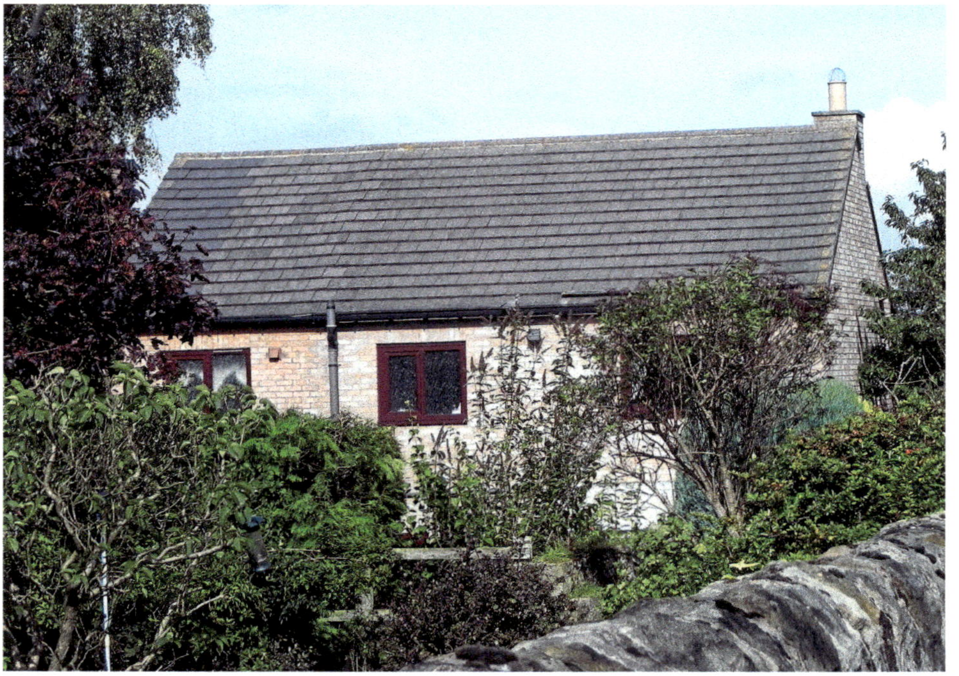

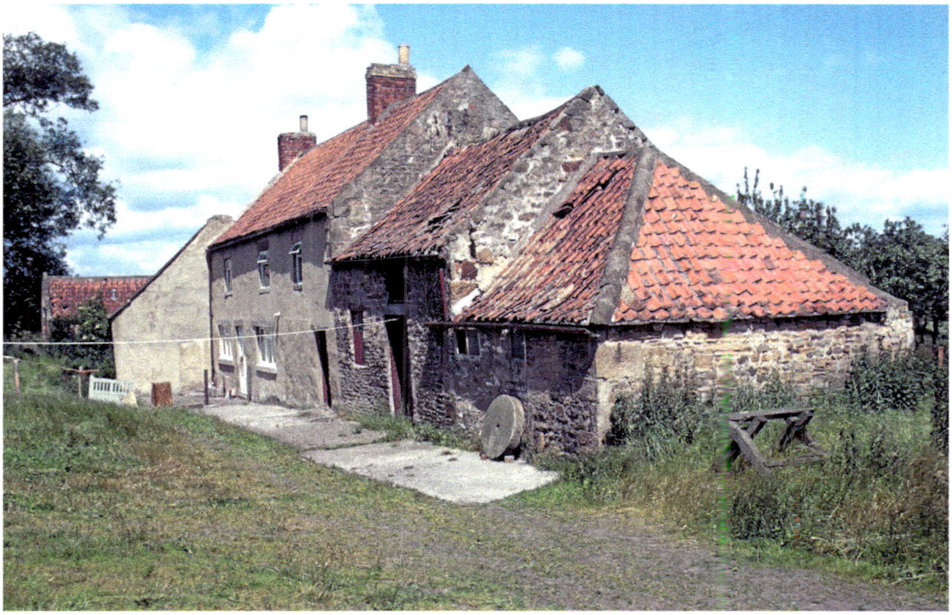

Broom Water Corn Mill, near West Auckland, NZ 193 262
A fine linear arrangement of mill and mill-house, stable and store, of wood, stone and pantile construction – a superb example of local vernacular architecture. The buildings were subsequently restored, extended and converted to a farm shop with café, sometime before 2008, and if the architectural harmony of the original has been lost, the buildings have nevertheless been retained. Photographs 1972 and 2011.

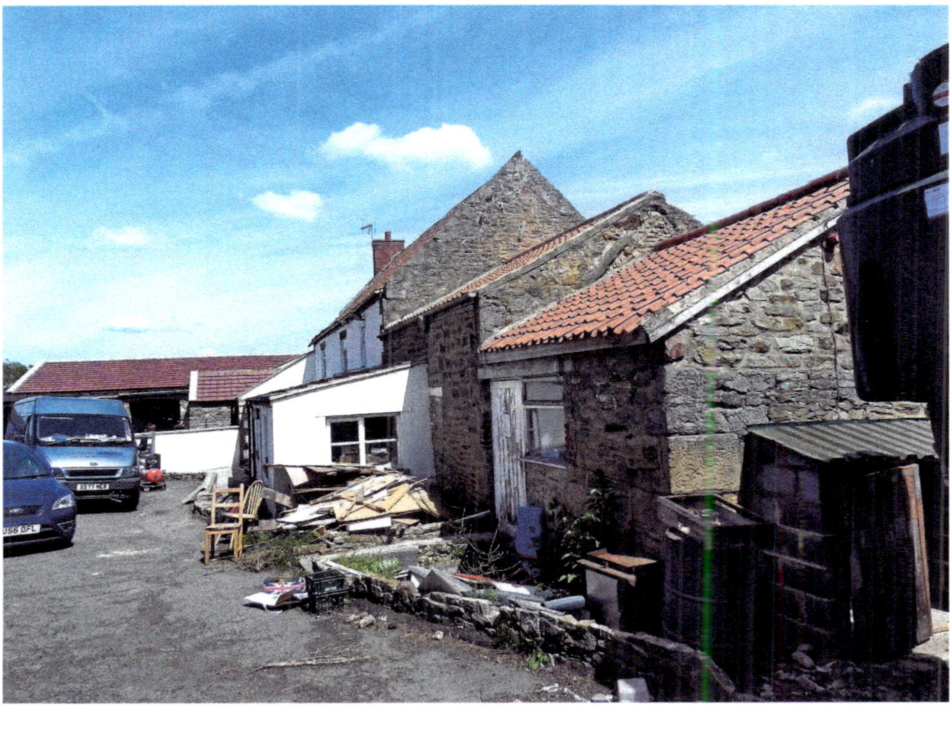

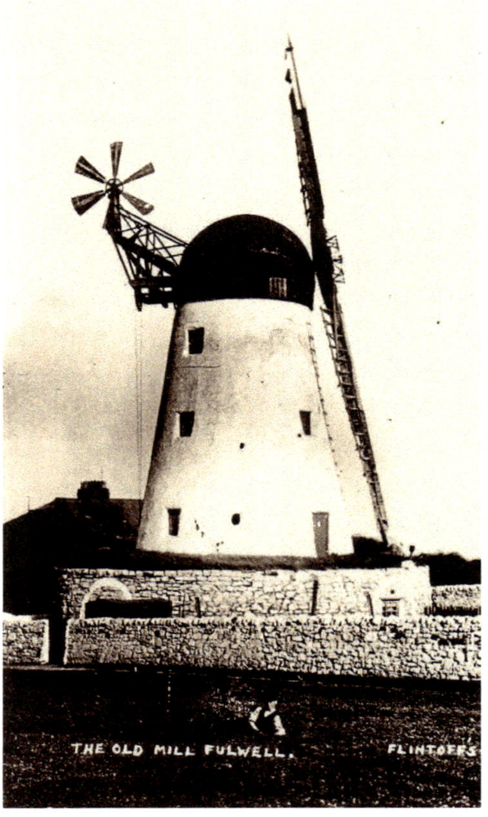

Fulwell Windmill, NZ 391 595

The present Fulwell windmill was built in around 1820, and remained in commercial use until 1949, although it had lost its sails long before then. Some external restoration was undertaken by Sunderland Corporation in the 1950s, and further works were carried out in the 1980s. A full restoration to working condition has since taken place and it is frequently open to the public as a working windmill. Photographs *c.* 1900 and 1974.

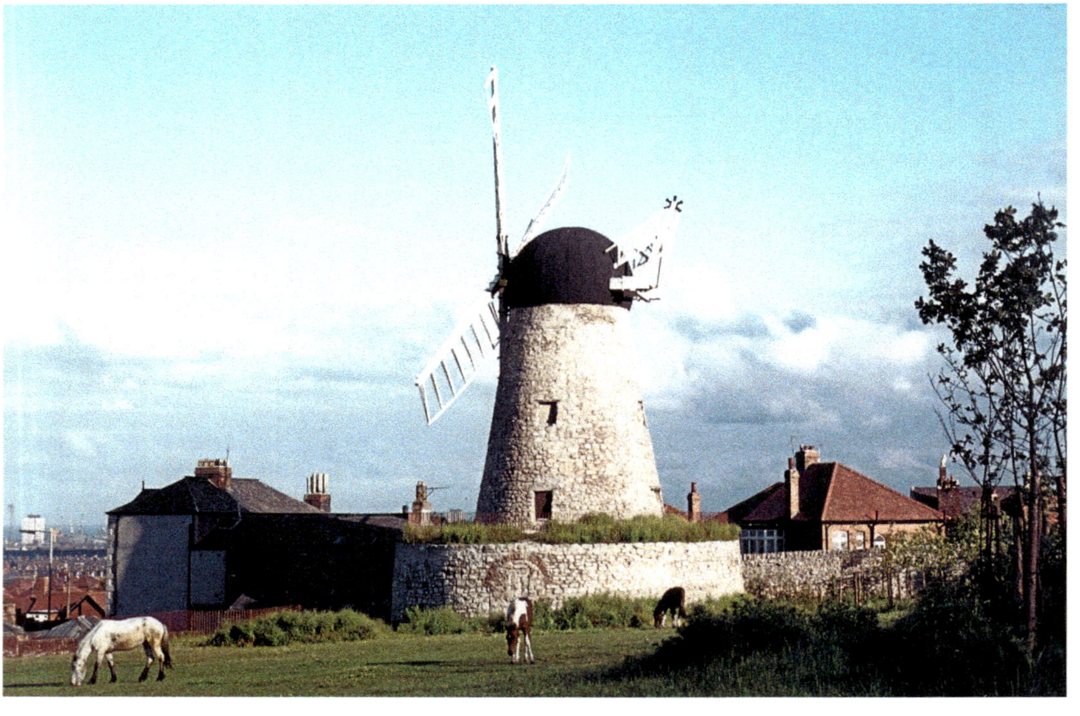

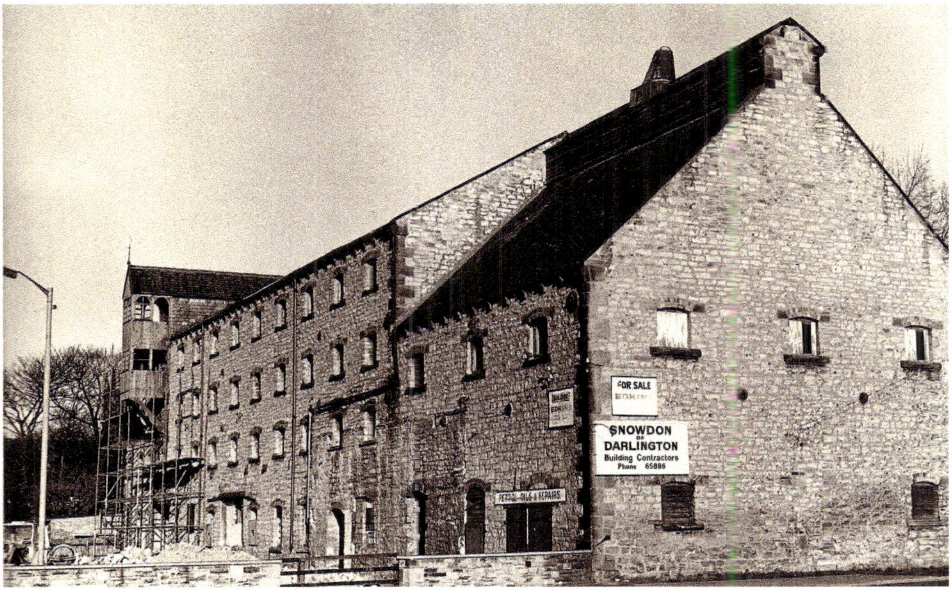

Houghton le Spring Brewery, NZ 341 497

This building, thought to date from 1874, was actually a maltings. It was closed down as such in 1925 but found a variety of subsequent uses – by skin merchants, a nightclub, and a garage and filling station. It stood unused and semi-derelict for a while in the 1990s but was then converted into 'much sought after' domestic accommodation in 1998/9. Photographs 1976 and 2011.

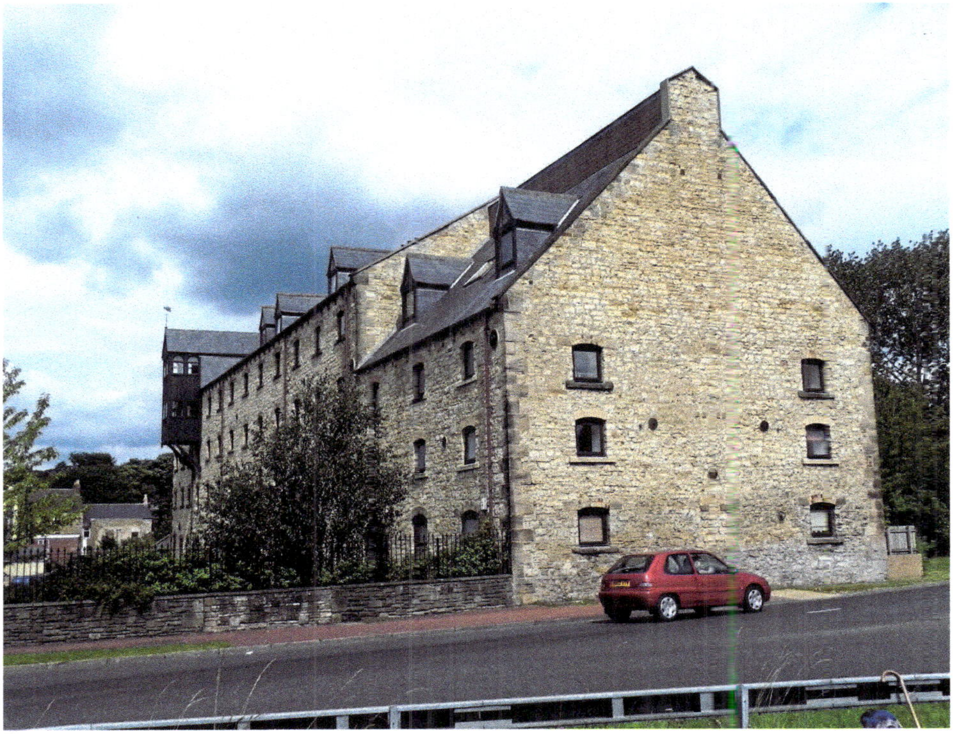

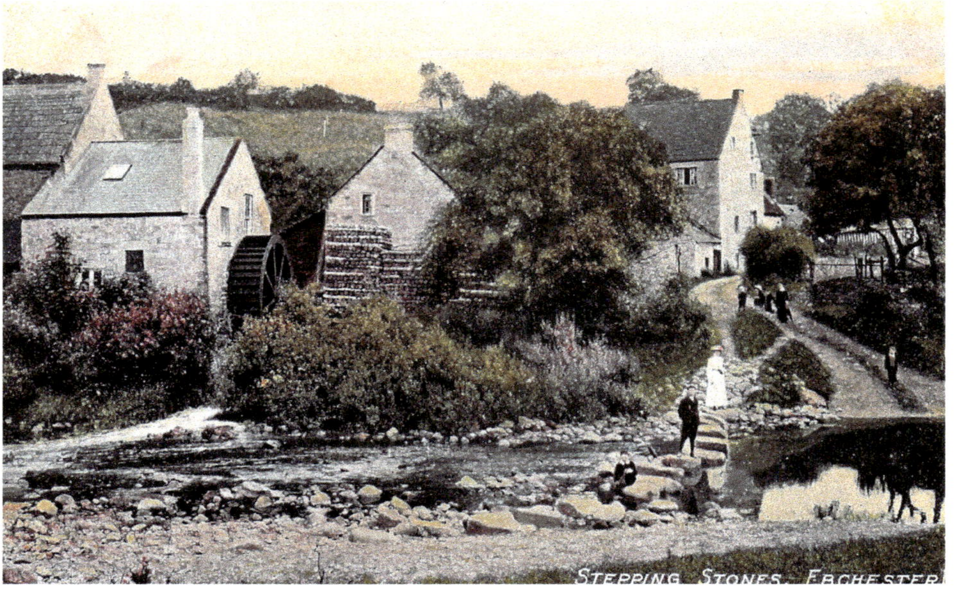

Ebchester Mills, NZ 104 558

This idyllic scene at Ebchester shows two of the three water mills that stood along the same half-mile of mill race taken off the River Derwent. In the left foreground a mill that variously served as a general sawmill, a bobbin mill and a poss-stick mill. Behind it stands the former Ebchester woollen mill, and well out of view, the local corn mill. The stepping stones clearly formed part of a popular Sunday afternoon walk. Only parts of the sawmill and woollen mills now remain, while the stepping stones had been replaced by wire-caged gabions by 1975 and more recently by a less flood-prone wooden footbridge. Postcard dated 1909; photograph 1975.

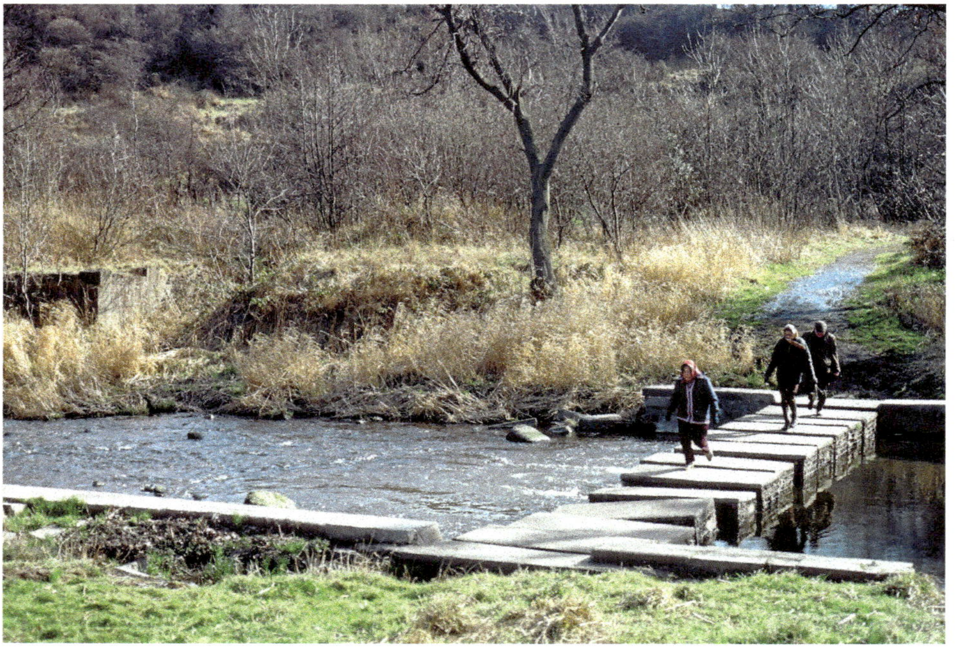

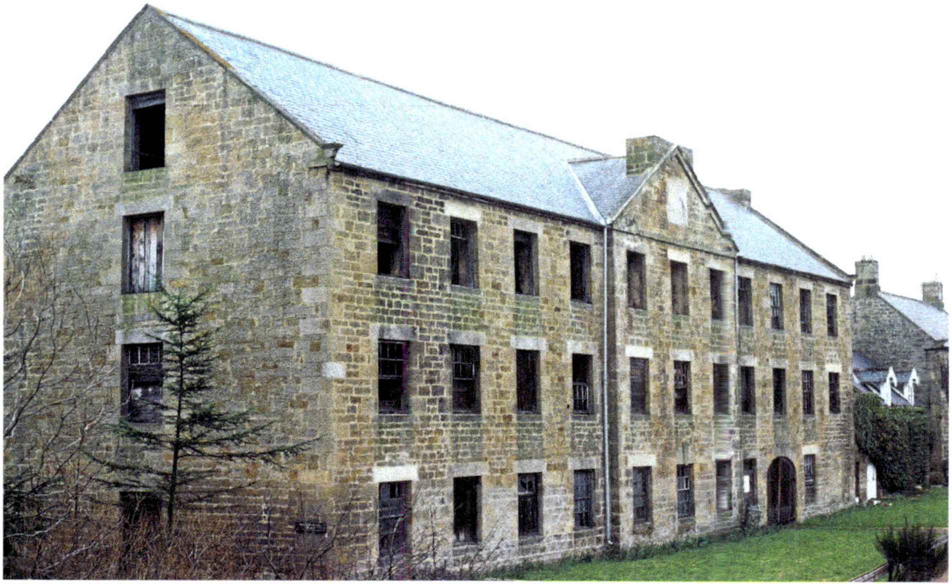

Netherwitton Cotton/Woollen Mill, NZ 101 903

Netherwitton Cotton Mill began production during 1787, but a crisis of confidence had descended upon the cotton industry by 1788, and the cotton boom that inspired the mill's creation was over. The mill seems to have closed in 1795, but was re-opened as a woollen mill around 1823, then converted to an estate sawmill in around 1930. The sawmill was relocated in 1972 and the mill building was then used for storage before being converted to quite fine domestic accommodation in 1989. Photographs 1979 and 2011.

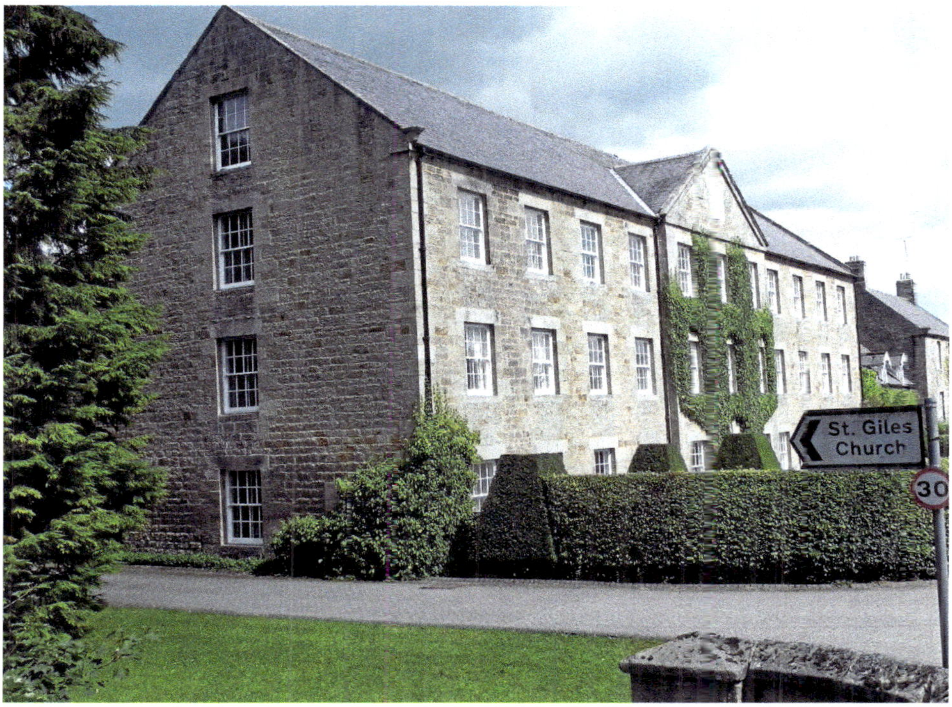

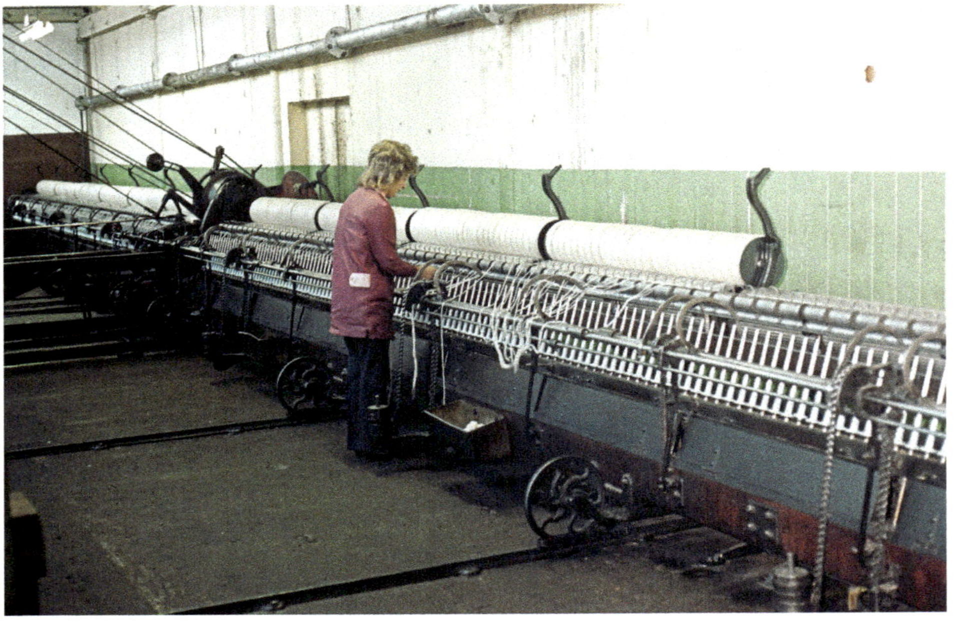

Otterburn Woollen Mill I, NY 887 927

Otterburn Mill's origins are unclear, but it was certainly operating in the eighteenth century and its international reputation for tweeds, rugs and blankets was established during the following century when the word 'Otterburn' became synonymous with rugs. It remained a fully functioning country woollen mill until 1976, after which date much of the spinning and weaving machinery was removed to a mill at Selkirk. The mill was re-opened in June 1997 as a museum, café, tourist information centre and shop. Photographs 1972 and 2010.

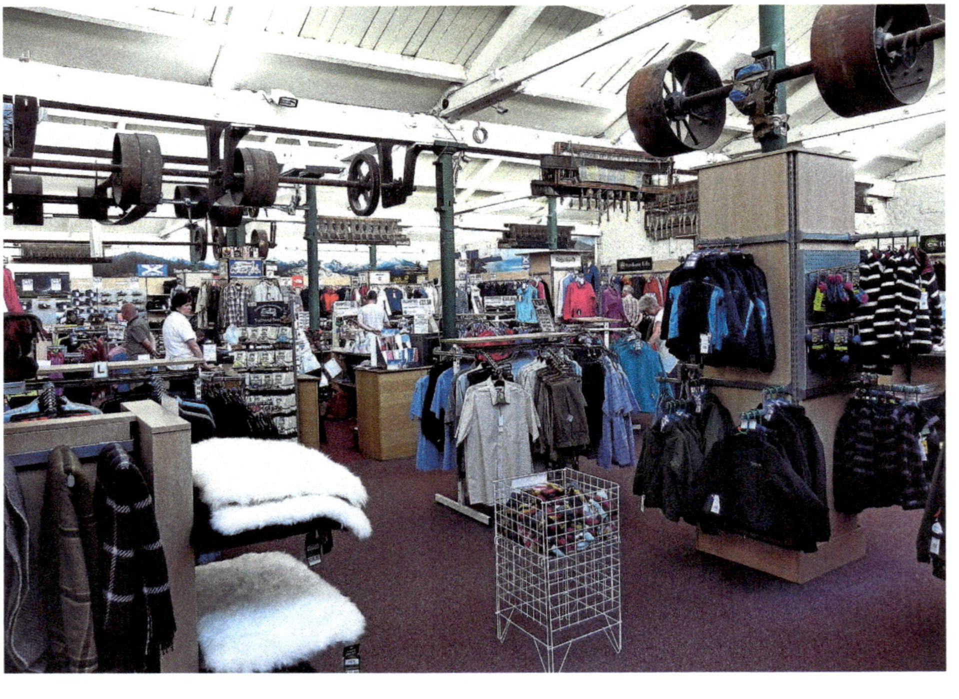

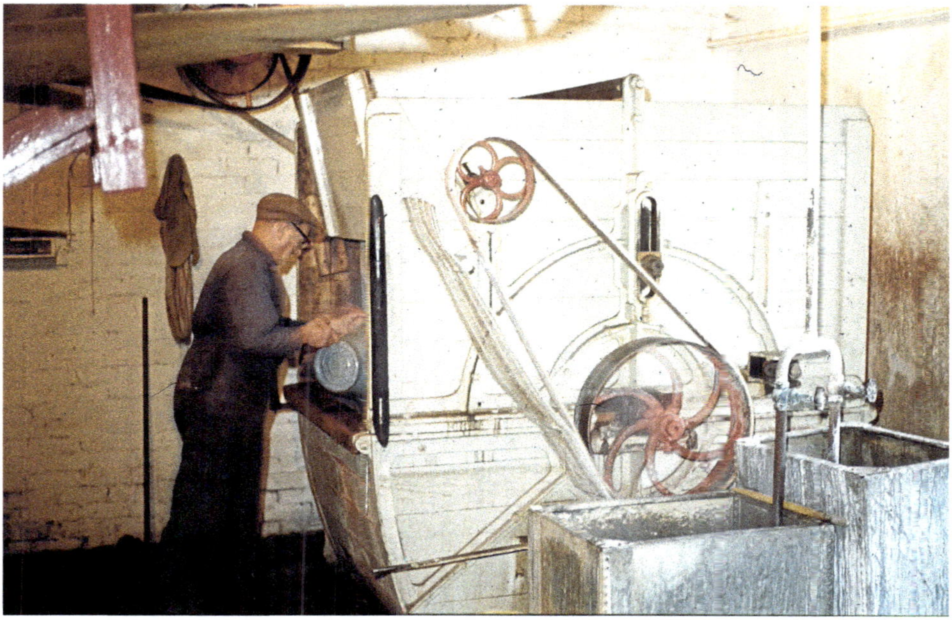

Otterburn Woollen Mill II, NY 887 927

Up to 1976, Otterburn retained a full range of woollen mill equipment and machinery, including spinning machines, carding machines, looms, dye becks, fulling stocks, tenter frames, a gig mill with Somerset teasels, etc. , a truly remarkable survival. When the mill re-opened in June 1997, it retained what little machinery had not been offloaded, and happily these relics, such as this scouring machine, remain available for public inspection. Photographs 1972 and 2010.

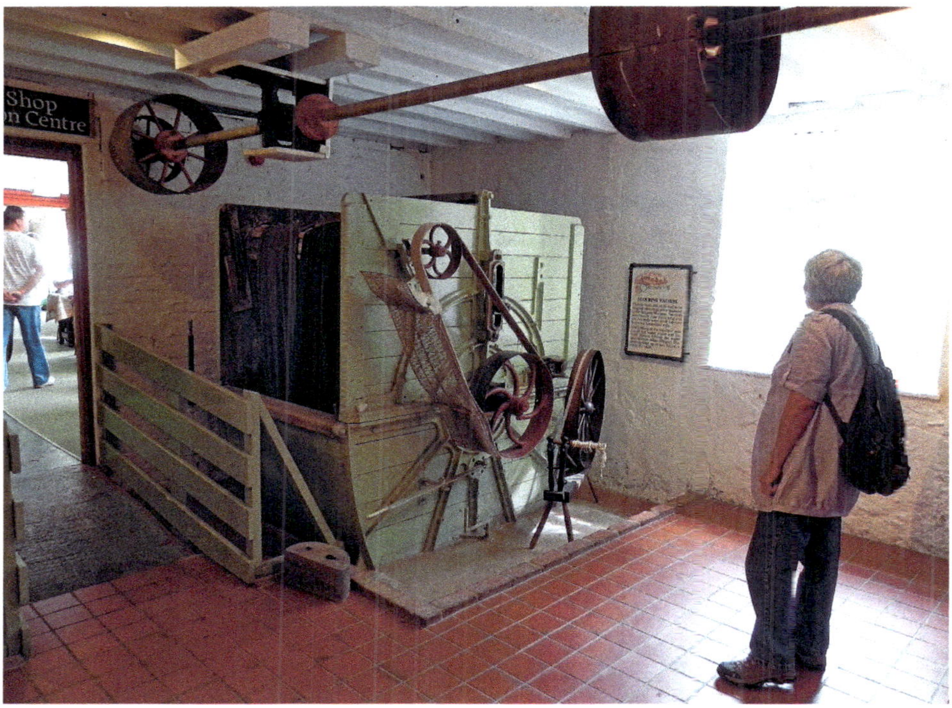

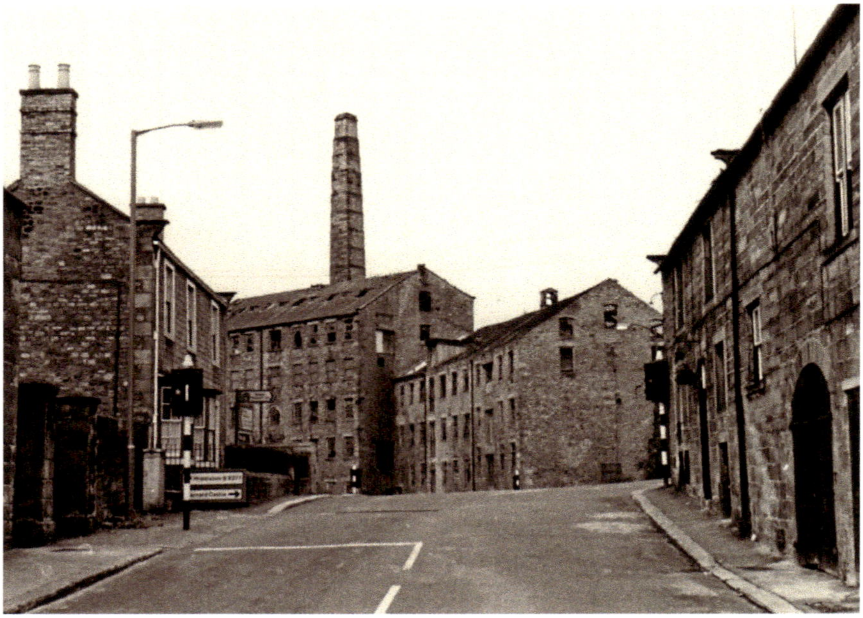

Ullathorne's Mill, Startforth, Barnard Castle, NZ 047 164

This former flax spinning mill, opened in 1760, became one of the largest shoe-thread mills in the country, employing about 100 men and 100 women and children by 1907. Flax was imported from Belgium, Ireland, France, and Russia, and the concern had an extensive export trade with Spain, Turkey, and the Colonies. The business closed down just before the Second World War, and for a while soldiers were billeted in the mill. Although a listed building, it was demolished around 1977. Now essentially a grassed area where a few mill fragments survive and a gaping hole in the townscape. Photographs 1973 and 2011.

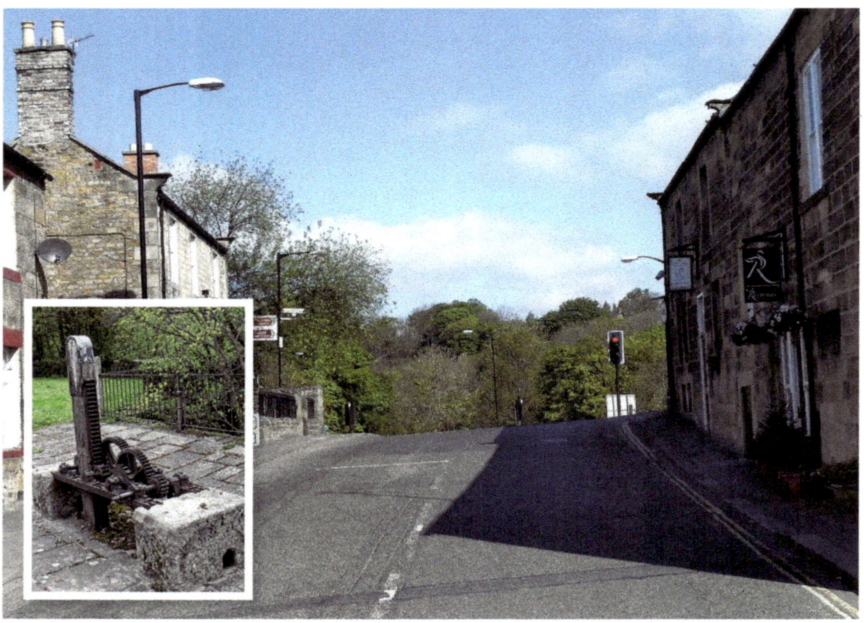

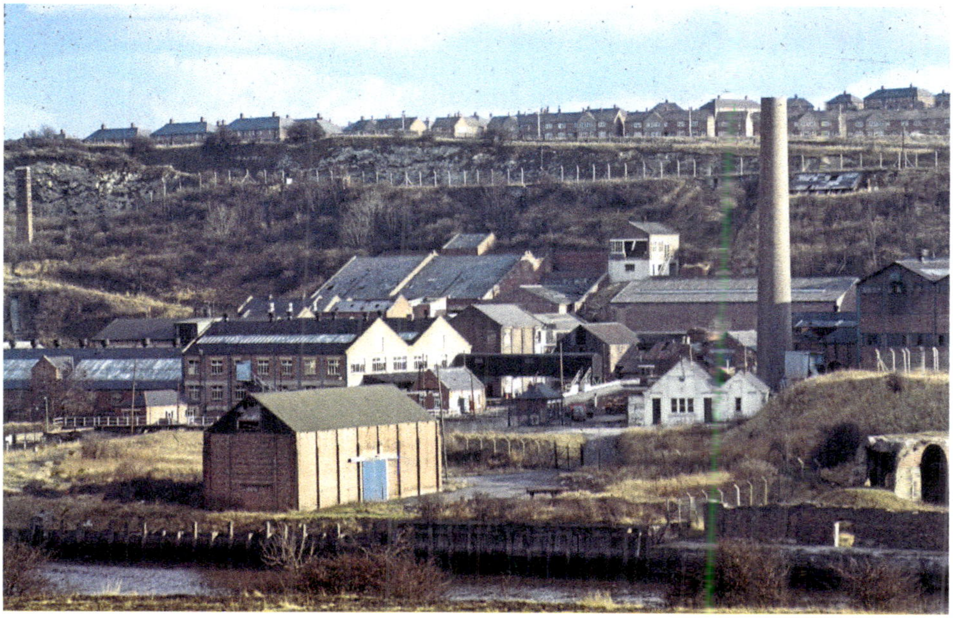

Hylton Paper Mill, Sunderland, NZ 360 574

This was the first paper mill in Britain to make extensive use of esparto grass for papermaking. Although initially dependent on the River Wear for import and export, it had a rail connection by 1852/53. It was said to have been 'an efficient mill ... in the forefront of technical innovation', but it closed in 1971. The site was subsequently cleared and much of it laid down to grass, but a rowing club headquarters was established by the river's edge. Photographs 1973 and 2011.

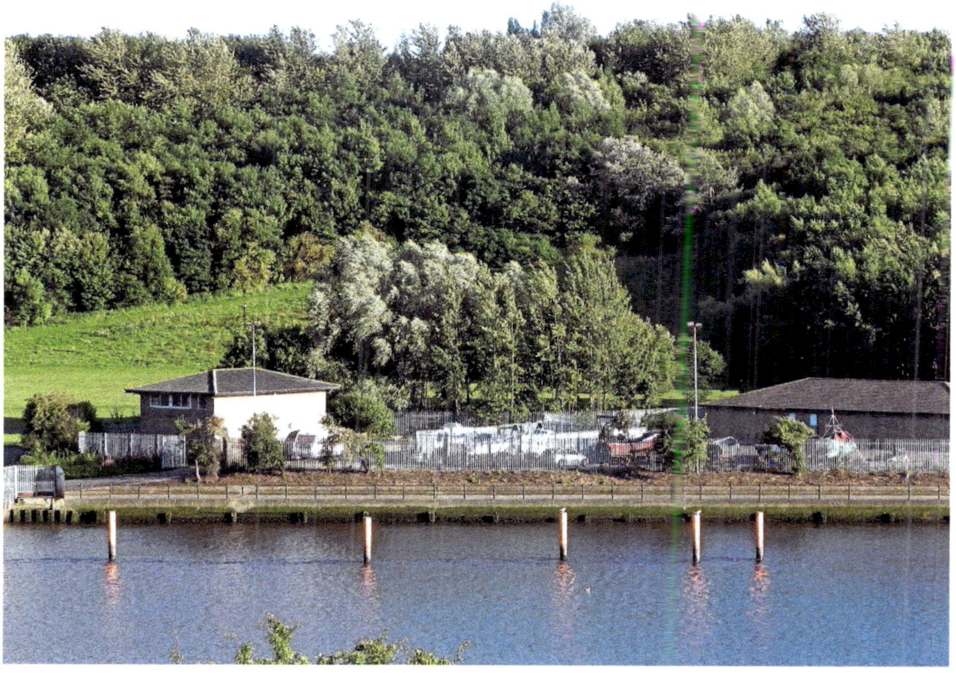

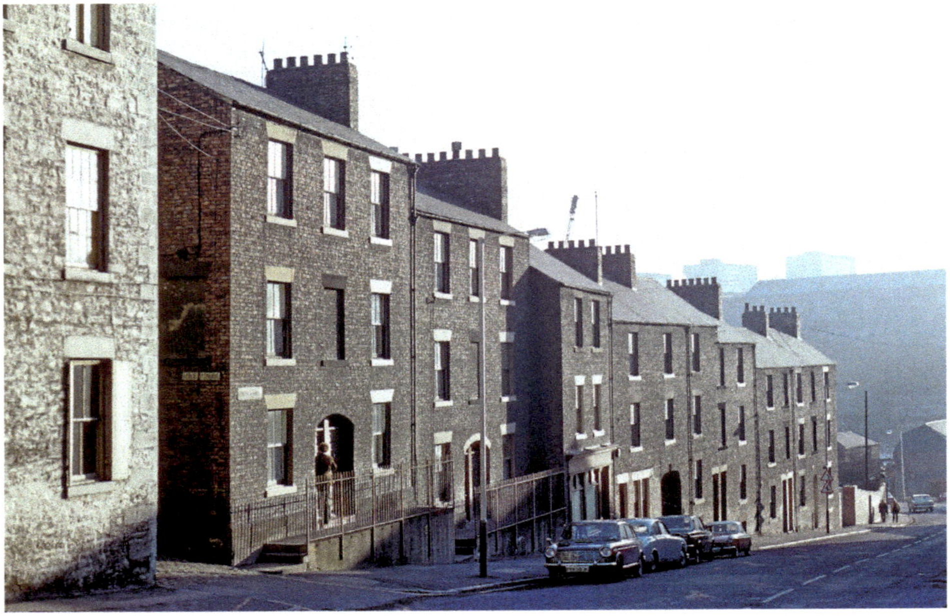

Leslie Terrace, Newcastle, NZ 246 636

These houses, running steeply down Forth Banks towards the Tyne, were described in 1827 as 'a double row of dwelling-houses, mostly occupied by workmen. Some of the higher houses ... near the top of the bank, are very neatly built'. They were indeed quite substantial dwellings, and the reason for their demolition is unclear, but the result has been unnecessary dereliction. The rather inelegant, (but presumably cheap) Tyne Metro Bridge of 1981 now hovers over the scene. Photographs 1972 and 2011.

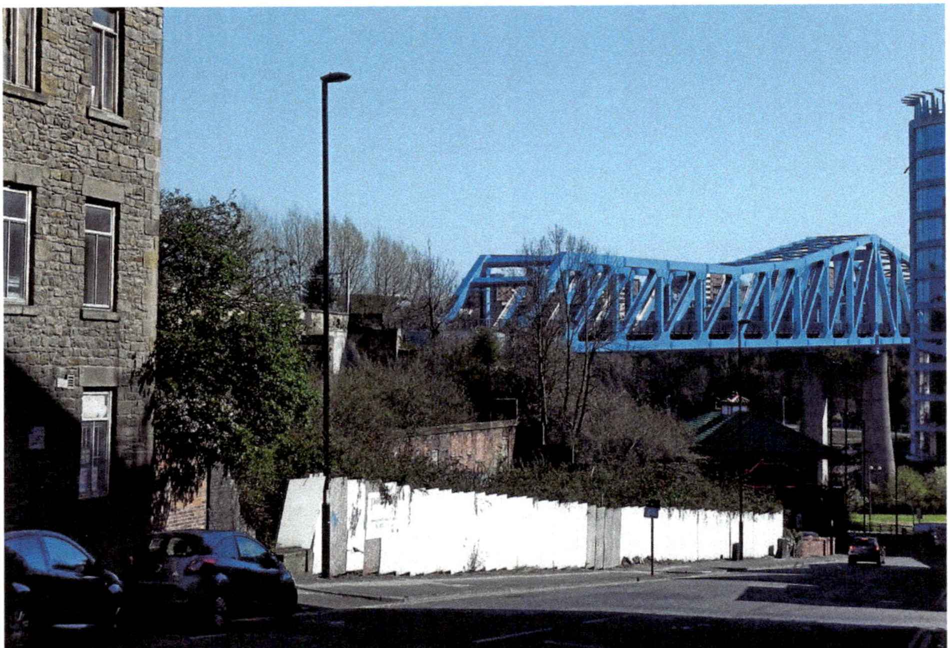

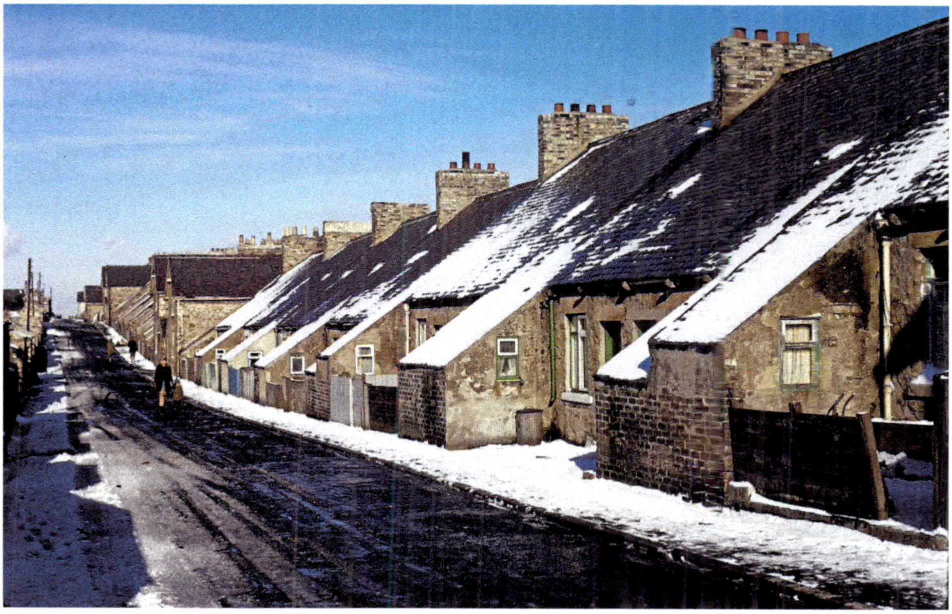

Pease & Partners Colliery Housing, NZ 167 377 and 139 386

Pease & Partners were major coal owners in County Durham, and they developed a particular style of terraced house for miners and their families. Wooley Terrace, in Stanley Crook was a good example, with cat-sliding roofs and small backyards, the latter sometimes later infilled to provide additional cottages. That terrace was demolished a number of years ago, but a similar terrace still stands at Sunniside Crook, and shows how such houses have been subsequently modified. Photographs 1973 and 2011.

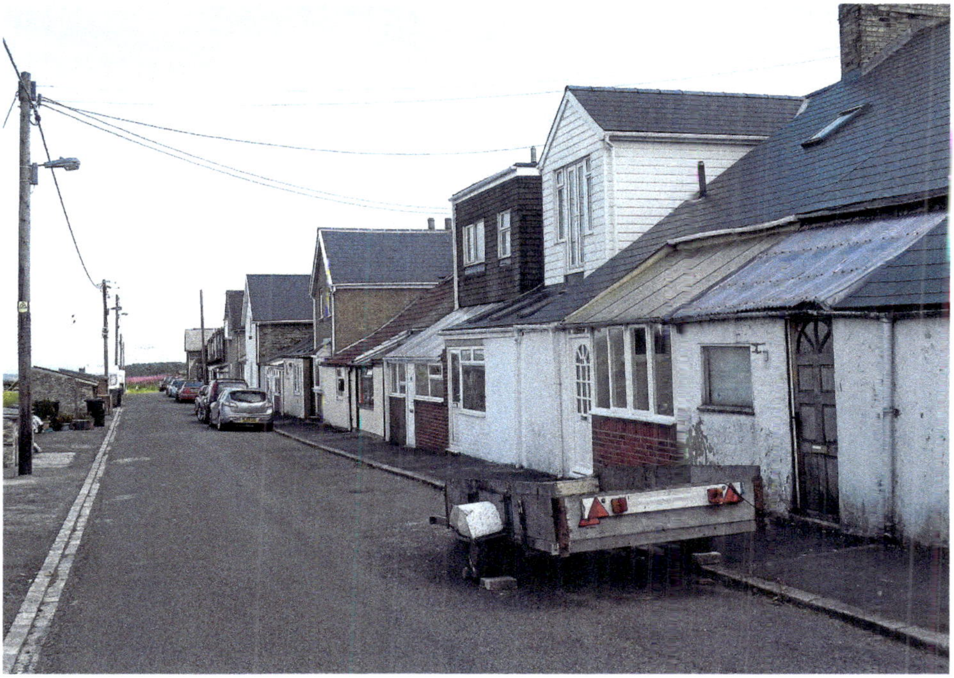

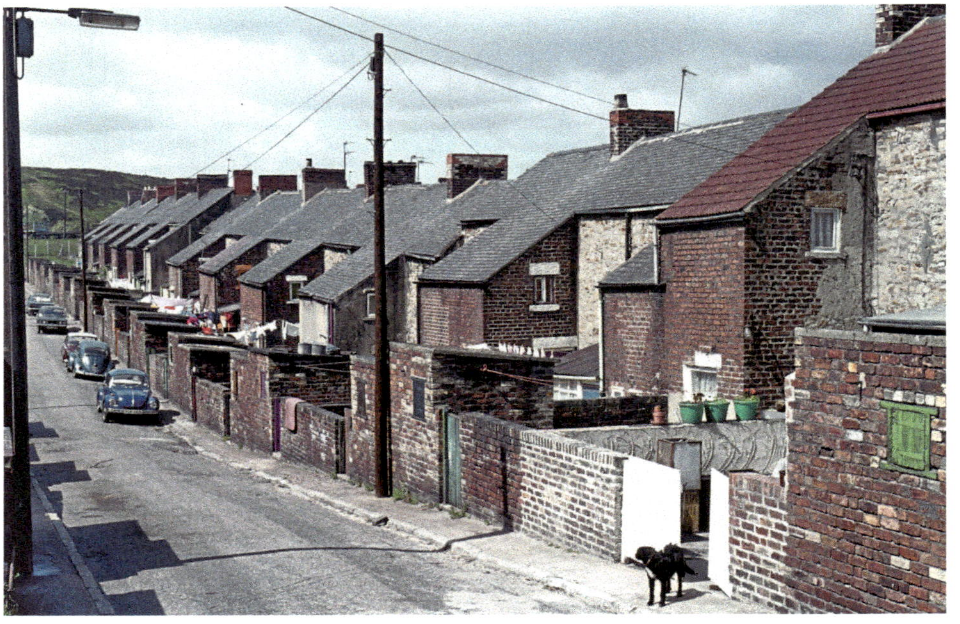

Waldridge Village, Back Lime Street, NZ 252 501

Waldridge was a typical small County Durham coal-mining village, whose colliery had opened in 1831 and closed in 1926; the present village replaced the original settlement on the fell above in around 1890. As can be seen, a degree of upgrading, and occasionally gentrification, followed the disposal of the houses by the NCB to its tenants. Photographs 1974 and 2011.

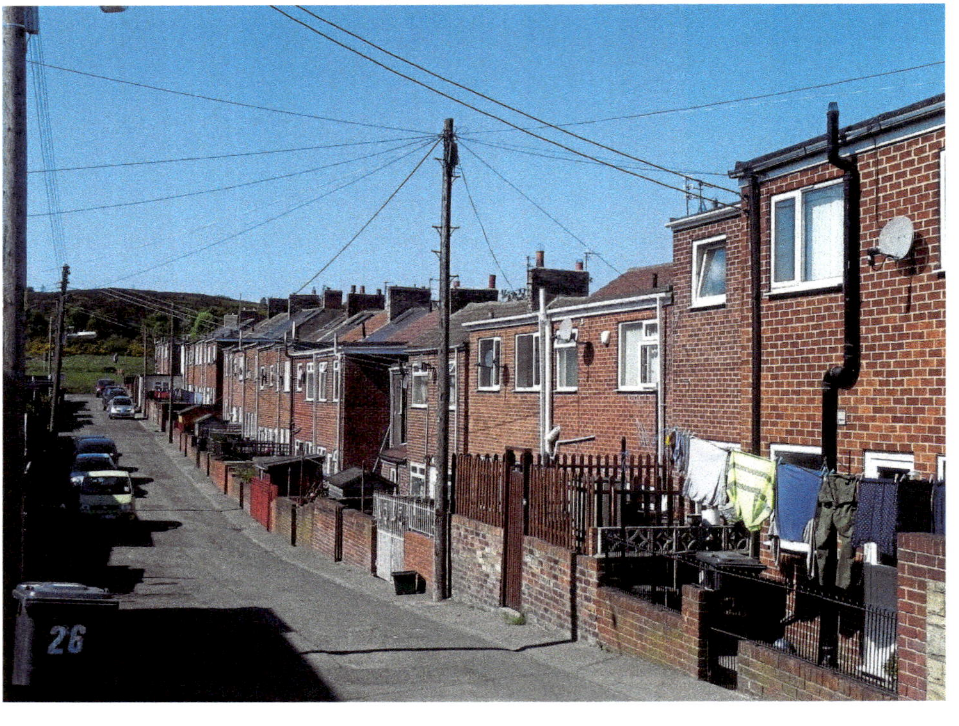

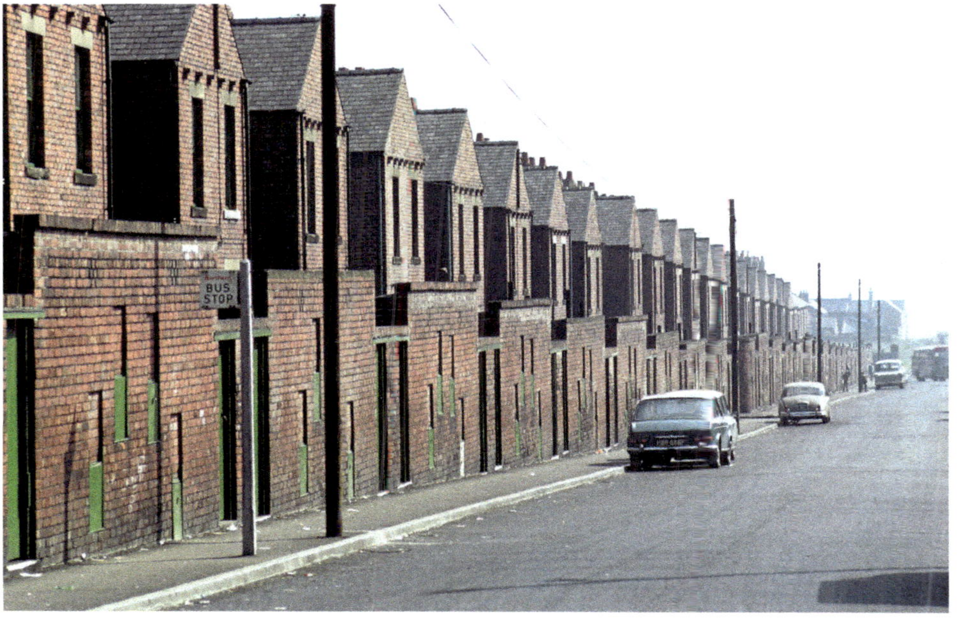

Quaking Houses Village, near Stanley, NZ 188 507

This small former mining village, the origin of whose name is uncertain, comprised four streets prosaically named First, Second, Third and Fourth Streets; extensions to the latter two streets, with large houses for senior pit workers, were however, named Woodside and Fellside. The houses illustrated, probably built in around 1920, were first photographed at a time when the entire village was threatened with demolition. It survived, but most of the coalhouses, outside toilets and ash middens were replaced by house extensions, garages and sheds, after the houses were sold to NCB tenants and others. Photographs 1972 and 2011.

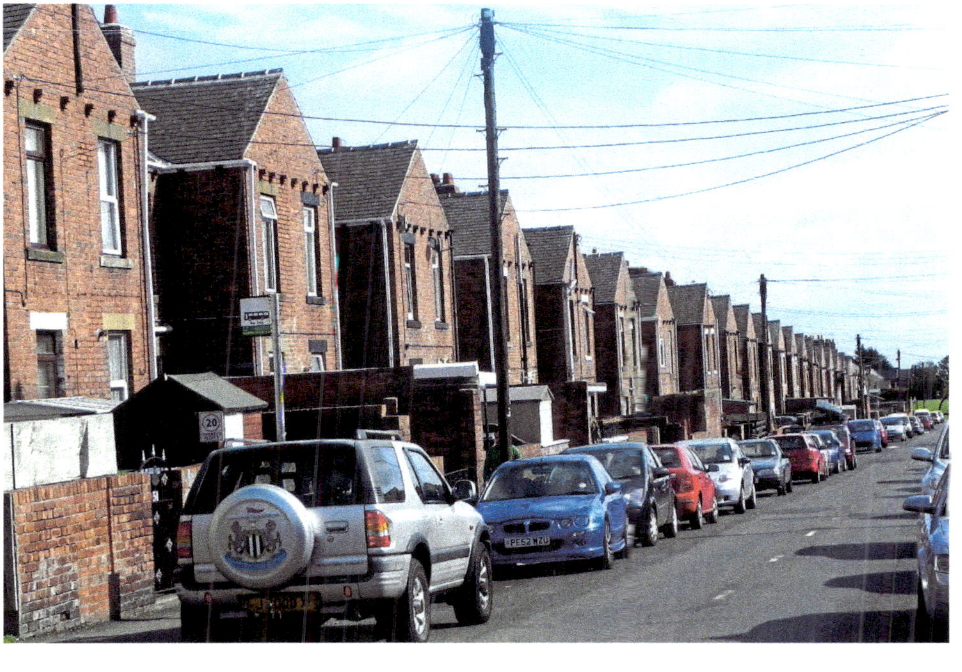

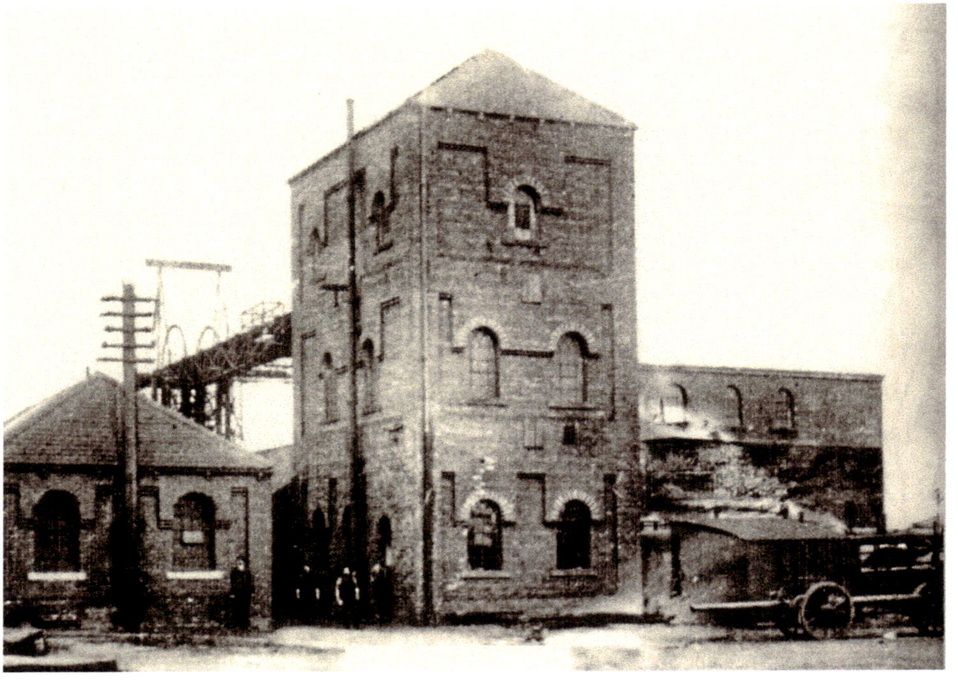

The Billy Pit, Quaking Houses, near Stanley, NZ 188 507

The William Pit at Quaking Houses, popularly known as the 'Billy Pit', was sunk in 1839, and finally closed in 1960. The large building in the illustration housed a vertical steam-powered winding engine, with a simple headstock beyond. The sun has well and truly set on the deep coal-mining industry of North East England, but the pulley wheel on the site of the Billy Pit, like those elsewhere in the region, provides a poignant reminder of its triumphs and tragedies. Photographs 1920s? (Derek Hall) and 2009.

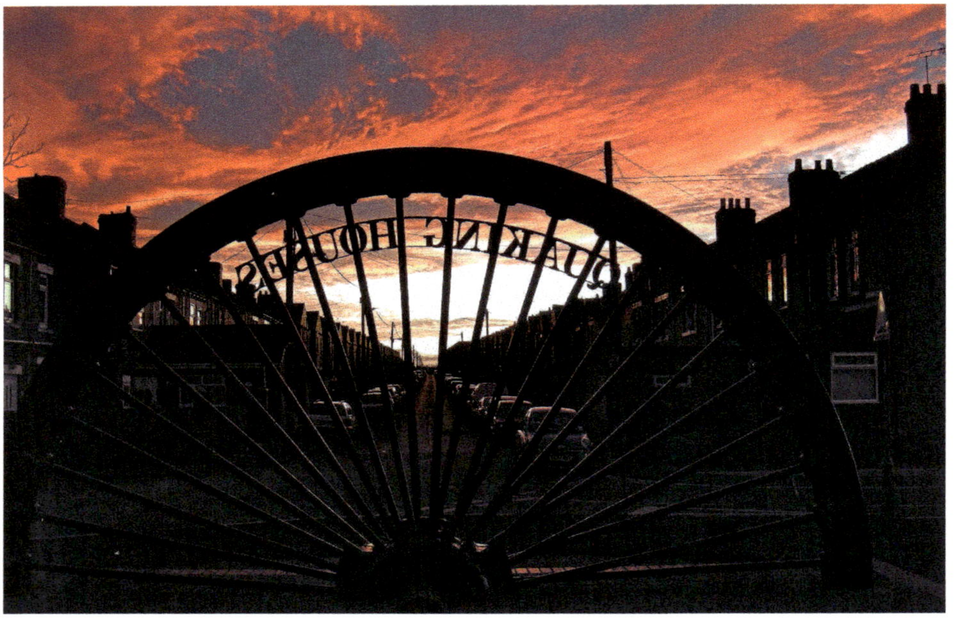

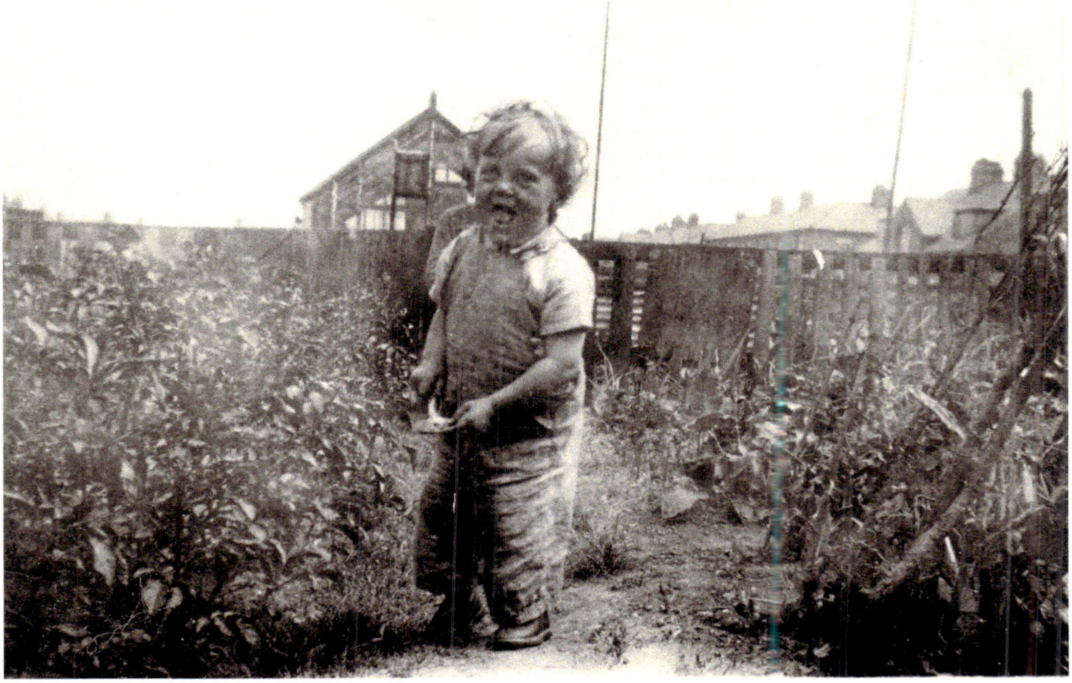

And Finally – The Author.
The author, digging for victory in the First World War in 1940, and still digging,, but for victory in the Village Show, in 1998 (Tessa Gray).

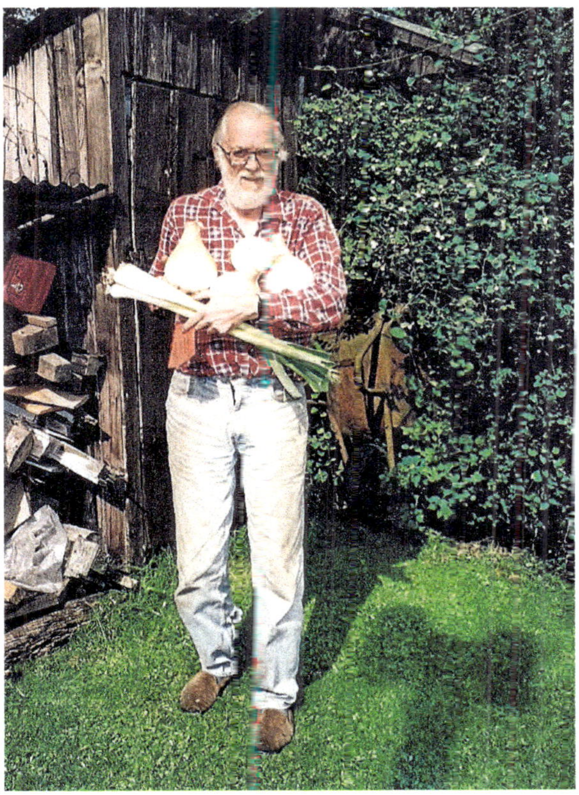

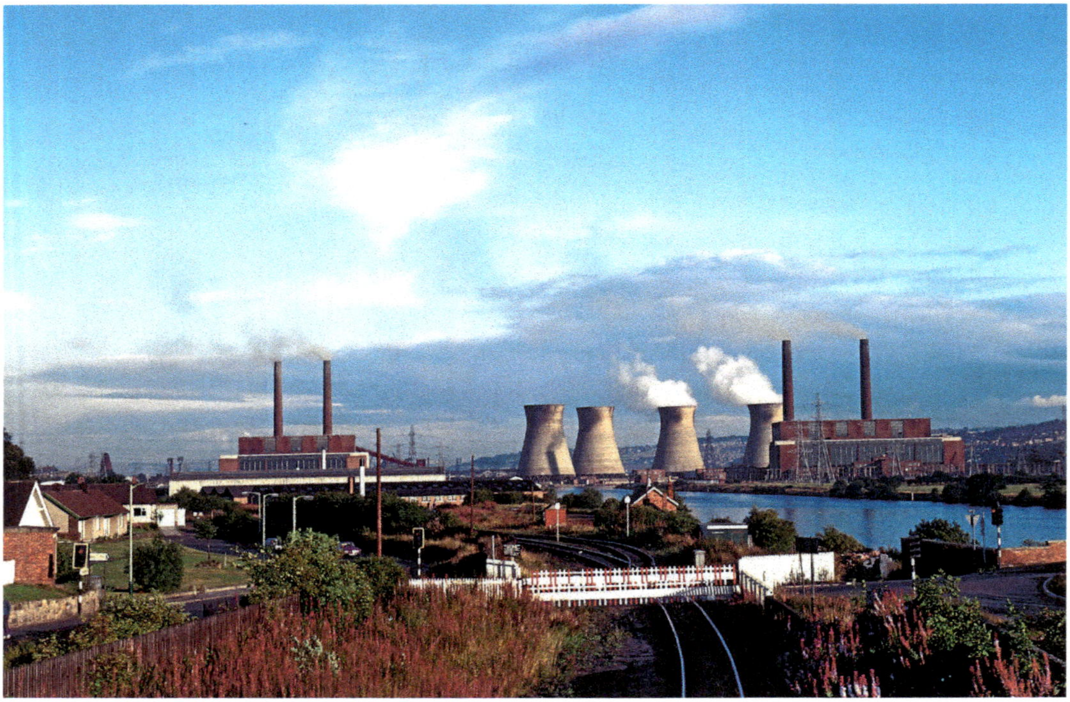

Never To Be Repeated View from Newburn, ESE from NZ 164 652
The two power stations have gone, the railway has gone, and the high footbridge over the railway that made this view possible has also gone, all since 1972.

Acknowledgements

Most of the photographs reproduced here were either taken by the author or are from his collection, but he is extremely grateful for those taken or supplied by friends and colleagues; their names appear in brackets within the captions. I am also much obliged to the many friendly strangers who allowed me access to their properties, and to the inventors of digital photography.